Migration — United Kingdom

Migration United Kingdom

A handbook on the taxation, exchange control and legal implications of coming to, investing in and leaving the United Kingdom

Edited by:

J.R. Poole

and

P.G.D. Kiers

1978

Springer-Science+Business Media, B.V.

Cover design: Pieter J. van der Sman

ISBN 978-90-200-0514-1 ISBN 978-94-017-4436-2 (eBook)
DOI 10.1007/978-94-017-4436-2

Originally published by Kluwer, Deventer in 1978
Softcover reprint of the hardcover 1st edition 1978

Foreword

The law and practice in this work is that at 10th January 1978. To complete this work in Autumn 1977, as originally intended, was impossible. Principally, this has been due to the changes in the Finance Act 1977, the various mini budgets and the exchange control changes, many of which are relevant to the subject matter of this work. Gratitude is expressed to the publishers for their patience. The Revenue has just revised its useful practice notes, IR 25 1977, dealing with the taxation of foreign earnings. The new IR 25 1977 modifies only slightly the IR 25 in Appendix 4.

It will be appreciated that in this work it is impossible to provide for exhaustive treatment of all the taxes. Complexity in some places has been set aside for simplicity and clarity. Any such selectivity consisting of various emphases and omissions rests solely on fallible judgment. It is hoped that some light nevertheless is cast on the basic facets relevant to migrants. Too often these facets are not dealt with appropriately, dealt with separately without any co-ordination or submerged in a plethora of exotic detail of interest to academics and theoreticians only. Further reading is suggested in the Bibliography.

Many thanks for assistance, constructive suggestions and encouragement are due (in no particular order) to Dr. J. Barry Bracewell-Milnes of Erasmus University Rotterdam, Dr. Nico Nobel of Nobel & Van Wierst BV, Dr. Albert Rädler, Edo de Vries of Gray's Inn and Jeremy Lamb of Comprehensive Financial Services.

Thanks are also due to Klaus Meyer Swantée, Malcolm Brookes, Bart van Hedel, Robin Christopher, Lindsay Duncan, Lawrence Freeman, Brett Patton, Harry Brown and Koen Bruyn.

Thanks are given to Her Majesty's Stationery Office for consent to print extracts from IR 20 and IR 25.

J.R. Poole

1st March, 1978

Table of Contents

Section I: Introduction

The aim of the work is to go through the maze of UK legislation and practice examining practically the fiscal, legal and EC aspects of particular relevance to an individual planning to come to the UK either to visit or become resident for one or other reasons such as taking up employment or for the purpose of retirement. The converse situation of the individual who plans to leave the UK temporarily or permanently is similarly catered for.

UK fiscal legislation and practice contains many complex and diverse facets. Moreover these are subject to change because of the social, economic and political pressures which exist in the UK. The diversity obscurity and impact of the relevant UK legislation and practice, as it affects the individual coming here from overseas, is not very welcoming. To an individual who is leaving the position is less obscure and from his point of view less satisfactory. To a large extent the general attitude (particularly with income tax) can be explained by concern shown by successive governments with tax avoidance (as opposed to evasion) especially where there is a foreign element in a seemingly domestic matter or where a foreign element can be artificially introduced. This particularly applies to the legislation relating to overseas employment, non-UK trusts, and non-UK companies.

The EC regulations are complex because of the balance of payments situation and strict not-to-be-underestimated surveillance is excercised by the Bank of England chiefly through the banks. Severe penalties can and are exacted for breaches of EC regulations. Nonetheless it is a basic EC rule that funds originally introduced by a non-resident in the EC sense are capable of re-export and are not in danger of being restricted or frozen (i.e. blocked) unless the individual concerned becomes resident for exchange control purposes. Recent EC rules have modified the position even further in favour of the individual.

Many of the problems of the migrant can be mitigated by appraising fully the technical rules, careful planning and timing. Preferably this should be done *before* arriving in or leaving the UK. In short there is no substitute for forward planning.

Both tax planning and tax avoidance are legitimate. Tax avoidance however is officially disapproved of. The highly technical and legalistic nature of anti-avoidance provisions (usually by way of detailed specific legislation) means that there are traps for the unwary. An individual temporarily resident in or even 'temporarily outside' the UK can well become enmeshed in such provisions quite unwittingly even where the aim of the operation was something other than tax avoidance. There is no question, as, is possible, in some other jurisdictions of the authorities knowing of a malpractice and choosing to tolerate the situation. Tax evasion is severely dealt with and heavy penalties can be levied.

In using this work as an outline to the various facets of becoming resident, or even domiciled, in the UK readers should before turning to the rest of the book, digest and relate to their own circumstances Section II together with the relevant parts of Appendices 1 and 2. The tax, EC, and social security implications will depend entirely on his or her types of residential and domiciliary status. Nationality rarely comes into the reckoning. Further the tests particularly for residence vary as between residence for taxation purposes, EC purposes and Home Office regulations and the various social security provisions.

The editors approach has been to try and leave aside where possible academic influences and present in a practical way the topics in separate sections so that an individual is at least able to anticipate any problems that may arise or will arise and consider the options available to minimise present and future difficulties.

The work is not intended to be an encyclopaedia of UK taxation. Rather it is a panorama of what is of particular relevance and interest to an individual coming to the UK and leaving the UK or where an individual has interests in the UK. Naturally certain UK taxes and aspects of UK taxation e.g. development land tax, stamp duty, are either not or only briefly dealt with. Such information is available elsewhere. There are separate sections covering the main topics. Some aspects of necessity are only touched on briefly – the basics of income tax capital gains tax and corporation tax. Those features high lighted are those of particular interest to the international readers . CTT is dealt with from an international view point. A few books of varying types are suggested in the bibliography. Domicil (a concept peculiar to the English-type legal systems) and Residence are dealt with at some length and the principal extracts from the extremely important Revenue publications IR 20 Non-residents and Residents: Liability to UK tax and IR 25 Taxation of Foreign Earnings and Pensions following FA 1974: are set out in Appendices 1 and 4 respectively. The latter has been slightly amended by FA 1977. Most situations are determined in accordance with the current practice. The Appendices contain other material and examples considered to be key ancilliary material.

The editors are aware that because of the breadth and the scope of the subjects the work purports to cover some subjects are not dealt with a length and some only superficially. The editors will be satisfied if a non-UK reader appreciates the fundamentals and their application to the facts of an individual situation.

In Section XI there are two check lists or aide-memoires which may be useful to the reader.

Visitors of all types to the UK although faced by a mass of legislation and practice will be assured of a welcome to the UK. The UK, particularly south east England, is now more than ever a cosmopolitan society. Historically the UK has benefited immensely from the experience of its citizens abroad and from outside influences and will no doubt continue to do so.

Section II: Domicil and Residence

A. General

From the start it must be grasped that domicil and residence (and also ordinary residence) are separate concepts. A foreign-domiciled individual who *visits* the UK must consider whether or not he becomes:

i) domiciled in the UK[1]
ii) resident in the UK[2]
iii) ordinarily resident in the UK[2]

Conversely, a UK domiciled individual who *leaves* the UK must consider whether or not he:

i) acquires a foreign domicil and thereby loses his UK domicil[1]
ii) becomes not resident in the UK[2]
iii) becomes not ordinarily resident in the UK[2]

Any combination between the above forms of status is possible. The individual's income tax CGT and CTT liabilities can be considerably affected by the permutation applicable.

Residence in the tax context should not be confused or identified with residence in the context[3] of UK EC (or any other sense).

It is impossible to over-emphasise the importance of the various forms of status. Most people living in the UK are domiciled in the UK and both resident and ordinarily resident in the UK.

Greatly over-simplified, the general tax position of such an individual is:

Income tax – He will be subject to tax on his worldwide investment income on the arising basis, i.e. when the income accrues to him.

CGT – He will be subject to CGT on realisation of any capital gains.

CTT – On his death his worldwide assets will be subject to CTT. The position is similar with lifetime gifts.

If an individual does not have one or more of the forms of status, then his position can be substantially different. This will be spelt out later in some detail. To gain an idea of the variations possible some brief examples are:

A foreign domiciled UK resident individual will be subject to tax on his foreign investment income[4] and foreign capital gains on the remittance basis, i.e. when he receives the income or the capital gains in the UK.

A foreign domiciled individual (provided he is not treated as domiciled in the UK) will only be subject to CTT on his assets that are situated in the UK.

A UK domiciled but non-resident individual will not be subject to UK tax on his foreign investment income. If he is also not ordinarily resident he will not be subject to CGT if he realises any capital gains.

A UK domiciled resident but not ordinarily resident individual will be subject to tax on his foreign investment income on the remittance basis, i.e. when he receives it in the UK.

DIVISION OF SECTION II

Parts B. C and D following deal in some detail with domicil, residence and ordinary residence respectively. At the outset it should be appreciated that there are no statutory definitions of domicil, residence and ordinary residence. Further, the case law on residence and ordinary residence has not provided enough of an administrative sub-structure. Accordingly, the UK Revenue has set out in its booklet IR 20 'Residents and Non-Residents', the Rules it administers. The principal parts of IR 20 are set out in Appendix 1 (B). Various extra-statutory concessions set out in Appendic 1 (C) must also be considered. Both the practice and extra-statutory concessions modify and extend the legislation and case law.

Potential residents and potential non-residents are dealt with in Part E. Part F deals with how the position can be effected by Double Tax Treaties.

B. Domicil

Domicil is a concept peculiar to the various different English-type legal systems of the world, such as England and Wales, Northern Ireland and many colonies, former colonies and territories overseas. Scotland, which has a Roman-Dutch legal system, also recognises the concept. It should be appreciated that there are other legal systems in the British Isles such as in the Isle of Man and the various Channel Islands. None of these form part of the UK for tax purposes. For the purposes of domicil these Islands are separate countries (or territories) from the UK.

Under English law, every individual has a particular domicil but this is not to say that English law does not recognise that under other legal systems the same individual may have a different domicil. Sometimes a 'double' domicil is provided for, e.g. see UK-USA Estate Duty Convention. It is impossible to provide a short comprehensive definition of domicil but one could say that an individual under English law is domiciled in the country (or a law district in a country) which he regards as his permanent homeland. Or to put it another way, it is the place where he intends to end his days.

Domicil is *not* synonomous with residence or nationality but they may well run together, e.g. an individual may have a French domicil, be a French resident and a French national.

Domicil is quite different from the French concept of domicile habituelle. Confusion is often caused by some Double Tax Treaties which head the article dealing with residence with the words 'Fiscal Domicile'.

There are various forms of domicil:

(1) *Domicil of origin:* This is acquired by an individual at birth and he takes his father's domicil. Everyone under English law has a domicil of origin.

(2) *Domicil of choice:* This is acquired by establishing both actual physical residence in a particular country (other than that of a previous domicil i.e. a domicil of origin, or the previous domicil of choice)) ***and*** an intention to remain there permanently. The intention to remain is paramount and there must be a weighty form of physical presence together with evidence of such an intention. To help show the acquisition of a domicil of choice any links with the country of the previous domicil should be severed, e.g. directorships, membership of clubs and associations and active business.[6] Conversely, as many links as possible should be made with the new country where it is intended to acquire a domicil of choice, e.g. by making a Will in local form to deal with the estate in the new territory or country, memberships of clubs, associations, active business interests, etc.[6] In other words there must be a clean break.

There is a presumption (which is rebuttable) against an individual having an intention to acquire a domicil of choice in a country (or territory) where the conditions, religion and customs are so different from those of his domicil of origin.

Often, an individual will have an intention to remain in the country of the domicil of choice for the rest of his life although when pressed will admit that the decision is not irrevocable, i.e. there could be future events which might cause him to change his mind. However, this may not be regarded as fatal to the acquisition of a domicil of choice. Nonetheless, it is not helpful. The right ingredients for a domicil of choice will be lacking if an individual intends to remain in the new country for a fixed period of time or alternatively there is an intention to leave at a future unspecified date.

Such a domicil can always be abandoned for another domicil of choice. It is easier to lose a domicil of choice than a domicil of origin, but it should be appreciated that to show the loss there has to be a physical cessation of actual residence ***and*** an abandonment of the intention to live there permanently. In the event that a domicil of choice is abandoned without another domicil of choice being acquired, then the domicil of origin revives. When planning moves between countries, it is particularly important that an individual with a foreign domicil of choice and a UK domicil of origin who permanently leaves the country of his domicil of choice for another country should do so in such a way as to avoid the domicil of origin reviving i.e. there should be no period of 'limbo' between the two domicils of choice.

(3) *Domicil of dependency*[8]*:* This applies mainly now to young children. Under the English law a child is capable of obtaining his own domicil at 16 (or younger on marriage!).

Prior to January 1st, 1974, a woman always acquired on marriage the domicil of her husband (sometimes called a domicil of acquisition). On January 1st, 1974 the Domicil and Matrimonial Proceedings Act 1973[7] came into force. The basic objective of the Act was to enable a wife where appropriate (e.g. when separated from her husband) to acquire (or retain?) a different domicil from her husband. No doubt it was the intention of the legislature that there should be some physical severance between the husband and the wife but in the way that the Act has been worded there is no such provision. There are two basic positions:

a) *pre-January 1st, 1974 marriages*[8]*:* The general position is that such wives will have acquired the domicil of their husband on marriage and will retain it unless thereafter there is some act of severance. As of yet, there is no case law but it is considered that a positive act on the part of a wife will be necessary, e.g. if she takes an independent career which necessitates frequent separation from her husband and residence in a country other than that country where her husband resides and is domiciled.

b) *post-January 1st, 1974 position*[8]*:* It is not possible here to detail the various permutations that are now available but suffice it to say on marriage a woman will now only acquire the domicil of her husband if the two elements necessary for the acquisition of a domicil of choice (see 2 ante) are evident e.g. if an English girl married a Frenchman who worked for a private concern in the UK, then it might be difficult to show that she had acquired a French domicil until she went to live with her husband in France.

The CTT legislation specifically provides for the eventuality that sometimes a husband and wife will not have the same domicil.

(4) *Deemed domicil (for CTT purposes only):* FA s.45 (as amended) provides that a person will be treated as domiciled in the UK at a point in time if:

a) he was domiciled in the UK:

(i) on *or* after 10th December 1974 *and*

(ii) at any time within three years of a particular point in time

i.e. even if an emigrant leaves the UK and acquires under English law another domicil then for CTT purposes he shall be treated as having retained his UK domicil until a period of three years has elapsed from the date of leaving the UK (but see (c) below).

OR:

b) he was resident in the UK for tax purposes on or after 10th December 1974 *and* in *not less* than 17 out of the last 20 years, e.g. if a person has been resident in the UK for UK tax purposes (but in deciding this any place of abode that he may have available is ignored) for 16 consecutive years and is resident at the beginning of the following tax year then he is treated as being domiciled in the UK, i.e. his true domicil is ignored.[10]

OR:

c) Since 10th December 1974 he has become domiciled in the 'Islands' *and* prior to becoming domiciled there he was domiciled in the UK. The 'Islands' means the Channel Islands and the Isle of Man.

Domicil has now a greatly extended meaning for CTT purposes[9] and many people have been or are about to be caught (often unknowingly) in its web. A point to note is that the operation of s.45 may well be restricted by the existence of an estate duty treaty. FA 1975 Schedule 7, paragraph 7, provides for this in respect of deaths. An individual caught by s.45 (1) (c) can only escape by emigrating from the 'Islands' to a country other than in the UK. The modifications introduced by FA 1977 s.49 (set out in Appendix 5) apply only to very restricted circumstances. A foreign-domiciled person caught by s.45 (i) (b) if he wishes to avoid it has to become a non-resident of the UK for a period of one, two or three years where appropriate so as to break the sixteen year period.

Domicil in the strict sense arises by operation of law and the application of well established objective tests.[11] There is a presumption under English law that there is not a change in an individual's domicil. Mere statements by an individual of what *he* considers his domicil to be are frequently coloured by sentiments, confusion with nationality and/or residence, and even wishful thinking and so are unreliable. Quite apart from the statutory novelties of domicil introduced recently, it is often difficult to be certain about an individual's domicil which sometimes can only be ascertained long after the event. Great care should be taken before taking any course that depends on an exclusion through a foreign domicil.

Practice: As a practical matter, it is advisable for an individual who comes temporarily (even for an extended period) to the UK to establish to the satisfaction of the UK Revenue that he has retained his foreign domicil.[10] Failure to do so properly (or not at all) usually leads to delays if not difficulties at a later stage.[11] There are special tax returns for foreign domiciled individuals and the UK Revenue usually require a special domicil questionnaire to be completed.[12] Care must be taken over completion of any other Revenue forms and other statements made.[11] By way of conclusion on domicil, it is worth considering the facts of a recent case.

CIR –v– BULLOCK (COURT OF APPEAL 25th JUNE 1976)

The taxpayer had a Canadian domicil of origin. He was Canadian born and went to school and university in Canada. In 1932 he came to England and subsequently he joined the RAF. In 1946 he married an English girl. He retired from the RAF in 1959 and until 1961 when he inherited a substantial sum from his father's estate in Canada he worked in England. After 1961 he retired. During this period both he and his wife had made numerous visits to Canada but his wife disliked it and was not prepared to live there. Accordingly they remained in England and she purchased their UK residence. The taxpayer remained in England although he wanted to return hoping that he would be able to do this if his wife changed her mind or died before him. Before 1966 the taxpayer had given up hope of returning to Canada during his wife's lifetime.

The Inland Revenue claimed that he had lost his domicil of origin and had acquired a domicil of choice in England. The Special Commissioners held that the taxpayer had not established a domicil of choice in England but in the Court of first instance their decision was reversed. But the Court of Appeal unanimously decided that the taxpayer had retained his domicil of origin. Lord Justice Buckley said 'it seems impossible not to hold that the appellant has always maintained a firm intention to return to Canada in the event of his surviving his wife'.

This case is beneficial to taxpayers with foreign domicils particularly foreign domicils of origin who visit the UK. Conversely with individuals with UK domicils – particularly UK domicils of origin who leave the UK, then it does show how difficult it is for them to lose their UK domicils. Under F (No. 1) A 1974 s.45 (1) (c) the taxpayer in this case is treated as being domiciled in the UK for CTT purposes only. Not surprisingly the Revenue utilise this authority a lot in questions of domicil. Perhaps the most cogent word on domicils of choice are those of Scarman J in the Estate of Fuld deceased (No. 3) (1966) 2 WLR.

'A domicil of choice is acquired only if it be affirmatively shown that the propositus is resident within a territory subject to a distinctive legal system with the intention, formed independently of external pressures, of residing there indefinitely. If a man intends to return to the land of his birth upon a clearly foreseen and reasonably anticipated contingency, e.g. the end of his job, the intention required by law is lacking; but, if he has in mind only a vague possibility, such as making a fortune (a modern example might be winning a football pool) or some sentiment about dying in the land of his fathers, such a state of mind is consistent with the intention required by law.'

C. Residence

There is no statutory definition of residence and whether or not a person resides in the UK will be decided (often after the event) on the facts of his case. Nonetheless with a case it is extremely helpful to ascertain the facts to date and make assumptions as to the future so as to be able to plan ahead.

Before looking at the UK Revenue practice and the effect of provisions of Double Tax Treaties, it is prudent to look at the various factors that constantly occur when considering residence.

i) ACCOMMODATION AVAILABLE FOR OCCUPATION IN THE UK[13]

It has been established for a long time that if an individual visits the UK for one day in a tax year ***and*** has accommodation available for his occupation ***then*** he will be treated as resident in the UK. Who or what actually owns the accommodation is irrelevant – it may be rented, owned by a foreign company or even available through an informal 'understanding'.

The position is, subject to one exception, clearcut and straightforward. ICTA 1970 s.50 provides the one statutory exception[14] to this rule. It simply provides that where an individual is engaged in full time work abroad, then the question of whether or not he is resident in the UK shall be determined ignoring the fact that accommodation is available. It is important that no part of the work, other than incidentals, is carried on in the UK. 'Incidentals' is extremely narrowly construed. The position of non-working spouses is not catered for.[15]

This harsh rule is often ameliorated by Revenue practice and Double Tax Treaties.[16]

ii) Purposes of Visits to and Connections with the UK

Occasionally the reasons for visits to the UK can be material. Usually they are not and the fact of physical presence alone is the main factor.[17] Involuntary stays through illness or detention can result in residence. In hardship cases, the UK Revenue can be reasonable.

iii) Physical Presence in the UK and the Making of Visits to the UK[17]

A person will always be resident in the UK if he is present there for a period of six months or more (whether in one or more visits) in a tax year. Six months is 183 days. In practice, the days of arrival and departure are usually ignored. ICTA 1970 s.51[18] states that if an individual be in the UK for a temporary purpose only he will not be treated as resident if:

a) he was not physically present in the UK for a period of six months *and*
b) he was not in the UK with a view to establishing residence there.

Between the position of an individual being resident as a result of physical presence in the UK for a period of six months or more and the position of an individual who is physically present for a lesser period, there are numerous authorities. It is impossible to briefly deal with the authorities and much of their content appears in Revenue Practice. Two often quoted authorities are:

Levene -v- IRC 1927 2B 38: Individuals will be resident if their visits to the UK form part of the 'regular system of life' which the individuals 'made their abode and lived in the country for a period between four and five months each year. . .'.

IRC -v- Lysaght 1928 A.C.234: An individual with a previous history of residence in the UK emigrated. He retained a directorship of a UK company and visited the UK to attend monthly board meetings, staying for about a week on each occasion. It was *held* that he was both resident and ordinarily resident.

iv) Residence in the previous year

ICTA 1970 s.49[18] provides that every ordinarily resident (i.e. habitually resident) British subject or Irish citizen shall be treated as resident in the UK if he has only gone abroad for the purposes of occasional residence. This provision has no application to immigrants and it is clearly aimed at British subjects who emigrate or have nomadic tendencies. For them there must be a clean break unless it can clearly be shown that the reason for going abroad is not for purposes of occasional residence.

The general rules[17] are that an individual will be treated as resident in the UK (subject to any Double Tax Treaty) if he falls into one of the following categories:
a) If he is present in the UK for six months or more in a tax year
or
b) He has accommodation available for occupation in the UK and visits the UK for one day in a tax year. (The one exception to this rule is where he has a full-time occupation abroad.)
or
c) If he is physically present in the UK (with no accommodation) during four consecutive tax years for periods averaging three months or more per tax year.

It is quite possible for a person to be resident and ordinarily resident in several countries. Where this arises any appropriate tax treaty should be carefully perused.

The definition of the UK for residence purposes is extremely wide and covers England, Wales, Scotland, Northern Ireland and their territorial waters. Also included is the UK continental shelf (and the water above) in respect of exploration or exploitation activities taking place thereon or therein. The definition of UK is contained in FA 1973 s.38 the full text of which appears in Appendix 1A.FA 1973 s.38 is subject to the provisions of any double tax treaty.

Usually it is far easier to determine if an individual is resident than to determine if he is ordinarily resident.

D. Ordinary Residence

There is some difficulty in defining ordinary residence. There is no statutory definition and also no statutory differentiation between ordinary residence and residence.[19] Further, some learned Judges have suggested that they can see no difference between the two forms of status. There are, however, numerous references in the taxing Acts to the two forms of status so it seems clear that there is a difference.

IRC -v- Lysaght (1928 A.C. 234): '"ordinarily" means... established custom or practice or as a matter of regular practice or occurrence...' to be contrasted with "casual or occasional"'.

Thomson -v- Minister of National Revenue (S.C. Canada): 'expression "ordinarily resident" has a restricted significance. It is held to mean residence in the course of the customary mode of life of the person concerned and is contrasted with special or occasional or casual residence. The general mode of life is therefore relevant to its application'. (approved in *Miesages -v- IRC 1957 37 TC 493).*

It is clear that an individual can be ordinarily resident in the UK without being resident.[19] An individual might be abroad for a whole tax year in a hospital (or gaol!). Conversely, a visitor to this country who becomes resident in one tax year only will usually be treated as not ordinarily resident. It seems that less attention is paid by practictioners to determining whether or not an individual is ordinarily resident or not.

E. Shedding Residence and Becoming Resident

(1) Potential Non-Residents[20]

(i) Without full-time Work Abroad

The retention of accommodation available for occupation in the UK can result in the emigrant not only remaining resident but also ordinarily resident. Again, even if he has no accommodation available but his visits to the UK average more than three months each tax year over four consecutive tax years then he will be ordinarily resident (as well as resident).

It is advantageous for an emigrant to obtain a provisional ruling from the Revenue that he is not ordinarily resident. To do this he must satisfy the Revenue over his accommodation position, e.g. has he sold or let his UK home and bought one abroad and make a declaration that his visits will not exceed on average three months or more in each tax year over four consecutive tax years.

The provisional ruling is confirmed (depending on the facts of the case) after he has remained abroad for a period which includes a complete tax year. If he is not able to obtain this provisional ruling, then he is treated as remaining resident and ordinarily resident. His liability is adjusted if appropriate at the end of the third tax year. During this period he will not be however treated as resident if he does not visit the UK during one tax year.[20] Otherwise he is treated as being resident and ordinarily resident which is obviously very disadvantageous.

(ii) With full-time Work Abroad[21]

If an emigrant leaves to work full-time abroad, then provided certain criteria are satisfied he is treated as not ordinarily resident (and not resident) from the day following the date of departure.

(2) POTENTIAL RESIDENTS

If an individual having previously lived abroad comes to the UK to take up permanent residence, then he will be treated as resident and ordinarily resident from the date of arrival.[20] A visitor (who has no accommodation available) will be treated as ordinarily resident (as well as resident) if his visits to the the UK over four tax years average three months or more. If an individual comes to the UK to work for a short period of time (say two years) he will usually not be treated as ordinarily resident until he has (if ever) been in the UK for three years. Unless of course this was obvious from the start. If, however, he comes to the UK with no definite intention, then he is normally regarded as ordinarily resident from the beginning of the tax year in which the third anniversary of his arrival falls. If during this period of time the individual makes up his mind to stay for an extended period he will be treated as ordinarily resident from that time.

F. Double Tax Treaties

It is possible for an individual to be resident in two (or more) countries. Where two such countries have a modern Double Tax Treaty, it will contain provisions to determine the individual's residential status. Somewhat misleadingly some of the treaty articles dealing with this subject are headed 'Fiscal Domicile'.

A typical article is in the US-UK Double Tax Treaty. Article 4 (2) reads:

(2) Where by reason of the provisions of paragraph (1) an individual is a resident of both contracting states, then the individual's tax status shall be determined as follows:

(a) the individual shall be deemed to be a resident of the contracting state in which he has a permanent home available to him. If the individual has a permanent home available to him in both contracting states or in neither of the contracting states, he shall be deemed to be a resident of the contracting state with which his personal and economic relations are closest (centre of vital interests);

(b) if the contracting state in which the individual's centre of vital interests is located cannot be determined, he shall be deemed to be a resident of that contracting state in which he has an habitual abode;

(c) if the individual has an habitual abode in both contracting states or in neither of them, he shall be deemed to be a resident of the contracting state of which he is a national; and

(d) if the individual is a national of both contracting states or of neither of them, the competent authorities of the contracting states shall settle the question by mutual agreement.

1. See B post
2. See C post
3. Or for any other purpose e.g. Social Security
4. ICTA 1970 s.122 (2) (a) see Appendix 3
5. But he must be a British Subject or Irish Citizen ICTA 1970 s.122 (2) (a) see Appendix 3
6. See Section XI Checklist B 2.1
7. See Appendix 1A
8. Under proposed revisions to the UK-US Double Tax Treaty US National wives of UK domiciled husbands who were married prior to 1st January 1974 shall be deemed to have been married after 1st January 1974 for the purposes of determining her domicil on or after 6th April 1976. This proposal is restricted to income tax and capital gains tax. It effects only the domicil of dependency and as such a US National wife's domicil will now be determined in the normal way. It will be of interest to see if other tax treaties are similarly amended or new treaties include this sort of provision.
9. See Appendix 5. But see some of the exceptions e.g. FA 1975 Schedule 7 (3) in Section VI E.
10. See s.45 (i) (b) table in Appendix 5
11. The individual visiting the UK should consider Section XI Part A 1 & 2
12. See the forms in Appendix 2
13. See Appendix 1B paras. 28, 29 & 30
14. See Appendix 1A
15. See Appendix 1B para 12
16. See E post
17. See Appendix 1B para 20 and particularly para 21
18. See Appendix 1B paras 11, 16, 18, 19, 78 and Appendix 1C Extra-Statutory Concessions A.14 & D.2
19. See Appendix 1B paras 6, 7, 8, 10, 13, 19, 21
20. See Appendix 1B paras 19-27, 64, Appendix 1C Extra-Statutory Concessions A.14 & D.2 and Section X A 1 & 3
21. See Appendix 1B para 18

Section III: Income Tax – Outlines

A. Introduction

Income tax is generally levied on individuals although non-resident companies may in certain circumstances be subject to income tax as well. The tax is levied in respect of years of assessment; such a year begins on 6th April in one year and ends on 5th April in the subsequent year. For ease of reference, a year of assessment is referred to as a tax year. For the tax year 1977/78 the basic rate of income tax is 34% and details of the higher rates and personal allowances appear in Appendix 3.

Income tax is an annual tax. Its levy is proposed by the Chancellor of the Exchequer in the Budget Speech. This is then followed by a Finance Bill which incorporates the Government's proposal. The Provisional Collection of Taxes Act 1868 ensures that income tax can be levied during a period of 4 months after the end of a tax year, so as to allow time for the passage of the Finance Bill through Parliament. Before the end of that 4-month period the Finance Bill must have been enacted – or income tax cannot be levied! The income tax legislation is periodically consolidated. The most recent consolidation is the Income and Corporation Taxes Act 1970 ('ICTA 1970'). Unless otherwise mentioned, all statutory references in this Section are to ICTA 1970.

Matters of administration collection and procedure are dealt with in the Taxes Management Act ('TMA') 1970.

Tax administration is under the control of the Commissioners of Inland Revenue and for the purposes of administration the UK is divided into tax districts, each of which has an Inspector of Taxes. As is in the case of a number of other countries, assessments are issued by an Inspector and the tax is paid to a Collector of Taxes. Unpaid tax carries interest, at present at the rate of 9% per annum, generally from 30 days after the date of the assessment until payment.

No person is liable to pay income tax in any tax year unless in that tax year he is either resident[1] in the UK or he has a source of income in the UK. Everyone, whether resident or not, is taxable in respect of his income from UK sources. A non-resident may, however, be exempt pursuant to a Double Tax Treaty.

A resident is taxable in respect of his world-wide income, unless the remittance basis applies to him as explained later in this and the following Section.

For income tax purposes, the sources of income are divided into six Schedules, some of which are sub-divided into Cases.

The Revenue cannot charge tax under one Schedule where the income properly falls to be dealt with under another Schedule and if a profit or a gain does not fall within any of the Schedules, it escapes income tax – although it may be a capital gain and fall to be treated accordingly.

Each Schedule deals with a specific source of income:

Schedule A – Income from land in the UK.

Schedule B – Income from woodlands in the UK.

Schedule C – Interest payable on UK Government stocks or stocks of the Republic of Ireland and the stocks of foreign Governments where the interest is paid in the UK (including coupons collected in respect of bearer issues).

Schedule D – This is divided into six Cases:

Case I	– profits of a trade
Case II	– profits of a vocation or profession
Case III	– annual payments, interest, annuities, small maintenance payments and discounts
Case IV	– income arising from foreign securities (these have a restricted meaning of a secured debt and do not include equity interests in stocks and shares) other than foreign Government stocks
Case V	– income arising from all other types of assets out of the UK[2]
Case VI	– any profit or income gains not falling under any other Schedule or Case[2]

Schedule E[5] – Income arising from employment and pensions. Emoluments from employments are covered in these cases as follows[6]:

Case I	– UK and foreign emoluments of a person resident and ordinarily resident in the UK regardless of where the duties are performed. (Subject possibly to certain deductions).
Case II	– Emoluments of a person who is not resident[1] or, if resident, is not ordinarily resident[1] in the UK in respect of duties performed in the UK. (Subject possibly to certain deductions)
Case III	– Emoluments received in the UK by a resident. Tax will only be chargeable under Case III if it is not chargeable under Cases I or II.

Schedule F – Dividends and other distributions made by United Kingdom-resident corporations. See Section IX.

Income which falls under Schedule D Cases IV and V is taxable only if the taxpayer is resident[1] in the UK. In the case of a person *resident but not domiciled in the UK* such income is liable to tax on the remittance basis – i.e. tax is only paid on so much of the income as is brought into the UK.[2] Emoluments from an office or employment all the duties of which are performed wholly outside the UK are similarly treated when the holder of the office or employment is domiciled abroad and the employer is not resident in the UK.

B. The Schedules A to F

(1) SCHEDULE A - INCOME FROM REAL PROPERTY

This Schedule applies to annual profits or gains from land, including rents, rent charges and any other annual payments reserved in respect of or arising from, land, but not including mineral rents and royalties, which are taxed differently, nor income from land outside the UK.

Rents from furnished lettings can be assessed under Schedule A if an election is made within two years of the end of the chargeable period, otherwise rents from furnished lettings are assessed under Schedule D, Case VI.

For the purpose of tax under Schedule A, profits or gains arising to a person in any chargeable period are computed by taking the rents to which he becomes entitled in the period less the deductions referred to in ss. 72 - 77. No other deductions are allowed. Expenditure is allowable if it is made:

(a) in respect of maintenance repairs insurance and management (improvements or additions to the property are not deductible);

(b) in respect of services provided by the tax-payer for which he received no separate consideration;

(c) rates (see Section X 'Miscellaneous') and similar charges on the occupier which the tax-payer is obliged to pay;

(d) any rentcharge ground rent or similar annual or other periodical payment, including rent to another landlord.

The liability under Schedule A is charged by reference to the rental income, etc., to which the owner becomes entitled in the year of assessment rather than on the income from such sources which he has actually received. As a general rule, expenditure incurred on a lease cannot be deducted from income from another lease, nor can a person who is entitled to rent under a lease deduct expenditure on repairs incurred by reason of dilapidation of the premises which occurred before he became so entitled. These positions can however be mitigated in respect of rents which are not actually received but are obtainable but only on a claim if:

i) the person owing the rent has defaulted and the claimant can show that he has taken all possible steps to enforce payment

ii) the claimant has waived payment reasonably and for no consideration in order to avoid hardship

Lease Premiums

Sections 80–85 contain provisions for the taxation of lease premiums. Where a lease is granted for 50 years or less and its terms require the payment of a premium, a fraction of D/50 of the premium is treated as if it were rent to which the landlord became entitled on the grant of the lease. 'D' represents the number of years comprised in the lease minus 1. There are a number of anti-avoidance provisions which prevent escape from tax on lease premiums either by granting a lease for a period which exceeds fifty years but contains provisions for its early termination, or requiring the tenant to carry out works (a sort of 'premium' in kind) or granting a lease at an undervalue and assigning it for a capital sum. When the lease is granted out of a superior lease which was also granted at a premium, the charge only applies to the difference between the two premiums.

Rent paid to non-residents

S.89 requires that where payment is made to a person whose normal place of abode is outside the UK then the tenant or collecting agent should deduct tax at the basic rate from the payment.

(2) Schedule B – Income from Woodlands

(3) Schedule C – Income from Public Revenue by way of dividend

These Schedules are of limited practical note and will not therefore be covered in this work. Investment in woodlands is encouraged by tax incentives to plant.

(4) Schedule D[3]

This extremely important Schedule is subdivided into six cases:

Cases I and II

Tax is charged on the profits of any trade, profession or vocation carried on in the UK but does not apply where such a trade, profession or vocation is carried on wholly outside the UK. In this latter case the income is foreign income and falls under Schedule D Case V in respect of which special rules apply and are dealt with later and in Section IV.

The tax treatment of trades (chargeable under Case I) on the one hand and professions or vocations (chargeable under Case II) on the other is virtually identical.

'Trade' is defined as including an adventure in the nature of trade so that the profits of a single transaction if it has the nature of a trading transaction will be taxable under Schedule D Case I if the transaction is carried out within the UK.

A non-resident who trades in goods manufactured abroad may be able to arrange his affairs so that he is trading *with* rather than *within* the UK and escape tax altogether. Subject to that, the profit from the purchase and re-sale of any asset which cannot be said to have been acquired for either investment or for the personal pleasure of the acquirer, will generally be taxed under Schedule D Case I.

Similarly, the profits of the sale of an asset which was acquired with a view to being re-sold at a profit. In the absence of a comprehensive definition of the concept of trade there will however, be numerous difficult borderline cases where it is uncertain as to whether or not a trading activity has been carried out.

Where a trade is conducted *with* rather than *within* the UK, the source of the income is outside the UK and in accordance with the principles mentioned earlier, there will be no charge to UK income tax on the non-resident who trades in that manner. A trade is carried on where the operation takes place from which the profits in substance arise, and it follows that those operations should be carried out abroad. Thus, for example, the manufacture of goods and the greater parts of the sales contracts should be carried out abroad and the contract itself should be made there. Thus an agent employed in the UK should do no more than collect orders for acceptance or rejection by the principal abroad and should therefore have no power to accept orders himself.

The mere purchase of goods in the UK, whether directly or through an agent, for export, has long been held not to constitute trading in the UK.

Two particular types of trading receive special treatment:

i) Buying and selling securities

The ordinary investor will, of course, from time to time acquire securities, hoping to hold them in a portfolio with a view to ultimate realisation when a profit has been established. Generally the Revenue are slow to assess any such profit on a trading basis, mainly because if they did, a loss would have to similarly be allowed. However, if the scale of this type of activity increases then there may be an assessment on the basis of dealing in securities.

ii) Buying and selling land

The treatment of transactions in land is quite different and in practice a profit arising on a sale of non-income producing land which was not purchased with a view to occupation for personal use, will be charged to income tax, either as a trading profit or as unearned income under s.488 which is briefly mentioned in Section V. A sale of land may now also give rise to a charge to Development Land Tax which is outside the scope of this work.

Cases I and II deductions

The position is extremely complicated and generally expenses must be 'wholly and exclusively' carried out for the benefit of the trade, profession or vocation and not be restricted by s.130 which lists a number of non-deductible payments.

Case III

Interest, annuities (and similar annual payments) and discounts

The distinguishing characteristic of income charged under Schedule D Case III is that it is 'pure income profit' which increases the income of the recipient by the same amount as it decreases the income of the payer. It follows that if the recipient is to render some service, or otherwise incur expense of a Revenue nature, before he is entitled to the income, the income is not 'pure income profit' and accordingly not chargeable under Case III.

Most payments of income chargeable under Case III are to be made under deduction of tax at the basic rate. Generally, interest is paid gross but yearly interest paid by a company or to a non-resident is subject to tax at the basic rate ***unless*** the interest is paid on an advance by a UK bank, or by such a bank in the ordinary course of its business.[4]

Where tax is deducted at source, the payer, if an individual, will be entitled to keep the deduction for himself if he pays the annual payment out of taxed income. In all other cases, the payer will have to account for the tax to the Revenue. The recipient will not be assessable to tax at the basic rate in respect of the payment received. But for the purposes of income tax at the higher rates the payment is taken into account as the income of the recipient (and deducted in computing the income tax of the payer). It should also be borne in mind that as this type of income is unearned income, it will attract the investment income surcharge where the recipient is an individual. This is whether the individual is resident or not. If he is not resident in the UK then he may of course be protected by a Double Tax Treaty provision.

Cases IV and V – Income from foreign sources[2]

These cases are particularly important for the individual who is not domiciled[1] in the UK, for although he may be resident and ordinarily resident in the UK, such a person is assessed only so much of his foreign income as he remits to the UK.

Case IV applies to, what is termed under Case IV 'securities'. These have been defined as meaning a debt or claim the payment of which is in some way secured. The security would generally consist of a right to some fund or property for payment, e.g. a debenture or mortgage.

Case V applies to income from 'possessions' and this has an extremely wide meaning and covers all non-UK sources of income other than:

- Case IV 'Securities'
- Those foreign pensions taxed under Schedule E
- Emoluments taxed under Schedule E.

Case V includes all dividends from foreign shares, profits from trades, professions or vocations carried on abroad, foreign alimony and rental income from overseas property.

Case VI

This case charges to income tax any annual profits or gains not otherwise covered by any other case of Schedule D. Thus this case is the general 'mopping up' case of what is essentially a 'mop up' schedule. Casual earnings and income from furnished lettings have been held to be taxable under Case VI but its most frequent application flows from the number of specific statutory provisions pursuant to which a charge under Case VI is imposed. In the anti-avoidance legislation, the charge to tax is often made under Case VI.

Basis of Charge to Tax under Schedule D

Cases I and II

Tax is charged on the whole of the profits of a trade, vocation or profession carried on wholly or partly within the UK, whether or not the individual is resident in the UK. From 6th April 1974 an individual who is resident, ordinarily resident and domiciled in the UK and derives income from a trade, profession or vocation carried on *wholly* abroad will be liable to income tax on the whole of this income (whether remitted or not) less a special deduction of 25% of the income which will not be liable to tax. It will be remembered, however, that an individual who is so resident will be considered as trading in the UK so that the 25% deduction or as the case may be the remittance basis, will in practice only be available to a member of an overseas partnership. This is dealt with at greater length in Section IV later. It will be remembered that the expenses of travelling to the base of the overseas operation will only be deductible in a computation of trading profits for tax purposes if the overseas base forms part of the trade carried on in the UK and not of a separate overseas trading operation which constitutes a separate trade.

Tax is normally charged on a preceding year basis. Where a trader keeps his accounts on a yearly basis, tax is charged on a particular tax year by reference to the profits shown in the accounts for the accounting period which ended in the preceding year. Special rules apply where a new trade is set up and where an existing trade is discontinued. The preceding year basis is modified where a trader does not keep his accounts as aforesaid (or no accounts at all).

Case III

The income is taxable on the preceding year basis with special rules for opening and closing years (see s.119–121). Examples of Case III are bank deposit interest, annuities and annual payments.

Cases IV and V[2]

Tax is charged on the full amount of the income arising in the year preceding the actual tax year (year of assessment) whether or not the income has been, or will be received in the UK. The two cases where the remittance basis applies are given below. One of the results of that rule is that a new resident will be charged on income which he received during the tax year preceding his arrival, even though he was then not resident in the UK. The cases in which the remittance basis applies are:

a) Where the taxpayer is domiciled outside the UK or
b) Where the taxpayer is domiciled, resident but not ordinarily resident in the UK provided he is a British subject or a citizen of the Irish Republic.

Case VI

Tax is charged on the profits received during the tax year, i.e. the actual basis.

(5) Schedule E – Income from offices, employments and pensions[5]

This Schedule is of considerable concern to the individual coming to the UK to take up employment. The Schedule is divided into three Cases:

Case I

This covers the most usual situation of an individual who is resident and ordinarily resident in the UK. The charge to tax is on any salary in the tax year wherever it arises and whether or not it is received in or remitted to the UK. There is, however, an important exemption, which is dealt with in greater detail in Section IV. Where the duties of an office or employment are performed outside the UK, a deduction will be allowed of either 25% or 100%, depending on the length of the period of absence from the UK of the individual concerned. If the duties are performed abroad for a period of not less than 365 days, the salary will be effectively free of tax. If the duties are performed abroad during not less than 30 days (whether these days are consecutive or not) in any tax year a deduction of 25% will be allowed before computing the taxable salary (on a proportionate basis).

An individual who wishes to claim the 25% deduction, notwithstanding the fact that he will be outside the UK for less than 30 days, *may* still be able to do so if he carries out the duties of his overseas employment under a contract of employment separate from any employment in the UK.

A foreign domiciled employee who:

a) is employed by a non-resident employer and
b) performs his duties *wholly* outside the UK

will continue to be subject to UK tax on the remittance basis and similarly any such employee should also be interested in a separate contract of employment.

Foreign Emoluments

This term contained in s.181 (1) denotes:

'emoluments of a person not domiciled in the United Kingdom from an office or employment under or with any person body of persons or partnership resident outside and not resident inside the United Kingdom'

Any such employee will be taxed on 50% of his emoluments for an office of employment, the duties of which are performed wholly or partially within the UK unless the employee has been resident in the UK for more than 9 consecutive years in which case he will be taxed on 75% of his emoluments. The position of such an employee who performs all (or substantially all) of his duties abroad is summarised above.

These foreign aspects are given greater detail in Section IV.

Case II

This case applies where the employee is either not resident or not ordinarily resident in the UK in a tax year. The charge to tax is on so much of the salary as is attributable to the duties performed in the UK. If the salary qualifies as foreign emoluments (see above) then the same deductions as are mentioned above in connection with the corresponding situation under Case I are allowed.

Case III

This case provides for the remittance basis. Since 1974 the only person to whom Case III can apply is a foreign domiciled employee who is:

(a) resident in the UK
(b) is employed by a non-resident employer and
(c) is performing all of his duties abroad.

When discussing Schedule E earnings above, the word 'salary' is used for convenience but in the legislation the word 'emoluments' is used which is defined in s.183 (1) as including 'all salaries, fees, wages, perquisites and profits whatsoever'. FA 1976 contains extensive provisions, the effect of which is to charge to tax what is termed 'the cash equivalent' of almost every benefit provided by any employer for an employee. Any voluntary pension granted to an individual who has ceased to hold an office is charged under s.182. Nevertheless there are in fact 'fringe benefits' which give real benefit to an employee even though he pays tax on the benefit, e.g. provision of cars, health insurance, etc.

Expenses will only be deductible for tax purposes if they were 'wholly exclusively and necessarily' incurred in the performance of the job and related duties. Judicial interpretation has narrowed this concept down to the point where very few expenses may be so deducted.

Payments by an employer to provide retirement benefits for directors and employees are taxable under Schedule E unless the scheme is 'approved'.

After FA 1974 the Revenue published a booklet IR 25 and the relevant chapters of it are reproduced in Appendix 4 including a table showing the various categories for taxation under Schedule E. Whilst considering IR 25, it should be appreciated that their contents have been affected by FA 1977.

(6) SCHEDULE F – DIVIDENDS ETC. FROM UK COMPANIES

This Schedule was changed fundamentally with effect from 6th April 1973 when the imputation Corporation Tax system was introduced. The key features of the imputation system are described in Section IX.

C. Exemptions from Income Tax

The following types of income inter alia are exempt from income tax:

(a) The first £40 interest on deposits with the National Savings Bank and deposits with a Trustee Savings Bank – but not investment deposits. N.B.: Where, as is usual, the incomes of husband and wife are aggregated, each is entitled to the exemption – s.414.
(b) Accumulated interest on National Savings Certificates Issues – s.95.
(c) Some Social Security benefits – s.219
(d) Exit or terminal bonuses under agreed contractual savings schemes (the best known is the Save As You Earn (SAYE) arrangement) – s.415
(e) The interest earned on damages for personal injuries – s.375 (a)
(f) Scholarships – s.375
(g) Interest from certain specified UK Government securities, where the person beneficially entitled to the income is not resident or ordinarily resident in the UK – s.99. (Appendix 7 lists these securities).

N.B. – Building Society interest is not free of tax but is treated as having suffered basic rate income tax by deduction at source. But no claim for repayment of this notional deduction of income tax may be made by the depositor if his overall tax rate is less than the basic rate deemed to have been suffered by the deposit interest. It follows that when an individual pays higher rate tax, he will be charged on the interest received after grossing up at the basic rate.

D. The Unified System of Personal Taxation

The Unified System of Personal Taxation was introduced for the tax year 1973/74 and subsequent years. It marked the abolition of earned income relief and the assessment of surtax on incomes which exceeded a certain level. It applies to individuals, and to such companies as are not subject to Corporation Tax (see Section IX) because they are not resident in the UK. Now there is a single rate of tax called the 'basic rate' which applies to all income. The basic rate is fixed annually by Parliament and is for the year 1977/78 – 34%. In addition to the basic rate, higher rates of tax become payable by individuals when certain levels of income are reached. Again, these higher rates of tax can vary from year to year according to the Finance Act.

Investment Income Surcharge

The heavy discrimination against unearned income, e.g. investment income such as dividends, interest, (as opposed to earned income like salaries, fees, earnings) is maintained under the unified system. In addition to the higher rates of income tax an investment income surcharge on an individual's total investment income in excess of £1,500 at an additional rate of 10%. On investment income in excess of £2,000 the rate is increased to 15%.

Total Income

Before computing the liability to income tax and the investment income surcharge, the total income from the tax year of the taxpayer must be ascertained. The total income for any tax year is the aggregate of the income for that year computed in accordance with the rules attributable under each relevant Schedule for that year. The income will be that of the tax year except that tax under Schedule D, Cases I to V will be charged by reference to the income of the preceding tax year.

Charges on Income

Having ascertained the total income the next step is to deduct from this total income certain charges, e.g.

- certain annual payments which the individual has undertaken to pay
- loan interest: relief for loan interest is available in a few cases. Interest on loans used for defraying the cost of purchasing (or improving) a house or flat used as a principal residence is relievable to the extent that the loan does not exceed £25,000. Interest on loans used for purchasing or improving real property which is let at a commercial rent for at least 26 weeks in a tax year and is available for being so let in the rest of the tax year is relievable in full, but only against the income from that particular property. Other cases in which interest relief is available include interest on loans used for purchasing an interest in a partnership or, in certain cases, a close company. Interest relief should not be confused with the deductibility of interest on business loans which a trader requires for trading purposes. Such interest is deducted in computing trading profits in accordance with the normal rules (which are not discussed in this work).
- s.168 permits trading losses to be set off against the taxpayer's income for the same tax year or in the preceding tax year but subject to unlimited carry forward of such losses against such trading income. S.169 permits a relief if the loss is computed as a result of the grant of capital allowances.

Personal Income

Before computing the tax liabilities the taxpayers' personal allowances, if any, must also be deducted. Personal allowances are available for single and married persons and their children – the amount of the children's allowance depending on the age of the child. The personal allowances for the year ending 5th April 1978 are set out in Appendix 3. Having deducted the personal allowances, one is then left with the taxable income and the tax rates in force in the tax year as set out in Appendix 3 are applied.

Husbands and Wives

With husbands and wives the position of the following should be particularly noted:

i) Separate taxation for 'wife's earnings'

A husband and wife living together are treated as one unit for tax purposes. Accordingly, their incomes are added together and tax is payable on the total joint income as if it were the income of the husband. However, FA 1971 s.23 provides that where a man and his wife (who are living together) both agree they can elect for the wife's earnings (as opposed to investment income) to be taxed separately. 'Earnings' in this context means earned income as opposed to investment income.

Once the election is made the wife's earnings are charged to income tax as if she were a single woman, so that she receives the single person's allowance. For tax purposes, any other income which she has not earned is ignored in respect of her assessment to tax. The husband will also get the single person's allowance and any children's allowances and his wife's investment income will continue to be aggregated with his own. Once made, an election is valid until revoked. This election must be made within 12 months of the end of the tax year. The Revenue leaflet 13 (IR) sets out the position. Where one spouse is resident for tax purposes in the UK and the other is not, they are treated as not living together. In this case, there is no aggregation of income.

ii) Separate assessment for income

Even if there is no election in respect of the wife's earnings it is possible for the husband or the wife to apply to the Revenue for a separate assessment. *This does not reduce the amount of tax* which the husband and wife would have to pay but merely makes each spouse legally liable for the payment of his or her appropriate share of tax. Such an application must be made within 6 months before 6th July in the tax year for which separate assessments are required.

CHILDREN

A child's income above a certain level will reduce his parents' entitlement to child relief. If the income is paid to the child by the trustees of a settlement made by its parent, it is treated as the parents' income for tax purposes. Otherwise a child is entitled to the single person's relief as if he or she were an adult.

E. PAYE – Pay-As-You-Earn

Under the PAYE system, the employer deducts tax from his employees' Schedule 'E' income at source and remits monthly such deductions to the Revenue. If insufficient tax is deducted then the employer can be made liable.

The system is aimed at the collection of the employees' tax at source in such a manner that the whole of his tax liability is thereby discharged. In general, therefore, no assessment under Schedule E is made but the employee is entitled to demand one (which he will of course do in case of an overdeduction of tax).

The rate of tax payable under PAYE is also supposed to take into account any special deduction available under FA 1974 Schedule 2 (see Section IV). From experience to date, such special deductions are permitted by the Revenue through the PAYE system only after prolonged delays and lengthy enquiries.

At the end of each tax year a cumulative tax table is issued to each employer and it indicates what is to be deducted from each wage or monthly salary payment. Each employee has a code number and this is fixed by reference to the employee's overall tax position. A cumulative tax table is issued to the employer by the Revenue each year and, after establishing the code number, the table indicates the amount to be deducted from each payment.

F. Pension Schemes

Provision for a pension on retirement may be made, by:

(a) an occupational pension scheme set up by the employer for employees, or
(b) a private retirement pension plan financed by the individual. The taxpayer is entitled to participate in either type of scheme but cannot use both (a) and (b) in respect of the same employment.

Contributions to approved pension schemes by either the employer or the employee are deductible in arriving at the total assessable income of the taxpayer. Appendix 3 gives a brief summary of the conditions for approval and the permitted benefits.

From 6th April 1974, contributions by an employer are exempt from tax where they are in respect of the emoluments of an employee who is doing work overseas and who qualifies for the 100% special deduction or the emoluments for an employment overseas which are chargeable on the remittance basis.

An exempt approved scheme (i.e. generally an approved scheme set up under irrevocable trusts) pays no tax on its investment income. Thus the investment fund may obtain a rapid growth.

Pensions paid out of an approved UK scheme are liable to income tax under Schedule E and are taxed under PAYE. 90% of any pensions paid from overseas are taxed (if the recipient is resident in the UK) under Schedule D Case V.

There is a useful booklet issued by the Inland Revenue, entitled 'Occupational Pension Schemes', describing the tax treatment of such schemes and the methods of obtaining Inland Revenue approval.

1. See Section II on residence and domicil for tax purposes
2. Appendix 3, s.122
3. See Appendix 3, s.108
4. See Appendix 1, extra-statutory concession B13
5. See Appendix 3, s.181 et seq.
6. See Appendix 4

Section IV: Income Tax – Foreign Elements

A. Introduction

Section III briefly covered the panorama of income tax. The object of this Section is to consider the various foreign elements in some detail.

Major innovations in the system of taxation of foreign earnings[1] or emoluments of individuals were introduced by FA 1974.[2] One major aspect was the introduction of 'deductions' – either 100%, 50% or 25%. Where a deduction applies, the total earnings or salary are reduced by the percentage of the deduction and then the tax is charged on the remaining balance.

Particular attention is given to the changes introduced by the FAs 1974 and 1977[3] and these are dealt with in as practical a way as possible. There are still many points of detail with regard to these Acts that are unresolved in law and no doubt will be clarified in due course by Revenue practice. FA 1977 did not deal with the position of an individual in the UK who carries on his profession trade or vocation abroad and it is understood that changes in this area may be introduced in FA 1978.[4]

Finally, it is appropriate to consider what the UK means. For tax purposes, the UK includes England, Scotland, Wales, Northern Ireland and the Scilly Isles but excludes the Channels Islands and the Isle of Man. In addition, FA 1973, s.38 extends the UK so as to catch operations on the 'UK part' of the Continental Shelf underlying the North Sea. The full text of FA 1973, s.38 appears in Appendix IA.

B. Trades, Professions and Vocations Carried on Outside the UK

Where a trade, profession or vocation is carried on *wholly* outside the UK by a UK resident individual then the income of such trade, profession or vocation is (depending on the status of the UK resident) *either* liable to UK tax on the arising basis with the benefit of a 25% deduction[5] *or* subject to tax on the remittance basis (without any deduction).[5]

A trade, profession or vocation partly carried on in the UK is given the same tax treatment as one carried on wholly in the UK. Accordingly it does not qualify for either of these beneficial forms of tax treatment.

For tax purposes, it is impossible for a sole trader who is a UK resident individual to carry on his trade wholly abroad. A profession may be so carried on and it is possible (but only in exceptional circumstances) for a company resident in the UK to carry on a trade wholly abroad – but a company is in any case never subject to tax on the remittance basis in respect of income to which it is beneficially entitled, nor is it entitled to the 25% deduction. So invariably when one is considering a trade, profession or vocation carried on abroad this is in the context of overseas partnerships.

OVERSEAS PARTNERSHIP

The essential requirement of the overseas partnership is the fact that it is managed and controlled outside the UK. ICTA 1970, s.153 (1) provides:

'Where any trade or business is carried on by two or more persons in partnership, and the control and management of the trade or business is situated abroad, the trade or business shall be deemed to be carried on by persons resident outside the United Kingdom, and the partnership shall be deemed to reside outside the United Kingdom, notwithstanding the fact that some of the members of the partnership are resident in the United Kingdom and that some of its trading operations are conducted within the United Kingdom.'

Accordingly, if the 'control and management' of the overseas partnership is outside the UK then it is treated as being non-resident for tax purposes even though some partners may be resident in the UK. Indeed, there may even be a branch or agency of such partnership in the UK. However, if the desired object of any exercise is to obtain the 25% deduction or the remittance basis of taxation then any UK branch of the overseas partnership should be avoided. To ensure that the overseas partnership is treated as being resident outside the UK, the following should be taken into account:

(a) The partnership agreement should be signed outside the UK and provide (inter alia) that:
   - partnership meetings must be held abroad
   - any acts of partners on behalf of the partnership business in the UK are inoperative and ultra vires
   - a quorum is clearly defined.
(b) Preferably a majority of the partners should be not resident in the UK. If this is not possible, then voting control should if possible be vested in the non-residents.
(c) Regular partnership meetings must be held outside the UK and decisions clearly taken at them. Comprehensive minutes must be kept.
(d) Is the partnership under its proper law a partnership and not some form of limited company?
(e) Is the partnership on its own a commercially viable proposition i.e. does it appear to have commercial reality rather than being a tax avoidance scheme.

In addition to the above, it is essential that the trade should not only be carried on by an overseas partnership but also should be carried on wholly abroad, otherwise there is no question of the availability of either the 25% deduction or the remittance basis. The purchase of goods in the UK is innocuous, but no goods should be sold in the UK except under contracts made abroad, negotiated abroad and providing for payment abroad. In addition, any goods sold in the UK should be manufactured abroad.

If all those conditions are fulfilled then the 25% deduction is available to all individuals resident and domiciled in the UK. They should appreciate, however, that the cost of travelling to the base of operations of the foreign partnership will not itself be deductible. Frequently, this more than offsets the advantage of the 25% deduction.

Foreign-domiciled individuals are subject to tax on the remittance basis.[6] Such individuals, to avoid being liable to UK tax on their share of the partnership income, should keep their partnership income in a separate bank account outside the UK. 'Remittance' has a very wide meaning and this is discussed later in this section. The charge to tax on the remittance basis is under Schedule D Case V.

Double Taxation

This can often be of paramount importance and each case has to be studied on its own particular facts. Sadly, Double Tax Treaties do not often deal with partnerships and indeed in the OECD Model Agreement partnerships appear simply not to be catered for. As a general rule, a UK resident partner will not be able to claim any protection from Double Tax Treaties with regard to the UK Revenue.

Exchange Control

The requirements of the Exchange Control Act supplemented by Bank of England EC Notices are such that foreign earnings received by a resident of the Scheduled Territories must be brought to the Scheduled Territories. Fortunately the Channel Islands and the Isle of Man are in the Scheduled Territories for Exchange Control purposes but are not in the UK for tax purposes – hence the popularity of Jersey bank accounts to foreign-domiciled individuals.

Summary

Careful thought must be given before an overseas partnership is set up as it is by no means as simple as it appears at first sight. Leaving aside the numerous anti-avoidance provisions that can be applied, consideration has to be given to whether or not the operation is worthwhile in hard financial terms. In particular can the partnership afford to pay the expenses of the UK partners when they leave the UK to travel abroad and back? Appendix 4 contains extracts from IR 25 dealing with the taxation of foreign earnings and the various rules as to deductibility of expenses. With regard to the taxation of foreign partnerships, IR 25 is not amended by FA 1977.

C. Employment Overseas – 100% or 25% Deduction

The FA 1974[7] considerably changed the tax position of individuals who work abroad. Further amendments were added by FA 1977.[8] Now if a UK domiciled individual is resident and ordinarily resident in the UK *and* is in employment, then if he performs some or all of his duties outside the UK a special deduction of 100% or 25% is given from his emoluments (salary, director's fees etc.) in respect of his employment. The extent of the deduction depends on the length of stay outside the UK. These deductions are not to be confused with the deductions from foreign emoluments (See D post). Another point to be appreciated is that where a salary is assessed under Schedule E Case III (i.e. on the remittance basis) then the under-mentioned deductions of 100% or 25% do *not* apply. The new regulations are in effect since 6th April 1977.

(1) 100% DEDUCTION

To obtain the 100% deduction in a particular tax year the individual must be able to show that:

(i) some of the duties must have been performed wholly or partly outside the UK in that tax year,

(ii) the duties in (i) above must be carried out in a 'qualifying period' which consists of at least 365 days and falls wholly or partly in a tax year and,

(iii) if in substance some of the duties of the employment fall to be performed in the UK, the overseas duties cannot be merely incidental to UK duties.

The deduction is given for such amount of the salary from the employment overseas as is attributable to the qualifying period. Certain anti-avoidance provisions prevent the artificial attribution of emoluments to any qualifying period. Unfortunately FA 1977 is silent as to how the amount attributable to the qualifying period is to be calculated although it does state that terminal leave pay is to be included. In many cases it will be clear what is 'attributable'. It may be helpful, in cases where it is not clear, if there is a measure of agreement in writing between the employer and the employee.

A qualifying period is a period of consecutive days which are spent outside the UK or partly of days of absence from the UK and certain periods of time permitted to be spent in the UK. The manner of establishing the latter period is somewhat complicated and those to whom it matters should take specific advice against the background of their own particular circumstances. However, no combination of days of absence and intervening days can be treated as the qualifying period if:

(a) there are more than 62 intervening days (of non-absence) or,

(b) the total amount of days in the complete period spent in the UK equals or exceeds one-sixth of the total number of days in that period.

A day of absence is (by implication) defined as a day at the end of which the employee is absent from the UK.

(2) 25% Deduction

FA 1977 introduced a new category in that prior to FA 1977 it was usually not possible to obtain the benefit of the 25% deduction unless there was a separate contract of employment.

No Separate Contract of Employment

To obtain the benefit of the 25% deduction, the individual must be able to show (i) that some of the duties were performed out of the UK in the tax year, and (ii) that those duties were performed on not less than 30 qualifying days (which need not be consecutive) in the particular tax year. The proportion of the annual salary to which the 25% deduction applies is then determined on a time apportionment basis.

In this particular context a qualifying day is a day spent outside the UK which is substantially devoted to the performance of the duties of the employment or travelling for the purposes of the duties. A day of absence is defined in the same way as for the purposes of the 100% deduction.

Separate Contract

Where there is a separate contract in respect of overseas duties, the 25% deduction is available irrespective of the number of days worked overseas if *all* the duties of the employment are performed abroad *and* the employer is not resident in the UK.[9]

Expenses incurred Abroad

FA 1977, s.32 introduced new rules effective from 6th April 1977 where employees are resident and ordinarily resident in the UK and whose emoluments from an overseas employment are not foreign emoluments, i.e. because the employer is resident in the UK or the employee is domiciled in some part of the UK (or both).

A deduction is allowed in respect of:

(i) travelling expenses to and from the UK

(ii) expenses abroad and lodging outside the UK incurred or reimbursed by the employer for the purpose of enabling the employee to perform duties of the overseas employment

If any of those expenses are reimbursed by the employer, the reimbursement is not taxed as an emolument.

Some further relief is given in respect of travelling expenses where an employee is absent from the UK for a continuous period of 60 days or more for the purposes of performing duties of one or more employments abroad so as to enable the employee to:

(i) visit his spouse or child of his at the end of the period spent abroad
(ii) enable a spouse or child (under eighteen) to accompany the employee at the beginning of the period of absence or to visit him during it

If those expenses are borne by the employer, they are allowed as a deduction in charging the emoluments in the hands of the employee, provided that there are no more than two such journeys in each direction by the same individual in any tax year.

N.B. - The net effect of this provision and of the one summarised above is that the employee escapes tax on the benefit arising out of the travel expenses paid for or reimbursed to him, *not* that his taxable emoluments are reduced.

Aircrew and Seamen[10]

Aircrew and Seamen employed on journeys or voyages between a foreign port or airport and the UK will be treated as working outside the UK during a journey or voyage:

(a) beginning or ending outside the UK (but excluding any part of it which begins and ends in the UK) or
(b) any part thereof beginning or ending outside the UK of a voyage or journey which both begins and ends in the UK.

Appendix 4 contains Inland Revenue Booklet IR 25, a good part of which remains unchanged by FA 1977. However, it should be particularly carefully read with regard to the changes introduced by FA 1977 in respect of the above.

D. Schedule E - Foreign Emoluments

To the foreign domiciled individual these are perhaps some of the most important provisions. Foreign emoluments are the salary, fees, bonuses, etc. of an individual not domiciled in the UK from an office or employment with any person, body of persons or partnership resident outside and not resident in the UK.

CASE I - FOREIGN EMOLUMENTS

If the employee is both resident and ordinarily resident in the UK but domiciled outside the UK, he will receive a deduction of one half of the foreign emoluments for the first 10 years of his residence. Thereafter the deduction is reduced to one quarter.

The foregoing applies if the individual performs the duties of his employment wholly or partly in the UK.

CASE II – FOREIGN EMOLUMENTS – 50% OR 25% DEDUCTION

If an individual is not resident or, if resident, not ordinarily resident in the UK, he is charged on so much of his emoluments as relate to duties performed in the UK. Where such an individual performs duties both outside the UK and in the UK, the emoluments from these duties are apportioned. Incidental duties performed in the UK are deemed to be duties performed outside the UK where the employment in substance requires no UK duties.

It will be appreciated that whether or not a person has foreign emoluments then if in substance part of his duties fall to be performed in the UK then he will be subject to tax under Case II in respect of that part of his duties. If his emoluments are foreign emoluments he will receive a deduction of 50% or rarely, if appropriate, 25%.[12]

CASE III – DUTIES PERFORMED OUTSIDE THE UK – REMITTANCE BASIS

Case III charges any emoluments received in the UK by a UK resident. To that extent there is an overlap between Cases I and II on the one hand and Case III on the other, but tax is not chargeable under Case III on emoluments falling under Cases I or II. The result, therefore, is that Case III is a remedial case which only comes into operation in respect of a foreign domiciled individual who is resident in the UK (irrespective of whether or not he is also ordinarily resident) who receives foreign emoluments from an employment the duties of which are carried on wholly abroad.

GENERAL POINTS

FA 1977 introduced several new rules:

- Where foreign emoluments qualify for the 50% deduction (or 25% if appropriate) (i.e. when the duties for which the foreign emoluments are paid are not performed wholly abroad) then the individual will not be able to obtain any of the other type of deductions under C above i.e. 100% or 25%.
- In C above reference was made to certain anti-avoidance provisions[13] which are aimed at preventing the excessive apportionment of emoluments to a period in respect of which a deduction is available; similar provisions apply where an individual is employed under two contracts of employment, the emoluments of which are taxable under Case I and Case III of Schedule E respectively.

The principal criterion to be taken into account with regard to apportionment is what is reasonable with regard to the nature of time devoted to duties performed both outside and in the UK and in other special circumstances.

E. Multiple Schedule E Employments

Foreign domiciled individuals should of course be employed by an overseas company in respect of their UK duties, so that they are entitled to a 50% (or 25%) deduction from the emoluments from those employments in computing the charge to UK tax. It will also be advisable for such an individual to have a separate Schedule E emolument (or emoluments) with another overseas company (or companies) the duties of which are performed wholly outside the UK. The emoluments of this second employment (or third or fourth, as the case may be) will be taxable under Schedule E Case III *only* if these emoluments are remitted to the UK. In such a case it is essential to keep these emoluments quite separate in a separate bank account from any other income which is subject to UK tax on the arising basis. If, however, it is the intention of the individual to utilise all these funds in the UK, i.e. he is going to remit them to the UK anyway, it will probably be to his advantage to have the emoluments subject to tax under Case I on the arising basis with the benefit of the 50% deduction. Before deciding upon a particular course of action and putting it into effect, the arithmetic must be done.

Generally, with regard to the normal UK domiciled and resident individual, the question of separate contracts has become less important except in the case where the individual may not spend the minimum of 30 qualifying days outside the UK.

F. Foreign Pensions, Provident Fund Payments and Golden Handshakes

A resident ordinarily resident and UK domiciled individual will be subject to tax on his overseas pension on the arising basis (i.e. whether or not he remits it to the UK is irrelevant). He will however be entitled to a deduction of 10% before the charge to tax.[14]

A foreign domiciled individual who is resident in the UK will only be liable to tax on his overseas pension if he remits it to the UK i.e. receives it in the UK. He will not receive any deduction, as the remittance basis and deductions are mutually exclusive. A resident but not ordinarily resident British subject or Irish citizen will also be subject to tax on the remittance basis.

The charge to tax arises under Schedule D, Case V, unless the pension is payable in the UK through a Commonwealth government department or representative organisation when the charge to tax arises under Schedule E.

Clearly where an individual is not resident in the UK, there is no question of any liability to UK tax in respect of the overseas pension. Similarly there is no claim to tax on provident fund or similar compensation monies applicable to service overseas provided that these payments cannot be construed as being 'golden handshakes'. Particular rules apply to golden handshakes and these are dealt with in some detail in IR 25, chapter 4, which is reproduced in Appendix 4. Two points, however, should be emphasized:

(i) where a 'golden handshake' is paid to a director who was in receipt of foreign emoluments, it is not taxed if the service included foreign service of sufficiently long duration (three quarters of the whole period of service or, in the case of long employments, a lesser proportion). Where there was no such foreign service, only 50% of the 'golden handshake' is taxed.

(ii) ICTA 1970 s.188 (3) provides that the first £ 5,000 of any 'golden handshake' is free of tax

G. Overseas Investment Income and Remittances

Such income is taxable if at all under Schedule C or Schedule D cases IV and V. For a charge to tax to arise, the individual must be resident in the UK before either the arising basis or remittance basis can apply. The main category of individuals who can benefit from the remittance basis are foreign domiciled individuals.

(1) Schedule C

This applies to all interest and dividends payable in the UK from the public revenue of any foreign government or foreign public authority or body. ICTA 1970 s.94 provides that the person who makes the payment (usually a paying agent or the Bank of England) must deduct tax at the basic rate from the interest. The position is similar with bearer bonds. ICTA 1970 s.100 provides that tax shall not be withheld where the owner of the stock is not resident in the UK.

(2) Schedule D Cases IV and V

Case IV income is income arising from securities outside the UK unless such income is otherwise liable to tax under Schedule C above. In this context the word 'security' means any debt or obligation where the payment is in some way secured e.g. a debenture or mortgage stock. Thus, although the word in its general use includes stocks and shares, for the purpose of this case it has a special limited meaning.

All other forms of foreign income, other than income within Schedule E, is taxable under case V. The basic differentiation between case V and case IV are academic.

Remittances[6]

Clearly, a person who is living in the UK and has all his money abroad will have to make remittances for the purposes of defraying his living expenses. If he remits income which is taxable on the remittance basis, it is equally clear that he will be taxed on the amount remitted; it is thus in his interest to ensure that what he remits is money which is not so taxable.

In order to be able to do so he must be able to show that what he has remitted could not be income taxable on the remittance basis. It follows that any such income should be kept in a separate bank account abroad; remittances from a bank account containing a mixed fund of income taxable on the remittance basis and other money may render him liable to taxation, as he will not be able to show that what he remitted was definitely not income which, if remitted, would be liable to tax.

Provided that the taxpayer has taken the precaution of being able to identify his remittances by means of separate bank accounts, he will be allowed to remit capital, or income taxable on the arising basis, in view of the income taxable on the remittance basis, without incurring any charge to income tax on unremitted income.

The temptation to escape tax by borrowing in the UK against unremitted income and repaying the loan abroad should be resisted; there are anti-avoidance provisions which will deem any such borrowing to constitute a constructive remittance.[6]

Where income is chargeable on the remittance basis under Case V of Schedule D, the charge to tax appears to be restricted to a charge on money remitted; thus the importation of goods purchased with money which is so taxable would appear to escape taxation as long as the goods are not sold in the UK. That does not, however, apply to goods purchased with income chargeable under Case III of Schedule E, as such income is deemed to be remitted whenever it is effectively enjoyed in the UK.

H. Avoidance of Double Taxation

The discussion following is restricted to those provisions which aim at giving a relief in circumstances where an individual is subject to taxation in respect of the same income in the UK and also in some other country. Where the other country is one with which the UK has concluded a double tax treaty, the provisions of that treaty will regulate the liability to tax in either country; where no such treaty is in force, the statutory provisions relating to unilateral relief will apply.

The discussion below is restricted, as respects both unilateral relief and treaty relief to such of the provisions as apply to individuals.

(1) Unilateral Relief

Unilateral relief against UK tax is only given to a resident of the UK except that credit may be allowed by way of unilateral relief:

(i) for tax paid under the law of the Isle of Man or any of the Channel Islands, if the taxpayer is resident either in the UK or in the Isle of Man or one of the Channel Islands, and
(ii) for tax paid under the law of any country on emoluments from an office or an employment the duties of which are performed wholly or mainly in that other country, against Schedule E income tax on the same emoluments, if the taxpayer is resident either in the UK or in the other country.

The relief is given by way of credit against UK tax. The effect is that the taxpayer will never pay less than the higher of the two amounts due by him to either the UK or the overseas fiscal authorities, and there are a number of situations in which he will pay more. That is brought about on the one hand by certain special rules which apply for the purpose of computing dividends, and income or capital gains taxable on the remittance basis, and on the other by certain limitations on the amount of credit available for set-off.

Where the Remittance Basis Applies

For the purpose of calculating the credit available for set-off against UK tax in respect of income or chargeable gains taxable on a remittance basis, the amount remitted is increased by the foreign tax payable in respect thereof. UK tax is calculated by reference to the aggregate amount so calculated and credit for foreign tax is given against the total UK tax liability.

Dividends

Similarly, for the purpose of calculating the amount of credit available for set-off by way of unilateral relief on any dividend, the amount of the dividend is increased by any underlying tax which is to be taken into account and the UK tax liability in respect of the dividend is computed by reference to the amount so increased. 'Underlying tax' is a rather technical and complicated concept, which will not be treated in detail but which, in the broadest possible terms, means that not only foreign tax paid on a dividend, but also on the profits out of which the dividend was paid, may be taken into account for the purposes of unilateral relief.

Limitation of Credit

There are two limitations on the credit available for set-off against UK tax. In the first place, as may be expected in the context of set-off, the credit may not exceed the tax payable in the UK. Secondly, the credit is limited to the difference between the liability to UK tax which the taxpayer would have in respect of the whole of his income on the one hand and in respect of the difference between that income and that portion of it on which unilateral relief is available on the other. e.g.

Thus if in a particular year of assessment a tax payer has an income of £ 6,000 from sources within the UK and in addition £ 2,000 from a foreign source, the credit will be limited to the difference between the amount of tax which would be charged in the UK on £ 8,000 on the one hand and on £ 6,000 on the other.

This limitation is to be calculated separately per source of income abroad.

(2) Treaty Relief

Needless to say, a resident of a particular country who derives income from sources within another country will have to examine the text of the individual treaty, if there is one, between the two countries before he can ascertain whether, and if so to what extent, treaty relief is available to him in his particular circumstances. The summary below deals with the OECD model double tax agreement which forms the basis of many tax agreements. As with unilateral relief only the provisions relating to individuals are dealt with. The seemingly inapplicability of the OECD model to partners is not dealt with. Emphasis is given to the effect of the OECD model on residence, the liability to tax of individuals carrying on a trade, profession or vocation in a country other than that of their residence and on income accruing from an office or employment.

Definitions

Residence

The OECD model defines the term 'resident of a contracting state' as a person who, under the law of that state, is liable to taxation therein by reason of his domicil, residence, place of management or any other criterion of a similar nature. However a person who is liable to tax in a particular country in respect only of income from sources within that country is not within the definition. A free translation of this provision is to the effect that a person is resident of a country for treaty purposes if he is resident in that country for the purposes of its domestic tax legislation.

As there is no reason why a person should not be a resident of both countries under that definition, the treaty goes on to give four rules for the purpose of eliminating dual residence. They are as follows:

(a) For treaty purposes, a person is deemed to be a resident of the country in which he has a permanent home available to him. If he has a permanent home available to him in both countries, he is deemed to be a resident of that country with which his personal and economic relations are closest (which country is referred to as his centre of vital interests).

(b) If his centre of vital interests cannot be determined or if he does not have a permanent home available to him in either country, he is deemed to be a resident of the country in which he has an habitual abode.

(c) If he has an habitual abode in both countries or in neither of them, he is deemed to be a resident of the country of which he is a national.

(d) If he is a national of both countries or of neither, the fiscal authorities of the countries concerned will settle the question of his residential status by mutual agreement.

Enterprise of a Contracting State

The above expression, which is used throughout the treaty, means an enterprise carried on by a resident of a contracting state.

Permanent Establishment

This concept is of particular importance in connection with the treaty provisions dealing with business profits. The concept of permanent establishment is defined as a fixed place of business in which the business of the enterprise is wholly or partly carried on, and includes in particular a place of management, a branch, an office, a factory, a workshop, a mine and a building site which exists for more than 12 months.

In addition, an agent who has, and habitually exercises in a particular country, authority to conclude contracts in the name of the enterprise and whose activities go beyond the mere purchase of goods or merchandise for the enterprise, also constitutes a permanent establishment unless he is a broker, general commission agent or other agent of independent status acting in the ordinary course of his business.

Certain facilities are excluded from the concept of permanent establishment. They include facilities used solely for the purpose of storage, display or delivery of goods, the maintenance of a stock of goods for the purposes of storage, display or delivery or for processing by another enterprise, and a fixed place of business used solely for purchasing goods, for collecting or supplying information and for research purposes.

Business Profits

The profits of an enterprise of a contracting state are taxable only in that state unless the enterprise carries on its business in the other state through a permanent establishment situated therein. In that case, so much of the profits as is attributable to that permanent establishment may be taxed in the other state as well. It is to be noted that in any such case the rules for the grant of unilateral relief will apply if the enterprise is carried on by a person who for tax purposes is resident in the UK.

The profits attributable to a permanent establishment are calculated on the assumption that it is a separate enterprise dealing with its head office on an arm's length basis. Expenditure incurred for the purposes of the permanent establishment, including general overheads, are allowed as a deduction in computing the profits attributable to the permanent establishment. Activities for which the treaty contains special provisions are governed by those provisions and not by the Article summarized under this heading. Such special provisions apply to income derived from the operation of ships and aircraft in international waters, from personal services (both by self-employed persons and under contracts of employment), and from the activities carried on by directors and artists and athletes.

Independent Personal Services

The services referred to in Article 14 of the model treaty are not exhaustively defined. The defining paragraph states that the services include independent scientific, literary, artistic, education or teaching activities as well as the independent activities of physicians, lawyers, engineers, architects, dentists and accountants.

Income obtained from the activities of artists and athletes is within Article 17 and not within Article 14.

The income derived from such services or other independent activities of a similar character is taxable only in the country of residence of the person who performs the services, unless he has a fixed base regularly available to him in the other country for the purpose of performing his activities. If he has such a fixed base, any income attributable to the fixed base may be taxed in the country in which that state is situated, but it is to be noted that, unlike the Article dealing with business profits, there is no notional profits to be attributed to the fixed base.

Dependent Personal Services

Article 15 deals with salaries, wages and other similar remunerations derived by a resident of a contracting state in respect of an employment, but Articles 16 and 17 except from the ambit of Article 15 directors fees and the activities of artists and athletes.

The rule as respects salaries within Article 15 is that so much of the remuneration derived by a resident of one contracting state in respect of an employment as is derived from the exercise of the employment in the other contracting state may be taxed in both states, unless:

(a) the employee is present in the other state for an aggregate period not exceeding 183 days in the fiscal year concerned, and
(b) the remuneration is paid by or on behalf of, an employer who is not a resident of that other state, and
(c) the remuneration is not borne by a permanent establishment or fixed base which the employer has in that other state.

If all those three conditions are fulfilled, the employee is taxable only in the country of his residence as respects his salary or other emoluments.

Directors' Fees

Where a resident of one contracting state is a member of the board of directors of a company which is resident in the other contracting state, the directors' fees derived from that membership may be taxed in the state in which the company is resident. In the result, therefore, such a director receives no assistance from the treaty whatever.

Artists and Athletes

Income derived by entertainers and other artists, musicians and athletes from their personal activities as such is unprotected by the treaty, and the model treaty now contains a paragraph the net effect of which is that the interposition of a company to which the income accrues does not help. An artist who is a resident of a country which has concluded a treaty with the UK in which this provision appears should, therefore, consider the incorporation of an employing company in a country which has a treaty with the UK from which the provision is absent.

1. See Appendix 3
2. See also Section III
3. FA 1977 ss.31-34 and Schedule 7
4. Some rather rarified suggestions have been made in an Inland Revenue press release. There is still fiscal discrimination against the self-employed.
5. FA 1974 s.23 and ICTA 1970 s.122 – See Appendix 3 and also the extracts from IR 25 in Appendix 4
6. ICTA 1970 s.122 – See Appendix 3
7. FA 1974 s.21 and Schedule 2 paras (1) and (2)
8. FA 1977 ss.31 and 32 and Schedule 7
9. FA 1977 Schedule 7 para 3
10. FA 1977 Schedule 7 para 7
11. ICTA 1970 s.181
12. It is unlikely that he could be resident *or* ordinarily resident (but not resident) in the UK for nine consecutive years
13. FA 1977 Schedule 7 para 4. Note the definitions of control in para 4 (5)
14. FA 1974 s.22 (1) or if re Nazi persecution 50% – s.22 (2)
15. See also Section II F

Section V: Special Situations

The aim of this section is to briefly touch upon various provisions and aspects that UK tax planners have to consider. Most provisions concern the individual but some corporate provisions and general aspects have to be noted.

The UK legislation contains many anti-avoidance provisions. Many of these not only catch the guilty but also unfortunately impede and/or catch the innocent, often to the commercial detriment of the individual or the company concerned. This of course does not assist the UK economy. Ignorance of provisions is no excuse. The residential status or domicil of the individual or the purpose of the exercise can sometimes affect the application of a provision. Clearance procedures exist with some provisions but considerable information must usually be divulged.

The Revenue's powers to obtain information must also be considered. In certain cases UK resident individuals are obliged to disclose transactions in their tax returns. In some cases disclosure of individual's transactions by third parties is mandatory. In other cases the Revenue can request disclosure of information. ICTA 1970 s.481 is perhaps the most demanding in terms of effort required and time spent. Under this section specific or general enquiries can be made upon UK banks, accountants, solicitors and tax consultancy organisations in connection with the best known anti-avoidance provision ICTA 1970 s.478 (see post). The production of satisfactory answers to such enquiries is usually extremely time consuming.

A. ICTA 1970 s.478 – Transfer of Income Abroad

(1) The preamble to this all-embracing provision reads:

'... For the purpose of preventing the avoiding by individuals ordinarily resident in the United Kingdom of liability to income tax by means of transfers of assets by virtue of or in consequence whereof, either alone or in conjunction with associated operations, income becomes payable to persons resident or domiciled outside of the United Kingdom...'

All the terms in the preamble are widely defined. Some aspects to be grasped are: *the individual* who makes the transfer need not be the same individual who is assessed. The individual has to be ordinarily resident and resident but he may not have been so ordinarily resident or resident at the time he made the transfer;

the person to whom the transfer is made is usually a company or a foreign trustee. Any company formed outside the UK is treated as resident outside the UK. Possibly such a 'person' does not include a foreign partnership;

any *associated operation* may be carried out by some other person or individual than the individual who is assessed;

assets are property or rights of any kind. Such assets can possibly be created on the transfer – the original transfer or any subsequent transfer.

(2) CHARGING PROVISIONS

Subsection (1)

'...Where by virtue or in consequence of any such transfer, either alone or in conjunction with associated operations, such an individual has, within the meaning of this section, power to enjoy, whether forthwith or in the future, any income of a person resident or domiciled out of the UK which if it were income of that individual received by him in the UK, would be chargeable to income tax by deduction or otherwise, that income shall, whether it would or would not have been chargeable to income tax apart from the provisions of this section, be deemed to be income of that individual for all the purposes of the Income Tax Acts...'

'Power to enjoy' is defined in s.478 (5) and includes all forms of entitlement and benefit, receipts or enjoyment of income or the ability to manipulate the income of the 'person'.

S.478 (6) provides further that the definitions in s.478 (5) shall be considered in the light of:

'...the substantial result and effect of the transfer and any associated operations and all benefits which ...may accrue to the individual (whether or not he has rights at law or in equity in or to those benefits)...'

The term is defined very widely and covers every conceivable situation including where an individual is a:

- beneficiary of a foreign trust and the trustees of such foreign trust receive income;
- shareholder in a foreign company which has income. Or a subsidiary (or sub-subsidiary) of such foreign company which has income;
- shareholder in a UK company which owns a foreign company which has income.

Apart from the exceptions (which are touched upon later) it should be noted that there are no restrictions on this section's ambit. It applies to investment companies and trading companies alike. The size of any shareholding in a foreign company is irrelevant. Theoretically, it could apply to a UK resident and ordinarily resident shareholder in a UK company which has foreign subsidiaries which have income.

In practice the section is not applied to such a situation.

Whether a foreign company pays tax or not is irrelevant. The fact that it does, can or cannot distribute dividends is also irrelevant.

A frequently recommended scheme to avoid the 'power to enjoy' provisions is a two-tier structure. At the top of the structure is a discretionary trust. The trustees of the trust own the shares in an underlying company which accumulates the income. The argument, which has some legal strength, is that the discretionary beneficiaries who are resident and ordinarily resident in the UK do not have power to enjoy the income of the underlying company. Whatever the legal merits of this argument, the UK Revenue do not accept it. Another similar argument revolves around the use of assurance policies. For practical purposes in both these forms of scheme there is a s.478 risk.

Sub-section (2)

'. . . Where, whether before or after any such transfer, such an individual receives or is entitled to receive any capital sum the payment whereof is in any way connected with the transfer or any associated operation, any income which by virtue or in consequence of the transfer, either alone or in conjunction with associated operations, has become the income of a person resident or domiciled outside the United Kingdom shall, whether it would or would not have been chargeable to income tax apart from the provisions of this section, be deemed to be the income of that individual for all the purposes of the Income Taxes Acts.

In this Subsection 'capital sum' means:

a) any sum paid or payable by way of loan or repayment of a loan, and
b) any other sum paid or payable otherwise than as income, being a sum which is not paid or payable for full consideration in money or money's worth. . . .'

The purpose of this sub-section is to catch those situations where an individual may not have the power to enjoy the income of the trust or company but has received a capital sum from the trust or company. If there is a 'power to enjoy' it is not a relevant point as far as sub-section (2) is concerned. Indeed, in one way, as far as the UK Revenue is concerned, it is more remunerative to charge an individual under sub-section (2) than sub-section (1). This is because 'the income of the person' is deemed to be the income of the individual for all purposes of the Income Tax Acts! This means that once the charge has arisen the assessment is made for the current UK tax year and the past six UK tax years. For future years, the income will also be deemed to be the individual's.

There is no correlation in the section between the sum assessed and the size of the 'capital sum' received. In a recent case, the Court sought to restrict the charge to tax under this subsection.

(3) 'INCOME'

The word income appears several times in the section but nowhere is it defined and indeed there are judicial dicta to the effect that there is two (if not more) different forms of 'income' concerned. From the practitioner's point of view such considerations are time consuming, unrewarding and invariably expensive. As things stand at present it seems clear that the UK Revenue maintain that the income assessable – as the law stands – is under s.478 (1) or (2) is the total income of the 'person' i.e the trust or company. This view is backed by many of the authorities. Let's look at the effect of this in an example.

B. has a 10% shareholding in a foreign company which has deposit interest of £ 100,000. In Law B could be assessed on the total of the income.

In practice the UK Revenue fortunately tends to make proportionate assessments. In the above example the assessment would probably be made on a total of £ 10,000.

Another aspect must also be considered. There seems to be nothing to prevent different individuals being assessed in respect of the same income. Again in practice, the UK Revenue avoids difficulties by making proportionate assessments. With companies proportionate assessments can be based on shareholdings. With trusts, particularly discretionary trusts, the Revenue usually 'request' sight of ancillary documentation such as memoranda of wishes or letters of intent.

From previous chapters, it will be noted that certain UK resident individuals will only be subject to UK tax on foreign income on the remittance basis. Where such income is paid to a foreign 'person' and s.478 can be applied such income is taxable upon the arising basis and no longer upon the remittance basis.

Domicil, for the purposes of the individual concerned is *irrelevant* for s.478 purposes.

(4) QUANTUM OF INCOME ASSESSABLE

There are no statutory provisions determining how the income is quantified. Is it the income as shown by the accounts, the income receipts after deduction of any expenses or what? This subject received attention in the case of Lord Chetwode v. IRC which eventually reached the House of Lords. It is worth briefly examining the facts of the case.

There was a foreign trust under which Lord Chetwode, the settlor, was entitled to the income. The Bahamanian trustees of the trust owned and investment company which owned income producing assets. It is not clear why the settlor retained the right to the income of the trust nor why it was conceded on his behalf that he had 'power to enjoy' the income of the investment company. The main point in issue was the quantum of the income.

In the High Court Mr. Justice Megarry supported the Special Commissioners' viewpoint that income meant 'gross income or receipts less collection charges' i.e. management expenses etc. were ignored.

The Court of Appeal rejected this view stating that the 'income' within s.478 attributable to an individual included trading income as well as investment income and the obiter dicta of Mr. Justice Megarry to the effect that the income of trading companies should be computed separately had no authority. 'Income' in the context of an investment company was the company's profits i.e. the excess of receipts over outgoings and outgoings included tax and interest liabilities. The taxpayer should not be charged on a notional income that was greater than the company received. The basis of assessment must be on the accounts of the company in the local form they are drawn up in.

On 16th February 1977 the House of Lords rejected the view of the Court of Appeal holding that deductions for UK tax purposes were either authorised or they were not. With dividend income there were no deductions and the dividends received were the 'income' referred to in the section.

(5) Apportionment of Income

Once the quantum income is identified various points should be appreciated:

- UK tax at the basic rate will not be assessed (s.480 (1)) where it has already been paid on the income.
- Relief for foreign tax may be limited to the extent that relief will be given had the individual received the income direct.
- The position with regard to the UK tax credit paid on UK dividends is not catered for. The tax credit is not a withholding tax. In practice it is understood that the UK Revenue gives credit for it as such despite the fact that s.478 and s.480 preceded the introduction of the imputation system of corporation tax.
- Where an individual has income assessed upon him under s.478 it is expressly provided that it cannot again form part of his income for tax purposes.

(6) Exceptions s.478 (3)

If an individual shows to the UK Revenue either in writing or otherwise that either

a) the purpose of avoiding taxation was *not* the purpose *or one* of the purposes of the transfer of assets *or*,
b) the transfer and any associated operations were bona fide commercial transactions and were not designed for the purpose of avoiding liability to taxation,

then s.478 shall not apply. In both cases it is desirable to show that the avoidance of UK tax was not a purpose. 'Tax' means UK tax including estate duty, capital transfer tax but does not include exchange control. Clearly the second exception is less restrictive than the first.

Of course if one is preparing a bona fide commercial scheme it is difficult to consider how one does not take into account how to mitigate UK tax action. However it has been suggested that although a tax saving might result from the transaction it is of foremost importance to determine whether or not it is a bona fide commercial scheme and that any incidental tax saving may be ignored.

The situation is not satisfactory.

(7) SUMMARY

One of the most interesting aspects of this section is that although it has been in force in one form or another since before World War II, relatively few cases have come before the Courts. This is even after in the last few years extensive fact-finding searches under ICTA 1970 s.481 have been carried out. This is probably a tribute to its effectiveness. Despite this, it is often not taken sufficiently into account particularly where it is clear the exemptions do not apply.

B. Capital Gains Tax and Foreign Companies

FA 1965 s.41 provides in certain circumstances for capital gains of non-resident companies to be assessed upon individuals in the UK. There are various conditions to be satisfied:

- the non-resident company must be, if it was resident in the UK, a close company (see Section IX G);
- when capital gains accrue to the company the individual must be (i) resident or ordinarily resident in the UK *and* (ii) domiciled in the UK.

In such cases the proportion of the capital gain to accrue to a shareholder is equal to the share of the assets he would receive on liquidation of the company. S.41 (2) provides that the apportionment shall not take place if the amount that would be received on liquidation is less than one-twentieth of the company's assets.

There are various exceptions to the application of the section:

- Foreign currency profits accruing following the 18th November 1967 devaluation;
- proportions of the chargeable gain distributed by way of dividend distribution or capital on liquidation within two years from when the chargeable gain accrued;
- chargeable gains accruing on the disposal of property (real or moveable) used for the purposes of a trade carried on in the UK by a branch or agency *and* such gain was charged under other provisions;
- chargeable gains in connection with the disposal of assets connected with a trade carried on outside the UK whether or not the assets are subject to local tax.

In the event that a shareholder is not reimbursed by the company for the capital gains tax paid by him then the amount paid is allowed as a deduction in computing the gain obtained by the individual when the shares are eventually sold or the company liquidated.

A point to be particularly watched is that two charges to CGT can arise in respect of the same gain e.g. the usual apportionment is made and the gains are distributed on liquidation or otherwise more than two years later. The timing of disposals of shareholdings and distributions of any 'gains' must be watched carefully.

Relief is only given for losses inside the same company.

C. Capital Gains Tax and Foreign Trusts

(1) FA 1965 s.25 provides that a trust will be resident in the UK for CGT purposes (and therefore liable to CGT) *unless* the general administration of the trust is carried on outside the UK and the trustees or a majority of them are not resident and not ordinarily resident in the UK.

The harshness of s.25 was slightly alleviated by FA 1969 which added to s.25 the proviso that where the UK trustees are professional trustees (i.e. their business is trust management) then the general administration of the trust will be deemed to be carried on outside the UK where the property derives from an individual not domiciled in the UK and not resident and ordinarily resident in the UK.

Clearly UK resident or ordinarily resident trustees of foreign trusts are not advisable. Particularly with foreign trustees who are individuals as the sudden demise of a foreign trustee can have awkward consequences.

There must be many trusts unwittingly resident in the UK for capital gains tax purposes.

(2) FA 1965 s.42 contains the basics for taxing the capital gains of foreign trusts. For s.42 to apply there must be a trust where the trustees are not resident and not ordinarily resident in the UK *and* the settlor is (or was when he made the trust) domiciled resident or ordinarily resident in the UK.

So if the settlor has a foreign domicil then there are no CGT connotations. If not the approach taken by s.42 is to apportion any capital gains on to UK beneficiaries who are domiciled *and* resident or ordinarily resident in the UK. The apportionment is made in a just and reasonable manner according to the beneficiaries' interests in the trust property. This may be a life interest, a reversion or such similar interest and in such cases apportionments are made according to the values of the interests.

There are special rules for discretionary trusts. If in a three year period ending with the year in which the chargeable gain accrues a beneficiary *receives an income distribution* from the trust, then he is considered for apportionment purposes to have an interest in the trust property equal to an annuity of an annual amount equal to one-third of the total payments. Where a beneficiary *receives a capital advance* (which contains an element of a capital gain) then the capital gain is treated as accruing to the beneficiary when he receives the advance.

Three further points should be noted:

- there are special rules for pre 6th April 1965 trusts;
- there is no relief for losses (s.42 (6));
- if the trustees pay the CGT then the payment is not treated as a payment to the beneficiary (s.42 (5)).

D. Delayed Remittances

ICTA 1970 s.418 INCOME
FA 1965 a.40 CAPITAL GAINS

Where a UK resident:
(i) is liable to UK tax in respect of foreign income or foreign capital gains, *and*
(ii) is able to satisfy the UK Revenue that he cannot transfer the funds to the UK (despite reasonable endeavours on his part) because of the laws or executive action of the country where the funds are (e.g. local exchange control),

then the funds which cannot be remitted will be deducted from any assessment. When the funds are (if ever) received, then the assessment will be made in that year.

E. ICTA 1970 s.482 Migration of Companies

Unless the consent of HM Treasury is obtained it is unlawful for a UK resident company (i.e. not just a UK registered company):
a) to cease to be resident in the UK;
b) for the whole or part of its trade or business to be transferred abroad to a non-resident;
c) to cause or permit a non-resident body corporate which it controls to create or issue shares to any person;
d) to dispose of shares or debentures in a non-resident body which it controls to any person (other than in respect of a director's qualifying shares).

This often unconsidered section has extremely wide application touching upon many international operations. Various points should be appreciated:
- s.482 only applies to bodies corporate;
- the penalties are extremely heavy – of a criminal type and they apply to all parties – including professional advisors;
- the objective of the section is more economic than fiscal.

Various forms of general consent are issued by HM Treasury. An emigrant if he owns all the shares in a UK company can apply, subject to EC regulations, to 'export' (i.e. remove the company's control and management) from the UK.

F. ICTA 1970 s.460 – s.468 Transactions in Securities

Where a person obtains a 'tax advantage' from one or more 'transactions' in securities, then he may be assessed to income tax under Schedule D case VI. Extremely briefly a 'tax advantage' is the saving of corporation or income tax – it does not apply to capital gains tax or stamp duty. 'Transactions in securities' includes the sale and acquisition of shares in companies, reconstructions, schemes of amalgamation, formations and liquidations of companies. The most common application of these provisions is to prevent the use of a company to accumulate income i.e. the profits are undistributed and then the shares in the company are subsequently disposed of.

A clearance certificate may be obtained from the Revenue in respect of any transaction. The Revenue must be advised on all relevant facts and be satisfied that the main object of the transaction was commercial rather than tax savings.

G. ICTA 1970 s.487 Sale of Income Derived from Personal Activities

Prior to the inception of this provision, it was quite common for individuals such as pop stars with substantial incomes to form management companies inside which the income derived from their activities accrued. The shares or debentures in such companies being subsequently sold by such individuals for capital sums. The object of this provision was to prevent such schemes from operating. Such a capital sum received in respect of the sale of earnings is chargeable to income tax and assessed under Schedule D case 6. It is treated as earned income and is not subject to the investment income surcharge.

This is a typical UK Revenue 'blunderbuss' provision and can catch many situations where an individual receives a capital sum from the sale of a business which derives its value from his personal duties performed for the company. Rather surprisingly the section does not seem to be relied on very much by the UK Revenue in practice.

H. ICTA 1970 s.488 Artificial Transactions in Land

This provision is aimed at taxing the situation where an individual receives a capital profit from selling property (land and/or buildings) that he had purchased with a view to disposing of later at a profit. The provision can also effect the sale of land held as trading stock and property which had been developed with the intention of selling it at a profit.

Such a 'capital' profit can be treated by the Revenue as income and assessed to tax under Schedule D Case 6 i.e. income tax is payable and not CGT.

The Revenue tend to treat this broadly drawn provision as applying to all but pure dealing situations. Particular attention is given to any tax mitigation resulting from the sale of shares in a close company, the consideration for which derives indirectly from the increase in value of property held by the company. The vendor of shares in, for example a property dealing company, may ask for the purchaser of the shares to procure that the company disposes of the land by way of the company's normal course of trade, i.e. no investment situation arises. The purchaser of such shares in the company has to consider his position extremely carefully before giving such an indemnity.

In addition to s.488, the position of development land tax will have to be considered. This is, even by UK standards an extremely complicated tax, and it is not touched upon in this work.

Section VI: Capital Transfer Tax ('CTT')

A. General

The ambit of CTT is wide and it is not confined to the UK. CTT applies to both gifts made inter vivos and also to transfers on death. Subject to a few exemptions and reliefs CTT can affect many situations some of which at first sight may not have any CTT implications. This section considers CTT in the international context rather than detailing its computations and local UK aspects. CTT was introduced by F (No. 1) A 1975 and unless otherwise stated all references in this Section are to that Act.

Two basic points must be grasped:

(1) all UK situated assets with one or two exceptions (the UK does *not* include the Channel Islands and the Isle of Man) are subject to CTT *irrespective* of the domicil or residence of the individual owning them;

(2) the worldwide assets of an individual domiciled[1] (or treated as being domiciled under S.45) in the UK are subject to CTT. Worldwide assets can include interests under trusts.

Accordingly, the concept of domicil[1] and its application[2], particularly in its extended meaning applied under s.45, is extremely relevant for CTT purposes. The new legislation contained in FA 1977 s.49 will to a minor extent, restrict the application of s.45 to emigrants to the Channel Islands and the Isle of Man. The full text of s.45 and FA 1977 s.49 appear in Appendix 5.

Estate Duty was the predecessor of CTT. Estate Duty applied only to assets passing on an individual's death, interest in trust property and gifts made within 7 years of death. CTT however applies to gifts ('lifetime transfers') of assets made by a person once his £ 25,000 nil rate margin (or slice) has been exceeded.

It should be noted that at the lower levels there are two basic rates of CTT.[3] For lifetime transfers made more than three years before death, there are lower rates (up to a cumulative total of £ 310,000) than for transfers on death and lifetime transfers made within three years of death. After the cumulative total of £ 310,000 has been exceeded for lifetime transfers (made more than three years before death) the same rates apply as for the other forms of transfer. The rates are steeply progressive with no indexing provisions for inflation.[3] After the £ 25,000 nil rate margin has been exceeded each successive transfer is subject to tax in slices at higher rates. The overall rate of CTT applicable on the death of an individual will depend upon the total of his lifetime transfers and the assets that are transferred on his death.

Two further points must be noted:

a) the £ 25,000 nil rate margin applies to all individuals and also to certain trusts formed prior to 27th March, 1974. These trusts are generally (but not particularly accurately) referred to as discretionary trusts;
b) with many lifetime transfers there will be disposals for Capital Gains Tax ('CGT') purposes and no relief is given in a CTT computation for any CGT liability that may be payable. This is of course unless the transferee elects to pay the CGT.

The CTT legislation gives particular attention to trusts (often called 'settlements'). The CTT legislation pertaining to trusts is extremely complex and in this section only the international aspects are briefly touched upon. The entire effect of the CTT legislation pertaining to trusts is probably not yet fully appreciated – certainly not outside the UK.

For those not familiar with trusts they are creatures of the Anglo-US legal systems. There is no brief and all embracing definition of them. One of the best is:

'a trust is the relationship which arises wherever a person called the trustee is... compelled... to hold property for the benefit of persons... or for some other object permitted by law in such a way that the benefit accrues not to the trustee but to the beneficiary...

The key to understanding the trust concept is to appreciate the duality of the legal interest of the trustee (or trustees) and the beneficiaries non-legal (but nonetheless enforceable) interests. Trusts can play an important part in international financial and tax (particularly CTT) planning.[4]

B. Terminology

Some CTT terms have already been touched upon; some important definitions are:

Transfer of Value S.20 (2)

A transfer of property (not being excluded property) made by a person (the 'transferor') as a result of which the value of his estate immediately after is less than it would be but for the disposition. ***But*** there is no transfer if it can be shown that the transaction was not intended to confer any gratuitous benefit on any person and it was at arm's length.

There are two forms of transfers of value – lifetime transfers or transfers on death. Such transfers are chargeable *or* exempt.

Chargeable transfer S.20 (5)

Any transfer of value made by an individual after 26th March, 1974 other than an exempt transfer.

Exempt transfer
Any transfer of value that is specifically exempted from CTT.

Transfer on death S.22 (1)
The transfer of value which an individual is deemed to have made immediately before his death. It is equal to the aggregate of his assets less any liabilities i.e. the net value of his 'estate' at death. The first transfer on death can only arise on or after 13th March, 1975.

Estate S.23 (1)–(2)
An individual's estate is the aggregate of all the property to which he is beneficially entitled and this can include certain interests in trusts. Excluded property (see post) is not included in the estate of an individual.

Excluded property S.24, Schedule 5 para 2 (1) (a), Schedule 7 para 3
This property does not form part of a person's estate and it is not chargeable to CTT because of its special nature or because of the status of the person entitled to the beneficial interest. The full text of these provisions is given in Appendix 5.

Distribution payment Schedule 5 para 11 (7)
Any payment (including the transfer of assets other than money) from a discretionary-type trust which is not
(i) income for UK income tax purposes (or would be if the recipient were resident in the UK);
(ii) a payment in respect of costs or expenses.

Capital distribution
An actual or deemed distribution payment (see above) made from a settlement when there is no interest in possession (e.g. a life interest) in whole or part of the trust property from which the payment was made.

Interest in possession
There is no statutory definition of an interest in possession in trust property. But from the wording of the Act and Revenue Practice it is clear that there is such an interest where a person is entitled as of right to the income of the trust property or to the use and enjoyment of the trust property. However, there are doubtful cases with some trusts and this is unsatisfactory.

Accumulation and maintenance settlements Schedule 5 para. 15 (1)
Settlements where one or more beneficiaries, on or before attaining the age of 25, must become entitled to an interest in possession and the income from the trust property has been accumulated insofar as it has not been paid out for the maintenance of such a beneficiary.

Disposition

This term is not defined in the Act but includes all forms of transfers of interests in property of any kind including excluded property. Disposition also includes the various deemed forms of transfer.

C. Chargeable Transfers

Before considering the CTT exemptions, deferrals, exclusions etc., it is pertinent to consider briefly, by way of contrast, the position of a UK domiciled individual. This will emphasize the necessity for careful CTT planning.

A UK domiciled transferor prior to making a gift must also consider and make provision for any liabilities (other than CTT) that he may incur, e.g. Stamp Duty, CGT and any fees. He will receive no relief from CTT in respect of any such liabilities. The transferee can of course choose to pay any of these liabilities that the transferor may have incurred on the making of the gift. This, of course, merely reduces the value of the gift for CTT purposes.

Two basic situations can arise:

Transferor pays the CTT

Primarily, subject to contrary agreement, it is the transferors liability. In such a case, the value of the gift being 'net', must be grossed-up e.g. a mother decides to give her daughter £ 100,000 in cash. The tax which the mother has to pay on £ 100,000 is £ 15, 689, so the real cost of the gift to the mother is £ 115,689.

Transferee pays the CTT

Grossing-up is not necessary here as the transferee, by paying the CTT, receives the gift gross, e.g. a father decides to give his son £ 100,000 in cash and the son agrees to pay the tax. Here the CTT on £ 100,000 is £ 11,875 and the son pays this, leaving him with £ 88,125 net. If the father wished instead to give his son £ 100,000 clear then he must actually give £ 115,689 and so the son then has £ 15,689 in CTT to pay. See the previous example.

N.B. in the above examples:

(i) any exemptions are ignored, *and*

(ii) it is assumed that the £ 100,000 or so is the first chargeable transfer and that the transferors do not die within three years of making the gifts. In such an event, the CTT rates would be higher.

As gifts are taxed at progressive rates with generally even higher rates on death and on transfers made within three years of death then a UK domiciled individual (or a foreign domiciled individual with UK assets) ought to plan his gifts carefully. But with such high rates of tax, it has been the experience of UK tax practitioners to date, that few UK domiciled individuals are prepared to make any substantial gifts that are not covered by exemptions.

Instead provision is often made for the payment of CTT on a death by the intended transferees with the aid of the proceeds of a life assurance policy effected on the intending transferor's life. The premiums on such a policy would normally be paid by the intending transferors and/or his wife and be covered by one or more exemptions (see post). These policies are not of course inflation proof.

The overall result is that to a great extent domestic UK CTT planning is now largely restricted to re-organising estates, utilising exemptions and deferrals (see post) and providing funding for discharge of CTT from the proceeds of insurance policies. With a foreign domiciled individual there is more room to manoeuvre and it is vital for him or her who is or will be resident in the UK to *plann well in advance.* Particularly where a foreign domiciled lady is going to marry a UK domiciled man. *This planning must be done* before a UK domicil is acquired or before he or she is treated as being domiciled in the UK.[5]

D. Exemptions and Deferrals

Most exemptions and deferrals are contained in Schedule 6.

PARA. 1: TRANSFERS BETWEEN HUSBAND AND WIFE

Transfers between husband and wife are exempt. This exemption applies to both lifetime transfers and transfers on death. It is not a requirement that the donee should receive the gifted property absolutely – he or she may only be entitled to the income from the property, e.g. he or she may only have a life interest in the property.

Clearly care has to be taken over the items transferred. Cash for example, will increase the donee's estate to the same amount as the donor's estate is diminished. The value of the property transferred is the market value at the time of the transfer.

One further example of this exemption does not receive sufficient consideration. Where the *donor spouse* is domiciled *in the UK* and the *donee spouse* is domiciled outside the UK, then the exemption does *not* apply in whole. In such a case the transfer is exempt only to the extent that the increase in the value of the donee's estate does not exceed £ 25,000. The logic behind this seems to be that if such a transfer was exempt then the foreign domiciled spouse could then convert the gifted property into excluded property (see post) and so it could escape the CTT net. Since 1st January, 1974, when the Domicil and Matrimonial Proceedings Act 1973 came into force, a particularly close watch has to be kept on the domicil position of both spouses. If both migrant spouses have the same domicil the deferral is still available. Difficulties may arise in practice as it will be often difficult to determine an individual's domicil to the satisfaction of *both* the UK Revenue and the individual concerned.

It will be noticed that this form of CTT relief is really more a deferral rather than an exemption. Indeed over utilisation of it in the case of UK domiciled spouse can lead to more CTT being payable in the long run as the estates of both spouses are 'bunched' together on the second death.

This form of deferral is exceptionally useful to emigrant spouses from the UK who can cover their CTT position during the vulnerable three year s.45 period by leaving their assets in their wills to each other. In addition or alternatively consideration could be given to the use of term assurance and for the acquisition of exempt government securities (see E (a) post).

PARA. 2: LIFETIME TRANSFERS OF UP TO £ 2,000 P.A. IN AGGREGATE

These transfers are exempt. If the exemption is not used or fully used in one year then the unused part can be carried forward for one year only when it can be added to that year's exemption. A year is the twelve months to 5th April, (i.e. the UK tax year).

PARA. 3: GIFTS UP TO AND INCLUDING £ 100 P.A.

Gifts of up to and including £ 100 p.a. made to any person are exempt. This exemption is separate and in addition to that given under para. 2 above. Any number of such gifts can be made.

PARA. 4: GIFTS OUT OF INCOME

Gifts out of income are exempt to the extent that they are part of the donor's normal expenditure, which after allowing for the gifts, leave him with sufficient income to maintain his usual standard of living.

PARA. 5: MARRIAGE GIFTS

These are exempt as to the amounts of:

(i) £ 5,000 if made by a parent of either party
(ii) £ 2,500 if made by a remoter ancestor than a parent of either party or by one party to the other party
(iii) £ 1,000 in any other case.

N.B. the gift has to be made before marriage.

S.47: Deeds of Family Arrangement

Certain dispositions are not treated as transfers of value:

(i) A disposition by a deed of family arrangement which alters the devolution of a deceased individual's assets which is made within two years of his death;

(ii) a disclaimer of an interest in settled property other than for consideration in money or money's worth;

(iii) a surviving spouse's election to redeem a life interest in residue made within one year of the grant of probate or letters of administration where there is an intestacy;

(iv) a disclaimer of a legacy in an estate (not being for valuable consideration) made within two years of death.

S.46: Dispositions for Family Maintenance

Certain dispositions by an individual are not treated as transfers of value if they are made in connection with, inter alia:

(i) the maintenance of the individual's spouse or

(ii) the maintenance education and training of children (including illegitimate children) up to the age of eighteen years or until they have completed their full time education which ever is the later.

Others

In addition to the above there are various other exemptions such as gifts to charities, political parties, for UK national purposes, for public benefit. Deferrals are available in respect of works of art and historic buildings and woodlands (the standing trees rather than the land). Most of these are not so important in the international context of CTT.

E. Exclusions

There are various forms of excluded property. The first four forms are dependant upon the domicil of the individual concerned.

(a) *Exempt British Government Securities*[6], Under Schedule 7 para. 3, such securities (issued and authorised under F (No. 2) A 1931 S.22 or F (No. 2) A 1915 S.47) are excluded property so long as the securities are in the beneficial ownership of a person who is neither *domiciled* nor *ordinarily resident* in the UK. A list of these appears in Appendix 7.

If the securities are in a settlement ('trust') and a foreign domiciled[1] and not ordinarily resident individual has an interest in possession in such securities then to the extent that the interest subsists in such securities, they are excluded property. If there is no interest in possession (e.g. as in a discretionary trust) then provided *all known* beneficiaries of the trust are neither domiciled nor ordinarily resident in the UK, then the securities will be excluded property. This exclusion can be utilised in many cases with UK or ex-UK (i.e. exported) trusts where the life tenant has a foreign domicil and is not ordinarily resident in the UK. Where there is a discretionary trust, then all known beneficiaries must satisfy the requirements for the exclusion and this will be often difficult to fulfil in the case of many UK connected trusts. Two aspects are often not appreciated in connection with this exclusion:

(i) It appears that the investment in the securities can be made a day before any 'disposition'.

(ii) It applies irrespective of the domicil of the *recipient* whether the disposition is inter vivos or on death.

An emigrant can utilise this exclusion because if in law he has acquired a foreign domicil *and* is not ordinarily resident in the UK, then this satisfies the requirements for the operation of this exclusion.

Para. 3 (3), provides that the normal legal domicil rules will be applied and *excludes* the application of S.45. So the emigrant can 'cover' the vulnerable S.45 three year period by investing part or whole of his assets in exempt government securities. Emigrants to the Channel Islands or the Isle of Man since 10th December, 1974 can also benefit from this exclusion.

This exclusion has little application to immigrants and residents of the UK. Most of these categories of individuals will usually at one time or other be ordinarily resident or even be domiciled in the UK.

(b) S.24 (2) Property situated outside the UK is excluded property if the individual entitled to it is an *individual domiciled outside the UK.*[6] The UK in this sense means the United Kingdom of Great Britain and Northern Ireland but does not include the Channel Islands and the Isle of Man. The situs of assets is discussed later. The effect of this sub-section (and some of the above discussed exemptions and deferrals) can be simply illustrated with some examples:

(i) A, a foreign domiciled individual living in England has £ 100,000 in a London Bank. A wishes to give this £ 100,000 to his nephew who has an English domicil. (The S.45 deemed domicil position should first be checked out!) A and B should each open bank accounts in the Channel Islands (or the Isle of Man). A should then transfer the £ 100,000 from his London Bank to his account in the Channel Islands. Then he should transfer the funds from his account to his nephew's Channel Islands Bank account. So effectively this gift will be made abroad from excluded property and so is outside the CTT net. If the gift *was made in the UK* then it would be subject to CTT. The domicil of the nephew is irrelevant.

The position may be similar for transfers on death except where a double tax treaty affects the position.

Clearly, it is preferable that a foreign domiciled individual should for CTT purposes keep his funds or assets in the UK as low in value as possible.

(ii) B is domiciled and lived in Scotland until he was 25. He then lived in England for five years. Then B emigrated to Gibraltar together with his 'fortune' and within a short space of time say one year, met D, a Gibraltarian, and married her. B has £ 100,000 in a London Bank and proposes to make a gift of it to D. Can he effect the transfer either as an exempt gift to his spouse or out of excluded property as per (i) above?

Firstly it is clear that B has a Scottish domicil of origin and just because he has lived in England for five years it does not mean that he has necessarily lost his Scottish domicil of origin. To actually show that he has acquired a domicil of choice in Gibraltar may be rather a difficult matter at that stage. But whether he has or not a Gibraltar domicil he is caught by S.45 (1) (a) and so is unable to take advantage of S.24 (2) as per (i) above, i.e. he cannot move assets out of the UK and thus convert them into excluded property.

Secondly, although it may be unlikely that B acquired a domicil of choice in Gibraltar, it is far less likely that his spouse acquired a Scottish domicil on her marriage.[7] So B cannot take advantage of the transfer between spouse exemption, except to the extent that his estate does not decrease more than £ 25,000. Plus, of course, if unutilised, the £ 2,000 annual exemption.

What then can he do? The first thing is to establish whether B has acquired a domicil of choice in Gibraltar of choice. At first glance, it would appear to make no difference because of S.45 (1) (a). But assume for a moment that B is domiciled in Gibraltar and also is not ordinarily resident in the UK. He could then take advantage of Schedule 7 para. 3 (1) exemption and give government exempt securities to his spouse which will be free of CTT. This exclusion is *not* subject to S.45. So the solution may be for B if he is domiciled in Gibraltar[8] to give his wife £ 100,000 worth of, for example, $5^1/_2\%$ Funding Stock 1982/4. The place of donation is irrelevant.

But if he has *not* acquired a domicil of choice in Gibraltar then his room to manoeuvre is very limited.

(iii) M, domiciled in Belgium dies with £ 100,000 in a London Bank and a portfolio of UK registered company shares. Clearly, these assets are transferred on his death and are subject to CTT.

But if an Isle of Man investment company owns these assets, then the only assets that devolve on M's death will be the shares in the Isle of Man company and any loan account with the company. As these assets are located outside the UK, they are excluded property within the meaning of S.24 (2) and so there is no transfer of value on M's death.

(c) Schedule 5 para. 2 (1) (a)[6] gives a variant on the exclusion in (b) above. This exclusion is of particular interest to trustees of existing trusts where the settlor (i.e. founder) was not domiciled in UK when the trust ('settlement') was made.

'Where property comprised in a settlement is situated outside the UK, the property (but not a reversionary interest in the property) is excluded property *unless* the settlor was domiciled in the UK at the time the settlement was made.'

This replaces the old Estate Duty exemption, the primary differences being that it is far clearer and there is *no* requirement that the proper law of the settlement should *not* be that of England, Scotland or Northern Ireland.

What constitutes a 'settlement' is defined broadly in Schedule 5 para. 1 (2) as 'any disposition whereby property is held in trust for persons in succession or for any person subject to a contingency: or held by trustees on trust to accumulate the income or with power to make payments out of income on discretion: or is charged with the payment of an annuity, '...'unless granted for full consideration in money's worth'.

A wide definition of 'settlor' is provided for in Schedule 5 para. 1 (6) '... includes any person by whom settlement was made directly or indirectly, and in particular (but without prejudice to the generality of the preceding words) includes any person who has provided funds directly or indirectly for the purpose of or in connection with the settlement or has made with any other person a reciprocal arrangement for that other person to make the settlement'.

There will be a number of trusts around the world which are subject to CTT even if there is no property in the UK, simply because the settlor was domiciled in the UK at the time of creation of the 'trust' (or the date of death in the case of a Will Trust).

This exclusion can be utilised if an individual considers that he is about to acquire a UK domicil, either through the operation of law or the deeming provisions of S.45. Also a UK resident – whether domiciled in the UK or not – may prefer to have his wealthy foreign domiciled Uncle make a foreign trust in favour of him and his family rather than receive the cash direct Quite apart from the CTT advantages, there may be other advantages, e.g. such a trust may be free of UK exchange control restrictions and would also have UK capital gains tax advantages.

(d) Schedule 7 para. 5 provides where an individual is domiciled in the Channel Islands or the Isle of Man and is beneficially entitled to the rights from UK War Savings or National Savings Certificates, Premium Savings Bonds, deposits with the National Savings Bank or any Trustee Savings Bank, certain other Savings Banks and contractual savings schemes under ICTA 1970 S.414 and S.415 respectively, then such rights are excluded property. For the purpose of Schedule 7 para. 5 S.45 is *not applicable.*

(e) There are also various other exclusions which are not relevant to this work, e.g. transfers on the death of persons in the armed forces, cash options under certain annuity schemes, reversions, overseas pensions, moveable property belonging to members of visiting forces visiting the UK, etc.

F. Trusts

INTRODUCTION

Prior to the introduction in March, 1974 of CTT the utilisation of trusts was a well established technique in UK financial planning. In the international context it was then important that the proper law of the trust was not a UK law and that the settlor of the trust was not domiciled in the UK. In particular, the discretionary trust was often used as tax savings could be made since no beneficiary had any fixed rights to income or capital. The trustees in such cases usually had extremely wide powers with regard to the application of the income and capital and investment. The most that a beneficiary of a discretionary trust could (in theory) expect or hope for was that some day the trustees might exercise their discretion in his favour. In the interim period the trust funds effectively remained in limbo which from the point of view of UK tax inter alia was highly satisfactory.

The effect of CTT on trusts since March, 1974 can be summarised in that few UK inter vivos trusts (apart from the odd accumulation and maintenance trusts) will be created. Existing trusts must be reviewed in depth. Later it will be seen that a trust with foreign trustees will be in a very disadvantageous position if the trust property is not excluded property.

The creation of new foreign trust is obviously of particular interest to the UK Revenue – especially where UK domiciled settlors are concerned. At first sight it may seem that the CTT provisions relating to UK trusts may not be relevant, e.g. where the trust property is excluded property under Schedule 5 para. 2 (1) (a) (see ante) but there are *many foreign trusts where this exclusion does not apply* in whole or part.

Accordingly it is pertinent to look briefly at how CTT is applied to the three basic forms of trust.

(1) ACCUMULATION AND MAINTENANCE TRUSTS (SCHEDULE 5 PARA. 15)

These are defined earlier and the basic position is that where payments are made to a beneficiary or beneficiaries out of the trust property of such a trust and the conditions are satisfied then such payment is not treated as a capital distribution for CTT purposes. But where the basic conditions are not complied with, a capital distribution can be regarded as being made equivalent to the value of the assets distributed. Such a calculation is made along the same lines as a distribution from a discretionary settlement (see post).

(2) TRUSTS WITH INTERESTS IN POSSESSION

General

The CTT position is clearly dealt with in Schedule 5 para 3(1) which provides that the individual who has the interest in possession is treated as being beneficially entitled to the trust property in which he (or she) has the interest i.e. the trust is made 'transparent'. On termination of the interest there is a deemed transfer of value equivalent to the value of the trust property in which the interest has terminated. CTT is payable unless:

(a) the individual with the interest in possession becomes entitled to the trust property (Schedule 5 para 4 (3)) or;
(b) the interest reverts to the settlor during his life or his spouse – provided the recipient spouse is domiciled in the UK. Schedule 5 para 4 (6) (a) or;
(c) some other exemption or deferral is available.

If the interest in possession terminates *and* there is a CTT liability then the individual who had the interest in possession is deemed to have made the transfer and the CTT is calculated by reference to his own personal rate.

Foreign Trusts with Interest in Possession

Where the trust property is not excluded property (i.e. because at the time the trust was made the settlor had a UK domicil and/or non-exempt UK situated assets are now held directly by the trustees) then on termination of the interest in the trust property by death or otherwise CTT will be payable unless any exemptions are available. Several courses of action can be considered e.g.

(i) if the individual with the interest in possession has a non-UK domicil and is not ordinarily resident in the UK then the trustees could consider partly or wholly investing in exempt British Government securities (see Exclusion A. ante);
(ii) if permissible under the trust instrument then the trust property could be advanced out to the individual with the interest in possession (. . . and then perhaps placed in a new trust. . .?);
(iii) if the problem is caused only by UK assets being held directly by the trustees then:
    (a) consider disposing of the UK assets or
    (b) if (a) is not applicable or desirable then the consideration should be given to the interposition of a non-UK holding company between the trust and the UK assets;
(iv) if the potential CTT threat arises because of the domicil of the settlor at the time of formation of the trust (or the date of death in the case of a will trust) then consideration should be given to ways of terminating the trust to counter the CTT threat.

    Though the foreign trustees personally may be beyond the reach of the UK Revenue in the event that they decide not to pay the CTT, the UK Revenue can

enforce a CTT laibility against any trust assets in the UK or against the beneficiaries or the settlor if he is still alive.
No course of action should be considered without taking into account other factors e.g. CGT exchange control.
Before any steps are taken the CTT arithmetic must be done.

(3) Discretionary Trusts

It is for convenience and not for accuracy's sake that trusts other than accumulation and maintenance trusts and trusts with interests in possession are termed discretionary trusts. Some trusts 'outside' the other definitions may have little in the way of discretionary provisions. Discretionary trusts which do not contain excluded property (Schedule 5 para 2 (1) (a) or Schedule 7 para 3 – see Appendix 5 and E ante) are treated differently for CTT purposes from the other two forms of trusts. Basically all actual capital distributions from a discretionary trust are potentially subject to CTT and there are various forms of deemed distribution. The three main forms of actual or deemed distribution giving rise to a CTT liability are:

a) a capital distribution (e.g. an advance) is made *other* than to the settlor or his or her spouse (provided that the recipient spouse is domiciled in the UK);
b) an interest in possession is created in the trust property;
c) an accumulation and maintenance trust is created (Schedule 5 para 15).

There are two different ways of calculating the CTT payable on capital distributions depending on whether the discretionary trust is made *before* 27th March, 1974 or *on* or *after* 27th March, 1974.

(A) Pre 27 th March, 1974 Trusts

The rate payable on capital distributions is that applicable to lifetime transfers and each trust is treated as a separate person.
In order to provide a measure of relief following the introduction of CTT and so as to facilitate the early termination of trusts, there is a reduced rate of CTT payable on certain capital distributions:

Transitional Relief on Capital Distributions:

Schedule 5 para 14 (2) grants transitional relief by way of a reduced rate of tax on capital distributions made within certain periods of time:

Date of capital distribution		*% of normal tax rate*
up to 31st	March, 1976	10 %
year to	March 1977	$12^1/_2$%
year to	March 1978	15 %
year to	March 1979	$17^1/_2$%
year to	March 1980	20 %

N.B. the transitional relief does not apply:

(i) where a person (who receives the benefit of the distribution) is *not* domiciled or deemed to be domiciled in the UK.

(ii) where the charge to CTT is in respect of annual deemed distributions (see post – Periodic Charges) made by non-resident trustees. If the trustees of a non-UK trust wish to take advantage of the transitional relief, the beneficiaries must be domiciled in the UK.

(iii) to post 26th March, 1974 trusts. This includes funds added to trusts formed before that date. (Each addition being treated as a separate trust).

(B) Post 26th March, 1974 Trusts

(1) Schedule 5 para 7 (2) provides the formula for calculating the rate of CTT liability on distributions *up to* a total amount equal to the initial value of the trust assets settled; *the numerator* being the CTT the settlor would have paid on a chargeable transfer equal to the initial value of the trust fund ignoring any exemptions; *the denominator* being the initial value of the trust fund.

(2) Schedule 5 para 7 (3) provides that distributions *over* the initial value of the trust funds are taxed at the rate that would be payable by the settlor if he had made transfers of values of the same amount after creating the trust i.e. the trust is treated as being transparent for CTT purposes.

Three further aspects should be emphasised:

i) the transitional reliefs do *not* apply;

ii) if assets are added to a settlement after 26th March, 1974 then these assets are treated as being in a separate trust;

iii) the cumulative total attributable to the settlor at the time the trust was created affects the trust both on creation and afterwards.

Periodic Charge

In addition to the above, Schedule 5 para 12 provides for deemed capital distributions of the entire trust property to occur on each tenth anniversary of the formation of a trust (whether or not it was made before or after 27th March, 1974) if there is no interest in possession at the time of the relevant anniversary. The tax paid is 30% of the amount that would have been charged if an actual distribution was made. Where the trust is outside the UK there will be annual charges (see post).

It is worthwhile emphasising the operative dates:

i) Ten year 'relevant' anniversary – no date prior to 1st April, 1980 is a relevant anniversary for the ten year periodic charge. A relevant anniversary is at the end of a ten year period beginning with the date of the transfer of value i.e. the formation date (or the deemed formation date), e.g. a trust formed on 18th May, 1962 will have its first relevant anniversary on 18th May, 1982.
ii) Annual charge on the anniversary (where the trust is administered outside the UK) – No anniversary date prior to 1st January, 1976 will be an occasion for the annual charge. Thereafter annual charges will arise.

Foreign Trusts

These are trusts which are administered outside the UK and the trustees or a majority of them are not resident in the UK. Where this is the case Schedule 5 para 12 (2) provides for an annual charge on each anniversary (see above) in each ten year period ending with a relevant anniversary other than the tenth and last year. An anniversary occuring in any year prior to 1st January, 1976 is excepted. The rate of the annual charge is 3% of the tax that would be payable on a capital distribution if it was actually made. On the tenth anniversary of the trust (or multiples thereof) or on an actual capital distribution credit will be given in respect of the tax paid in satisfaction of the annual charge. But the reduction because of the CTT credit already paid with regard to capital distributions is restricted to the amount of tax paid on capital distributions. Schedule 5 para. 6 (5) omits the necessity for *grossing up*. This means that the CTT does not have to be added onto the value of the trust property but is calculated on the value of the trust property i.e. it is a net calculation.

Summary

The effect of the provisions can be summarised in that it is extremely unlikely that many UK non-charitable discretionary trusts will again be formed. Most existing UK discretionary trusts are in the process of being terminated or converted into trusts with interests in possession or with accumulation and maintenance provisions. Transitional reliefs are restricted where there is a foreign element. Offshore trusts that do not contain excluded property i.e. are outside the Schedule 5 para 2 (1) (a) exclusion are very heavily penalised by the CTT annual charge. In many cases foreign trusts which do not and cannot (because the settlor had a UK domicil) obtain the benefit of any exclusion will usually be liquidated or brought on-share.

Although a trust may obtain the benefit of the exclusion under Schedule 5 para 2 (1) (a) it must be appreciated that this exclusion *does not apply where the trustees hold UK assets other than exempt UK government securities directly.* In such cases and others the trust assets will *not* be excluded property and the general rules apply.

G. Liability for CTT

LIFETIME TRANSFERS (S.25 AND S.27)

Primarily the transferor is liable and if he does not pay then the transferee can be liable – or any other party who takes an interest in the transferred property. If the property is placed in a trust then any person who receives a trust benefit can be made liable in the event of default of the settlor or the trustees.

If the transferor dies within three years of making the transfer, then the higher rates of tax apply and any 'extra' tax is payable by the transferee. If the transfer involves the making of a trust then the trustees are liable, then beneficiaries to the extent that they receive a benefit from the trust.

TRANSFERS ON DEATH

Apart from a liability that arises in respect of property comprised in a trust or in respect of gifts or trusts made or broken prior to 27th March, 1974, the personal representatives are liable in respect of the free estate. With an interest in possession trust the trustees are liable in respect of CTT thereon. Nominees or agents in the UK can (as in Estate Duty days) be made liable to the extent of property in their hands. In the event of non-payment an individual who receives a benefit from the estate or trust can be made liable.

TRUSTS

The trustees are primarily liable to pay CTT on chargeable transfers of value of trust property. If the settlor has not paid any CTT due on formation of the trust, then the trustees can also be liable. If the settlor dies within three years of formation of the trust, then the trustees can also be liable for tax at the higher rates. Any person who receives a benefit from the trust property or has an interest in possession in it can also be liable if the trustees do not pay any tax that is due. If the trustees are not resident in the UK then the settlor (whatever his domicil or residential status) can be made liable in respect of chargeable transfers of value made by the trustees during his lifetime. These provisions are particularly relevant where foreign trusts are concerned because there will be

(a) many trusts that do not only contain excluded property, i.e. the trustees hold UK assets directly
(b) many situations where it is not possible to ascertain the domicil of the settlor at the time the trust was made.

It should be noted that any tax unpaid on trust property gives rise to a 'charge' in favour of the UK Revenue so that if property is physically in the UK collection is no problem for the Revenue notwithstanding that the offshore trustees, settlor or beneficiaries are all outside the UK.

H. Disclosure Provisions

Revenue Powers Schedule 4 para 5

Any person can be required by notice in writing with thirty days to furnish such information for the purposes of F (No. 1) A 1975 as may be stated in the notice and such notice may be combined with a notice relating to income tax e.g. ICTA 1970 S.481 Notice.

A barrister or solicitor is not obliged in pursuance of such a notice to disclose without his client's consent any information subject to the following exceptions in respect of which a claim to professional privilege could be claimed. However, a solicitor may be obliged to disclose the name and address of his client. If that client is not resident in the UK and carries on a business comprising of the provision of facilities and services (relating to the formation of companies or trusts) for UK residents, the solicitor may be compelled to furnish to the UK Revenue the details of individuals in the UK for whom the client has acted.

Mandatory Returns Schedule 4 para 4

Where a person in the course of a trade or profession (other than a barrister) has been concerned with the making after 26th March, 1974 of a trust and *knows or has reason to believe that:*
(a) The settlor had a UK domicil *and*
(b) The trustees are not or will not be resident in the UK, then he *must* within three months of the formation of the trust *make a return* stating the names and addresses of the settlor and the trustees of the trust.

No return is required in respect of will trusts or trusts in respect of which a return has already been made. The meaning of settlor in paras 4 and 5 is not restricted to the person whose name appears on the trust deed as settlor. A person who adds property to a settlement will be treated as a settlor.

I. Location of Assets

It is extremely important to ascertain the situs of assets so as to determine what is excluded property and where a debt is concerned whether it can be deducted from the UK or foreign property. Sometimes Double Tax Treaties can affect the location of the property.

LIABILITIES

Schedule 10 para 1 provides (except as otherwise provided) that liabilities shall be taken into account in determining the value of a transferor's estate. Para 1 (3) provides that a liability is only to be taken into account if it was incurred for a consideration in money or money's worth unless the liability is imposed by law. A liability which is attached to a property shall be (per para 2) taken in so far as is possible to reduce the value of that property e.g. if an individual owns a house in the UK which is mortgaged then the mortgage will reduce the value of the house and if it is more than the value of the house the surplus will be carried against the rest of his UK estate. Para 3 provides that where a liability is to a person resident outside the UK which *neither* attached to any UK property *nor* falls to be discharged in the UK then it shall reduce the value of property outside the UK in the first instance. These rules are exceptionally important where a non UK domiciled person has both assets in the UK and outside the UK. Subject to the above the situs of a simple contract debt will be where the debt is due to be discharged.

SITUS OF ASSETS

The general legal rules will apply except where varied by a Double Tax Treaty. For example cash in a bank account in the UK will be situated in the UK and cash in a bank account in Jersey will be situated outside the UK. Similarly, shares on a UK register will be UK situated and shares on a Jersey register will be situated outside the UK. But these situations are sometimes altered by a Double Tax Treaty e.g. the UK-South African Treaty. The situs of assurance policies (and their proceeds) in the first instance will depend on whether or not the policy contract is under seal. If it is not under seal then the situs will usually be where the policy moneys are payable. If the policy is under seal and payable in the UK then the policy (and its proceeds) will be situated in the UK. If a policy is under seal with a non-UK assurance company and is payable outside the UK then the policy (and its proceeds) will be situated outside the UK. These are the general and practical rules.

SUMMARY

By paying careful attention to the exact situs of assets and the attachment of debts, considerable CTT savings can be effected especially by individuals not domiciled in the UK.

J. Double Taxation

SCHEDULE 7 PARA 7 DOUBLE TAXATION RELIEF

Para 7 (6) provides that any estate duty treaty in force prior to enactment of F (No. 1) A 1975 shall continue in force substituting in effect CTT for estate duty. It is specifically provided that the deemed domicil provisions contained in S.45 shall *not* affect the interpretation of any such provisions. In other words where there is a comprehensive treaty S.45 does not apply. Where the deceased had a UK domicil with most treaties credit is given against UK CTT for any foreign duties paid on property located (or deemed to be located under the situs rules) in the foreign country in which the duties are paid.

SCHEDULE 7 PARA 8 UNILATERAL RELIEF

Schedule 7 para 8 used to provide that (irrespective of any treaty relief) where a foreign tax is either similar to CTT or is a tax arising on the death or gift inter vivos and both it and CTT are payable, then a credit shall be allowed against the CTT liability in respect of the foreign tax.

Para 8 was changed with effect from 6th April, 1976 by FA 1976 S.125. It now provides that unilateral relief will be given against CTT in respect of taxes imposed in any territory outside the UK in respect of a disposition if:

(a) the tax is similar to CTT *or* the tax is chargeable by reference to death or gifts inter vivos, *and*

(b) any CTT chargeable by reference to the same disposition or other event is also attributable to the value of that property.

Where the property is situated in the overseas territory and outside the UK, then the unilateral CTT credit will be equal to the overseas tax. If the overseas tax exceeds the UK CTT no UK repayment of the excess or extra UK 'credit' is available.

Where the property is outside both treaty countries *or* is situated in both of them (as can happen for tax purposes) para 8 (3) provides a formula for calculating the credit:

$$\frac{A}{A + B} \times C$$

A = CTT
B = Overseas Tax
C = Smaller of A or B

Where tax is imposed in two or more overseas territories in respect of property which is:
(a) neither situated in the UK nor in any of those territories or
(b) situated in both the UK and in each of those territories

then the formula above applies with:

B = the aggregate of the overseas tax
C = the aggregate of all except the largest of A and the overseas tax imposed in each of them.

1. See Sections II (A) (B), XI (A) (I) (2) and (B) (I) (2) (4)
2. See Section XI (B) (I) (2) (4)
3. Appendix 5 contains the table of rates
4. See post E (C) and F Section V (C) Section XI (A) (5) (6.4) (B) (8)
5. See Section II (A) (B), Section XI A, Appendix I (A)
6. See Appendix 5
7. It is difficult to see how she could have acquired a domicil of choice in Scotland as she has never lived there.
8. As Gibraltar is within the Scheduled Territories the gift can be made without any exchange control complications - see Section VIII.

Section VII: Capital Gains Tax ('CGT')

A. General

This tax was introduced by FA 1965, which has been amended by subsequent legislation. The ICTA 1970, the consolidated tax legislation, does not include CGT.

The tax applies to resident or ordinarily individuals[1] and resident corporations, except that individuals are liable to tax at the rate of 30% whereas corporations are liable corporation tax which is however calculated so that the effective rate is also 30%. The rules for arriving at quantifiable gains and losses are basically the same for both companies and individuals. Charities, retirement and superannuation funds, consular officials and visiting armed forces are exempt from CGT, notwithstanding that they are resident or ordinarily resident in the UK. The terms 'resident' and 'ordinarily resident' have the meanings as for income tax purposes (see Section II).

So far as a individual coming to the UK is concerned, it is important to bear in mind that chargeable gains are taxable in a year of assessment to an individual who is resident or ordinarily resident in the UK.[1] But see the Revenue Practice contained in extra-statutory concession D.2 (contained in Appendix I (C)) where the Revenue Practice is in certain circumstances to split a tax year.

In the case of individuals resident or ordinarily resident but not domiciled in the UK they are liable for chargeable gains arising in the UK but not for gains made outside the UK unless the proceeds are remitted to the UK.[2] In such an event they are taxable in the year of remittance and not in the year when the gain was made.

Losses made by a person resident or ordinarily resident but not domiciled on the disposal of assets outside the UK are *not* allowable as losses for use by way of deduction from other chargeable gains.[2]

Where a non-resident is carrying on a trade or business in the UK through a branch or agency, chargeable capital gains accruing from that trade and the disposal of its assets in the UK are liable to CGT.[3]

In appropriate cases the relevant double taxation treaty should be considered, for, where there is a non-resident element, then there may be provision in the treaty for exemption, for example, of the gains in the UK of the branch or agency, or even to determine the location of assets.

B. Chargeable Assets

All manner of property[4], wherever situated, including:
(a) Options, debts and all manner of incorporeal property.
(b) Currencies other than sterling.
(c) Property created by the person disposing of it – e.g. copyright of books, a building which a person has erected or goods which he has manufactured.

C. Exemptions and Reliefs

The following is a summary of the principal exemptions and reliefs:

(1) Gains arising from the disposal of a house or flat which is the principal private residence of the taxpayer are exempt.[5] Where a house is used partly for a trade or business, only a part of the gain is exempt, based on that part of the property which is used exclusively for private occupation. Where a house has not been entirely owner/occupied throughout the period of ownership (e.g., because it has been rented), then only a fraction of the gain is exempt, corresponding to the period of occupation – except that a period of absence not exceeding three years (or periods which do not, taken together, exceed three years) during which the individual had no other main residence is ignored in calculating what is to be deducted for absences. Further relief is given by the provision that during the last twelve months of the period of ownership, if the property is unoccupied then this period is to be ignored. Where a person has two or more houses, they may nominate one of them as being the principal private residence.

(2) Chattels sold for £ 1,000 or less any gain accruing from the disposal of such assets is not chargeable. If the consideration exceeds £ 1,000, then marginal relief is given by restricting the tax to half the excess over £ 1,000.
Similarly, there is a restriction on relief for losses, so that if a chattel is bought for more than £ 1,000 and is disposed of for less than that figure, the allowable loss which can be used against other chargeable gains is limited, so that the asset is treated as if it had been disposed of for £ 1,000 only.

(3) Replacement of business assets (such as buildings, plant machinery etc., – see FA 1965 S.33) – whilst there is no exemption from CGT for business assets as such, some relief may be claimed where business assets are sold and replaced by others. The relief consists of giving the trader the right to deduct the gain from the cost of acquisition of the replacement item and defer payment of tax until the assets are disposed of and not replaced – i.e., it is a 'roll over' relief. Trading stock does not qualify for roll over relief.

(4) Current assets (e.g., inventories and receivables) which are brought into account in arriving at the profits of a trade are exempt from CGT.

(5) Small disposals – if the total value of a disposal, or the aggregate of disposals, in a given fiscal year does not exceed £ 500 the gains made are not chargeable to CGT. Thus, an individual could buy shares in A and B companies for a consideration of £ 25 and £ 80 respectively, and if both holdings were sold in a particular fiscal year to give a total consideration of £ 480 (thereby giving a very substantial capital gain), there would be no CGT charge. Marginal relief is available where the disposal exceeds £ 500 since the tax is limited to one-half of the difference between £ 500 and the total consideration.

(6) If the disposals in any year do not exceed £ 500 any losses in the year will be reduced for the purposes of carrying forward to later years by the amount of the chargeable gains accruing in the year when the losses accrued.

(7) Wasting asset – a disposal of such an asset will not amount to a chargeable gain. Generally, an asset is regarded as being in this category if it has a predictable life of less than fifty years. Plant and machinery is always regarded as having a life expectancy of less than fifty years.

(8) Life assurance and deferred annuities – provided the gain is made by the original beneficial owner of the policy contract, any gain is exempt. The assurance can be effected on the life either of the premium payer or of some other person, provided he has an insurable interest therein, and the occasion of payment of the sum assured can be either by way of surrender or under the terms of the policy. However, a chargeable gain can arise where the contract or an interest therein is sold to a third party.

MISCELLANEOUS EXEMPTIONS

Private Motor Cars.

Fixed Interest British Government Stocks (when held for more than 12 months)

Realizations where the market value at the time of realization is under £ 100 and when made by individuals.

Savings Certificates, National Development Bonds and Premium Savings Bonds.

Winnings from betting or prizes.

Compensation or damages for any wrong or injury suffered by an individual or accruing to him in a professional or vocational capacity.

Works of art, etc. Gains which accrue on the disposal of works of art given or bequeathed to a body not established or conducted for commercial purposes, are exempt if the asset is thought to be of national or historic or artistic importance.

SPECIAL RELIEFS

(1) Alternative charge to tax.[6] The basic tax rate for individuals is at 30% on the

net gain. There is an alternative basis and this is often known as the 'Half Income Rule'. If the chargeable gains in a particular year do not exceed £ 5,000 and less tax will be payable if he is charged to income tax under Case VI of Schedule 'D' on one-half of the chargeable gain, then that is the rate that is applied. Where the gain exceeds £ 5,000 the Schedule 'D' income tax charge is based on £ 2,500 plus the amount by which the gain exceeds the sum of £ 5,000.

By bringing a gain under the Half Income Rule to a charge to income tax, it must be remembered that the proportion of the gain to be added to the individual's other income for that year and treated as a top slice of that income, and, moreover, as investment income. On the other hand, by treating a gain as a part of income, it will be appreciated that the amount of the gain can be reduced by personal reliefs – but not any life insurance relief.

Where husband and wife a living together, their gains are aggregated and added to their joint for the purposes of applying the Half Income Rule. Relief is then apportioned between them in proportion to their own individual gains.

(2) Delayed remittances – it is not unusual – e.g., for exchange control purposes – for a person who is technically liable to capital gains arising from the disposal of an asset abroad to be unable to remit the proceeds to the UK. In such case relief is given. This is described elsewhere.

(3) Retirement relief – if on or after age sixty, an individual disposes of his business which he has owned throughout the previous ten years, relief is given of £ 4,000 for every year by which his age exceeds sixty, up to a maximum relief of £ 20,000 at age sixty-five.

(4) Husband and wife – when, in any year of assessment, either of the spouses (who are living together) transfer assets to each other, the transaction does not give rise to a chargeable gain – nor an allowable loss – but the donee is treated as having acquired the asset for whatever was the base value (see below) of the asset in the hands of the donor.

D. Disposals

It is the act of disposal, whether for a consideration or by way of gift, which creates a chargeable gain.[7] The transaction is treated as taking place at the time when a contract is made, except that, if the contract is conditional, then the disposal is treated as taking place whenever the contract becomes unconditional. On the occasion of each disposal, the taxpayer, apart from the reliefs referred to above, has to compute whether a chargeable gain (or an allowable loss) has occurred.

Part disposals include the disposal of an interest or right in or over an asset to a limited extent, so that there remains an interest or right in the asset belonging to the individual or company.

There is also a disposal of assets by a person where capital sums are derived from special situations – such as:

(a) Monies, by way of capital, are received by way of compensation (e.g., under a policy of insurance) for damage, deterioration or destruction of assets.
(b) Capital sums are received in return for waiver of rights or forfeiture or surrender of rights.
(c) A consideration is received for the use or exploitation of assets.

Where hire purchase situations are involved and there is a sale, the property is treated as disposed of at the commencement of the hire purchase agreement, notwithstanding that, at that stage, the purchaser will not be the owner of the property.

The transfer and re-transfer of an asset by way of security for a mortgage, or on repayment, does not fall to be treated as a disposal or an acquisition – but, of course, if a person takes property subject to a charge or mortgage, then, to the extent that he assumes the liability attached to the property, this is treated as part of the consideration.

Where compensation or insurance monies are, within one year, expended on the acquisition of a replacement, any charge accruing from the receipt of such monies can be set off against the cost of the replacement.

A transfer of a capital asset to the trading stock is a disposal for CGT purposes and vice versa.

Unless covered by the exemptions where there is a company amalgamation, normally, the distribution of assets on the liquidation of a company is treated as a disposal.

Where a business is transferred to a company as a going concern and all the assets are exchanged for shares in the company acquiring the business, the transfer is not treated as a disposal, since the shares issued in consideration for the exchange are treated as having taken the place of the assets disposed of. There is, however, a capital gain where there is another consideration other than an allotment of shares.

In a take-over situation, where one company is offering shares or other scrip in exchange for the shares of another company, this is not regarded as a disposal provided certain conditions are satisfied.[8] The issue of bonus shares to shareholders is not a disposal.

E. Computation of Gains and Losses

FA 1965 Schedule 6 sets out the details but the basic principals may be summarized as follows: –

(1) In calculating a gain there is deducted from the consideration the acquisition cost of the asset (or the cost of producing it) together with expenditure which has been incurred for the purpose of increasing the value of the asset. Incidental costs on making the disposal are also allowable deductions, but must be related wholly and exclusively to the transaction – e.g., professional fees to an agent, legal advisor

and costs of transfer (including stamp duty). No deduction can be claimed where the expenditure has been otherwise allowed as a deduction in calculating a liability to income tax or corporation tax or, in the case of losses, it is covered by capital allowances. *No adjustment* whatsoever is made to take account of inflation. Insurance premiums paid on a policy to cover the risk of damage to or destruction of the asset are not deductible. On a part disposal of an asset, there are provisions for the apportionment of expenditure allowable as between the part retained and the part disposed of.

(2) In arriving at the consideration for a disposal of assets, there should be excluded any money, or money's worth, which is charged to income tax as income or which is taken as a receipt in computing a profit for income tax purposes.

(3) Assets held on 6th April, 1965 – the charge to CGT is on gains which accrue after 6th April, 1965. In the case of assets owned on that date and disposed of sometime after 6th April, 1965, only the proportion of the gain attributable to the period after 6th April 1965 is chargeable.

In the case of quoted shares or securities, the rule is that the gain, or loss, has to be calculated on the Stock Market Value as at 6th April, 1965, although the actual original cost price (if known) can be used if this would show a lesser gain (or loss). Where, as is often the case, shares are acquired on different dates and are disposed of on different dates, the general rule applies that the first into the portfolio is to be regarded as the first out of the portfolio.

For this purpose, 'quoted securities' mean stocks, shares, or debentures which, on the commencement date in 1965, were quoted on a recognized stock exchange in the UK or elsewhere and, also, mean the units of unit trust schemes where the prices are published daily by the managers.

In other cases, the market value of assets has to be equated with the price which they might be expected to fetch on a sale in the open market.

Other assets – e.g., not quoted securities – are for the purposes of the legislation taken to accrue at a uniform rate over the period of ownership, and the Time Apportionment Rules apply. Thus, if B is the number of years from the original date of acquisition to 5th April, 1965, and S is the number of years from 6th April, 1965, to actual disposal, then the fraction of the gain which is chargeable CGT is arrived at by applying the formula $\frac{S}{B + S}$

A right of election can arise, at the instance of the taxpayer, who can, if he wishes, elect to have the gain (or loss) based on a value ascertained as at 6th April, 1965. Such election must be made within two years by notice in writing to the Revenue, the time commencing to run from the date of disposal.

CGT is charged on the aggregate of the chargeable gains accruing to a person in a tax year after deducting any allowable losses. Unrelieved losses accruing in a particular year can be carried forward to future years.

F. Special Situations

(1) *Deferred payments* – where payment is made by instalment over a period in excess of $1^1/_2$ years, the first instalment commencing, at the earliest, at the date of disposal, then the chargeable gain, if any, can be paid by instalments over a period not exceeding eight years, provided that the individual taxpayer can convince the Revenue that, if he were to pay tax on the payment of the first instalment, he would suffer hardship. Otherwise, no discount is allowed in making the valuation for the postponement nor to cover the contingency that the instalment payments might not alle be received. If in fact, part of the consideration is not received, the Revenue will adjust the gain restrospectively and, if necessary, effect a repayment of tax.

(2) *Gifts* – the market value is taken as being that at the date of disposal by the donor, and it is the donor who is primarily chargeable to tax. However, if the tax is not paid by the donor within twelve months of the date of assessment, the Revenue has the right to proceed against the donee, who, in turn, is given the statutory right to recover the tax paid by him on behalf of the donor from the donor.

(3) *Inheritance* – the death of an individual is not treated as a chargeable disposal by him in respect of the assets which pass under his will or intestacy. However, the beneficiaries, on acquiring assets from the personal representatives or administrator of the estate, are treated as having acquired the assets at the market value at the time of death.

An elderly person who has assets with substantial gains attached to them will be well advised, all other considerations being equal, not to dispose of them in his lifetime – rather, to pass them by will to his or her heirs, who will then receive the assets free of CGT and will also have the past appreciation disregarded and will start at a new cost price, being that prevailing at the date of death of their benefactor.

If, however, the executor or administrator disposes of assets other than by way of transfer to the beneficiaries e.g., to pay debts or capital transfer tax, he will be liable himself for any gain that is thereby made between death and disposal.

(4) *Settled property* – this means any property which is held in trust[9], except where it is held by a person as nominee for another person or for another person absolutely entitled to it or who would be entitled but for being an infant or under a disability.

Insofar as the trustees of a settlement dispose of property, this gives rise to a chargeable gain, unless they are non-resident trustees, in which case they are exempt (see Section V (C)).

(5) *Partnerships* – partners are separately chargeable in respect of capital gains accruing to them on the disposal of any partnership assets – i.e., their dealings are treated as transaction by the partners and not by the firm as such.

(6) *Companies* – companies are liable to corporation tax only and not to capital gains tax, so that the amount to be included in the company's total profits is the total gain accruing to the company in the relevant year after deducting allowable losses. In arriving at gains and losses, the same principles are used as with the gains made by individuals, and the same reliefs are available, the major difference being that the chargeable gain is subject to corporation tax. The Half Income Rule is, of course, inapplicable to companies.
See Section IX (A).

(7) *Non-resident companies & Non-resident trusts*
See Section V (B) and (C)

(8) *Prospective Residents*
See Section XI (A) 4.4

(9) *Intending Non-residents*
See Section XI (B) 3.4

1. FA 1965 s.20 (1)
2. FA 1965 s.20 (7)
3. FA 1965 s.20 (2)
4. FA 1965 s.22 (1)
5. FA 1965 s.29
6. FA 1965 s.21
7. FA 1965 s.22
8. Subject to certain anti-avoidance provisions
9. FA 1965 s.25

Section VIII: UK Exchange Control ('EC')

A. Introduction and Administration

General

The UK legislation governing exchange control is the Exchange Control Act 1947 which in effect makes void transactions between residents and non-residents (these terms are defined later) without appropriate consent being obtained. The Treasury is empowered under the Act to administer exchange control but has delegated most of its powers to the Bank of England ('the Bank') which is responsible for the administration of the Act. It is pertinent to note that although the Treasury is ultimately responsible for both EC and Taxation (through the Inland Revenue) there is in practice no connection or exchange of information. Each of these bodies has its own regulations and each is independent of the other. The Bank in turn has delegated much of its powers to agents who carry out the most routine matters on the Bank's behalf. These agents (called 'Authorised Depositories') are Banks, Stockbrokers, Solicitors and sometimes Accountants. The delegation is carried out by sending official Notices containing the EC rules to its agents. These Notices are updated by supplements. Some routine transactions e.g. payment of minor non-resident invoices are within the powers of an agent but there are many which are simply outside the powers of the agents e.g. borrowings of foreign currencies by UK companies and allotment or issue of shares in private companies to non-resident shareholders. In such cases official Bank consent must be applied for before the transaction is effected. Because the Notices are basically of an administrative nature, the Bank often has a considerable degree of latitude over individual cases and the current practice should be ascertained before applying for any consents. Notices and current practice can change at very short notice.

Effect of UK EC

Investors in the UK and individuals present in the UK must consider the UK exchange control aspect of their investments and their personal positions as well as the fiscal position. Exchange control may affect financing and as a result any investment (in its broadest sense) is affected at one stage or other by exchange control. This section will comment briefly on the position of individuals in the UK.

Objective of UK EC

The principal objective of UK EC is to prevent uncontrolled movement of funds in and out of the UK and so purportedly protect the UK balance of payments. Movements of funds does not necessarily mean physical movements of funds in and out of the UK but more between individuals or concerns which are resident in the UK for EC purposes ('resident') and those who are not resident for EC purposes ('non-resident'). The word 'resident' in the EC sense has its own meaning and is quite separate from any other sense e.g. the tax interpretation. An individual can be physically present in the UK and yet be non-resident. Non-resident individuals' £ sterling bank accounts in the UK are usually called 'External Accounts'. Particular attention is given to

(i) Circumstances in which a resident may be paying to a non-resident more than the current value for an asset,

(ii) restricting credits to non-resident accounts. Subject to any authorised credits only non-resident funds, interest due and the £ sterling realised from the sale of foreign currency may be credited to non-resident accounts.

(iii) investment and transfer of assets to outside The Scheduled Territories by residents

(iv) the financing and control of UK companies which have non-resident shareholders.

Administrative Areas

For EC purposes the World has five parts: –

(i) *The Scheduled Territories:* This comprises of the UK (England Scotland Wales and Northern Ireland) Channel Islands Isle of Man the Republic of Ireland and Gibraltar.

Colloquially and inaccurately this is referred to sometimes as The Sterling Area.

(ii) *The Overseas Sterling Area:* ('OSA') The UK Commonwealth Countries (excluding Canada) some Gulf states, Jordan and South Africa. These countries together with the above mentioned Scheduled Territories comprised the Sterling Area prior to its break up in June 1972.

(iii) *The European Economic Community ('EEC'):* The Republic of Ireland is excluded from this category.

(iv) *Rhodesia:* This is an OSA country but the Bank effectively itself restricts all transactions between the Scheduled Territories and Rhodesia.

(v) *The Rest of the Non Scheduled Territories ('RNST'):* This is the balance of the World excluding the above.

B. Determination of Status

The residence of an individual is usually a question of fact. If an individual comes to the UK with the intention of residing permanently in the UK or for a period in excess of three years he will be designated resident in the UK which basically means that he must

(a) maintain all his Bank Accounts in £ Sterling,
(b) sell any holdings of gold,
(c) remit any foreign income to the Scheduled Territories,
(d) bring any foreign securities under the control of an agent (an Authorised Depository e.g. his bank)
(e) not make gifts to non-residents except within narrow limits,
(f) not be able to purchase assets outside the Scheduled Territories without complying with certain regulations.

The main restrictive regulation is that purchases must be made with investment currency which briefly entails a substantial premium (colloquially called 'the dollar premium') being paid. In these circumstances large scale portfolio investment outside the UK is almost prohibitive except perhaps through the medium of foreign borrowings. An individual may however be able to obtain a measure of exemption under EC 27 in respect of his non-UK source assets (see post).

If an individual does not propose to reside in the UK for a period of three years then he will be treated as non-resident for up to three years and then his status will be reviewed. Such an individual will be treated as remaining resident of the country in which he claims to be resident – usually where he was previously living. The country must be specifically named. Each case turns on its own facts and in practice the system generally works satisfactorily.

E.g. X is born in the United States and lives there until he was 18. X then works in Australia for a period of five years. X is then seconded by his Australian employer to the UK for two years. What is the EC status of X?

As X has not come to the UK for a period of three years or more he will retain his non-resident status. In what country will he be regarded as resident for UK EC purposes? As he lived in Australia for in excess of three years prior to his arrival in the UK he will be considered a resident of Australia for UK EC purposes.

NON-RESIDENT ACCOUNTS

The accounts of a non-resident are designated 'non-resident'. Such non-resident accounts can only be credited with other non-resident funds, the proceeds of sale of foreign currencies, interest on account monies etc. Resident funds can only be credited to non-resident accounts with specific consent or under a general consent e.g. salaries up to a limited amount.

Non-Resident Borrowings

Non-residents will find their borrowing powers from UK Banks and Institutions are restricted and/or subject to some form of Bank of England consent. For example UK £ sterling permitted borrowings for the purchase of a house or flat are generally limited to £ 25,000 per lender.

Residents Temporarily Abroad

These individuals remain subject to UK EC regulations irrespective of the fact that they are physically outside the Scheduled Territories – usually because they do not qualify as emigrants (see C post).

To avoid cases and hardship, the Bank is prepared to be sympathetic to applications for allowances from those who are going abroad for a short period only. This is especially so where the individual is going to an EEC or OSA country. Sympathetic consideration is limited to those who go abroad to work, i.e. not those on extended holidays. The application should be made by the individual's own bank to the Bank detailing, inter alia:

(i) the length of time to be spent outside the Scheduled Territories and in which country or countries;
(ii) the contract or engagement abroad;
(iii) the purpose of the application, e.g. to
  purchase accommodation;
  pay other living expenses e.g. school fees;
  purchase a car;
(iv) who from the applicant's family unit will accompany the applicant;
(v) the amount of currency required.

It should be noted that any such allowance will rarely exceed the £ 40,000 or £ 80,000 emigration allowance (see post).

If the applicant subsequently emigrates:

(a) any such special allowance will be deducted from the emigration allowance;
(b) the four year period of restriction will start running from the day the emigration form IE is signed.

Even if no such application is made permission should always be sought to open a bank account outside the Scheduled Territories to receive foreign salaries foreign earnings etc. On return to the Scheduled Territories such an account must be closed and the balance remitted to the Scheduled Territories.

Clearly it is preferable if possible to emigrate for EC purposes.

C. Emigration

If a resident about to leave the Scheduled Territories wishes to emigrate i.e.

become a non-resident then he must comply with the strict EC formalities. All potential emigrants must apply formally for redesignation as a non-resident and this will *only* be granted if the Bank is satisfied that residence abroad is intended (or is already in being) for a period of at least three years. The various concessions (outlined below) should be applied for by the individual through his bank. He will have to complete a long document (Form IE) which will detail his and his family unit's, assets, sources of income and contain a declaration as to his intended residence. 'Family unit' includes children up to eighteen years of age but does not include any of his or his wife's parents.

The normal resident, if he is emigrating to a RNST country (e.g. Canada) or OSA country (e.g. Australia or South Africa (see later for EEC countries)) will only be able to take with him and his family unit the following:

(i) an allowance of £ 40,000
(ii) their personal assets e.g. furniture etc.
(iii) their foreign currency assets and
(iv) certain (small) cash and travel allowances

Upon being redesignated a non-resident he will however be able to receive all his income wherever he likes. The income and capital element of a purchased life annuity can be transferred during the four year period except where the annuity is for a fixed term of years only i.e. not for life.

If the emigrant goes to an EEC country (e.g. France) then he will receive an allowance of £ 80,000 instead of £ 40,000. Where an emigrant has already received an allowance which is less than the current allowance he can make an application to have the balance between the original allowance granted and the current allowance released.

After deducting the allowance the balance of the assets in the Scheduled Territories will be restricted for a period of four years under EC Act 1947 s.40. The certificates to any UK securities must be lodged with an authorised depositary.

The restricted funds can sometimes be utilised in the UK. Non-residents can often make gifts to UK residents from them and usually are able to discharge UK liabilities e.g. air fares, educational medical and any expenses incurred during visits to the UK.

Single premium life assurance policies will usually be treated as ordinary investments and annual withdrawals of up to 10% are usually treated as income. If an endowment policy which was effected more than three years prior to redesignation matures or is surrendered during the period of restriction then the policy proceeds may be credited to the emigrant's non-resident account.

The allowance may be sent to the country of new residence not earlier than one month prior to departure. An emigrant can of course always extract assets during the four year period through the medium of investment currency; but this is extremely expensive. An alternative course of action is to try and arrange a loan (preferably in overseas £ sterling i.e. eurosterling) from a non-UK bank. The non-UK lending bank will invariably require a guarantee from a UK bank which will be given in consideration for a guarantee fee and a charge over the emigrant's restricted assets. The UK guaranteeing bank will require a very substantial margin so as to cover the discharge of the loan in investment currency within the four year period, interest payment and any currency depreciation. This can readily be arranged from the Scheduled Territories by the emigrant's local bank through if necessary its head office and its foreign branch subsidiary or associate bank will make the foreign loan.

If the individual owns a property outside the UK prior to emigration he can consider recouping the investment currency in whole or part by utilising his allowance in a reverse transaction. A reverse transaction is a means of receiving back the investment premium monies (wherever paid) by utilising the emigration allowance of £ 40,000 or £ 80,000. For example: A bought a villa for £ 100,000 in Spain (whilst resident in the UK) several years ago. Now he is emigrating to Spain with his emigration £ 40,000 allowance. If A wished to do a reverse transaction and the premium rate is 50% he could use his emigration allowance and switch it for £ 60,000 of the investment currency which exist in the value of the villa thereby receiving *restricted funds* in the Scheduled Territories totalling £ 60,000 a clear gain of £ 20,000. The 25% surrender requirement which was normally applicable to the sale of investment currency has now been abolished. Reverse transactions can be carried out at any time within the four year period and are clearly more attractive following the abolition of the 25% surrender requirement and the substantial increases in the emigration allowances.

Under current practice at the end of the four year period of restriction all restrictions are lifted and the emigrant can remit the funds to any country in the World (except Rhodesia).

D. EC 27 Exemption

Because of the above restrictive regulations the EC status of UK resident individuals and their assets receives so much attention. An individual of foreign nationality who has lived for a considerable period of time outside the Scheduled Territories can obtain a measure of exemption under EC 27 in respect of his foreign assets. There are stringent criteria and these must be carefully studied. It is often possible for an individual with dual nationality (one of which is British) to obtain the exemption. It is occasionally possible for UK nationals to be granted the exemption. If an individual with a foreign nationality has been granted a measure of exemption and then loses his foreign nationality then the Bank may wish to review his exemption.

If the criteria cannot be satisfied, then alternative courses of action should be considered prior to designation as a resident e.g. the formation of a foreign company or trust.

Once the exemption has been granted, it is possible for an individual to have at his UK bank both his ordinary resident account and his exempted non-resident account.

The exemption will normally cover assets overseas acquired before becoming resident e.g. foreign currency securities, foreign properties, foreign currency accounts (within or without the Scheduled Territories) but also covered are inheritances received after the individual has become resident in the Scheduled Territories.

But if the EC 27 exemption is granted there are the following restrictions which must be carefully noted:

(i) No gold can be held

(ii) Income from overseas pensions and salaries must be remitted to the Scheduled Territories and paid into non-exempt accounts

(iii) Funds switched out of foreign currencies into £ sterling in the Scheduled Territories cannot be switched back into foreign currency. This factor must be borne in mind when purchasing a house in the UK. On subsequent emigration, E post should be considered.

(iv) No £ sterling can be held in exempted accounts in the Scheduled Territories.

E. Repatriation

As an alternative to emigration it is possible for an individual (usually a foreign national) who was for many years resident outside the Scheduled Territories prior to becoming a resident to be 'repatriated'. Repatriation here is meant in the UK exchange control sense (rather than any other sense) from the UK rather than to a particular country. In such an event he will be able to take all his assets with him other than those which have been gifted to him (whilst he was resident) etc. within the past three years. He will also be able to take with him those assets derived from his earnings in the UK and from capital appreciation in the UK. A special Bank form – Form 'R' – has to be completed.

F. Conclusion

In the virtual absence of detailed legal criteria day-to-day matters are determined in accordance with the Bank's EC Notices. More weighty matters are dealt with by the Bank in the light of its current practice and policies. These can change at short notice. Special case can receive special attention. Substantial penalties can be exacted for breaches of EC regulations.

G. Visitors and Immigrants

See also Section XI (A) 6.

H. Emigrants

See also Section XI (B) 7.

Section IX: Corporation Tax

A. General

Introduction

All companies and unincorporated associations (other than partnerships) resident in the UK are chargeable to Corporation Tax whether profits are distributed or retained. Following the introduction of the new system of corporation tax in the UK, income tax at the basic rate is not now deducted from dividends.

The place of residence of a company is determined by reference to the place where the central control mind and management of the Company is situated. This is usually the place where its Board of Directors meets.

A company not resident in the UK is liable to Corporation Tax only insofar as it has trading income arising from a branch or agency in the UK or income arising from any property used or held by a branch or agency in the UK. A non-resident company will be liable to income tax in respect of its other income from sources within the UK, (subject to any Double Tax Treaty provisions).

The profits of a company that is resident in the UK are liable to Corporation Tax. But where dividends (and other income distributions) are received from another UK resident company relief is given to the recipient company in respect of the Corporation Tax paid by the dividend paying company on its profits.

Corporation Tax, unlike income tax, is levied on profits arising in a financial year, that is a year ending on any 31st March. The financial year 1976 means the year beginning 1st April, 1976, to 31st March 1977. The profits for a financial year are established by reference to so much of a company's accounting period(s) as coincides with a financial year.

Rates of Corporation Tax

The current rate of Corporation Tax is 52%. The rate is fixed by Parliament in arrears, e.g. the rate of Corporation Tax for the financial year 1974, i.e., the year ended 31st March 1975, was determined by F (no. 2) A 1975, which received the Royal Assent on 31st July 1975.

Only part of a company's capital gains are charged to Corporation Tax; the effective tax burden of a company paying the full 52% Corporation Tax rate is 30%.

Companies with taxable profits (including chargeable gains) in any accounting year not exceeding £ 40,000 pay Corporation Tax at a reduce rate (the 'small companies rate'). The rate for the financial year 1976 is 42%. The Corporation Tax rate increases gradually where the profit level is between £ 40,000 and £ 65,000. Companies with profits in excess of £ 65,000 pay tax at the full rate (currently 52%). Where a company has one or more associated companies the maximum and minimum profit levels indicated above are apportioned between the total number of associates.

Assessment of Corporation Tax

A company is assessed to corporation tax on the profits of its own accounting period, although, as stated above, the rate of tax is based on financial years. Where the accounting period does not coincide with the financial year, the chargeable amount liable to corporation tax has to be arrived at by apportioning the profits of the accounting period between the financial years in which the accounting period falls.

Thus where the period of account is twelve months and the company's accounts are made up to 31st December, 1976, a quarter of the profits will fall to be assessed in the financial year 1975 and three-quarters in the financial year 1976. For Corporation Tax purposes an accounting period cannot exceed twelve months. If a company makes up its Accounts for some longer period, the accounting period is deemed to end after twelve months and a new accounting period is deemed then to begin. The profits of the true accounting period are allocated between the two notional periods.

Corporation tax, on being assessed for an accounting period, is usually payable within nine months from the end of that period – or, where the assessment is made later, within one month from the date of assessment. Where companies were trading in the UK prior to 1st April 1965, there are different rules with regard to assessment.

Company Distributions

The full meaning of 'distribution' is given in ICTA 1970 s.233. It includes any transfer of assets by a company to its members except:

(a) to the extent that the member gives consideration for what he receives and
(b) on a liquidation

B. The Imputation System

The UK imputation system is one of the many imputation systems of Corporation Tax. The common denominator in these systems is that part of the Corporation Tax paid by the Company is imputed to the recipient of a qualifying distribution – usually a dividend. No income tax is deducted from the dividend.

ACT

The UK system is particularly ingenious in its method of collection of Corporation Tax in that when a company pays a dividend it must make an advanve payment of Corporation Tax ('ACT') equivalent to (currently) 34/66ths of the dividend. A tax credit is imputed to the recipient's dividend of (effectively) the same amount. But ACT should not be confused with tax credit – it may be its mirror image but it is not the same. The system described for dividends applies equally to other qualifying distributions. Figuratively, the position of a company ('X Ltd') and its shareholders can be expressed simply in three parts:

Cash Position

	£
X Ltd proposes to pay a dividend of	100,000
then	
X Ltd must pay ACT of	51,515
X Ltd must so have cash totalling	151,515

Tax Position

X Ltd has taxable profits for the year of	500,000
Corporation Tax thereon at 52%	260,000
Post-tax profits	240,000

But X Ltd will be able to take full credit for the £ 7,000 ACT paid. So X Ltd. will only have to pay mainstream Corporation Tax (when it is due) of £ 208,485

UK Shareholder's (owning 100% of X Ltd's Shares) Position

Receives dividend of	100,000
Plus tax credit	51,515
Total gross amount received (called 'franked payment')	151,515

If the shareholder is a UK resident he will be able to utilise the tax credit against any overall UK tax liability; he will be able to reclaim any excess. Non-residents, generally, are not entitled to a tax credit unless they are resident in a country with which the UK has a Double Tax Treaty under which provision is made for a tax credit. A non-resident is not liable to tax at the basic rate on the dividend, but as he has no tax credit he will clearly not be able to claim repayment of any excess of his credit over his UK tax liability – again, unless a Double Tax Treaty provides otherwise.

Recently revised Double Tax Treaties ameliorate the position by providing for portfolio investors to be paid part of the tax credit and for the balance of it usually to be treated as UK tax. But under the new UK-US Treaty, the direct investor can recover part of the tax credit. This was unexpected.

A US parent can recover half of the UK tax credits on dividends from its UK subsidiary less a 5% withholding tax. The withholding tax is calculated on the aggregate of the dividend and the half of the tax credit. Figuratively the position can be expressed:

Dividend from UK subsidiary	£ 100,000
Tax credit on above dividend £51,515	
one half thereof	£ 25,757
	£ 125,757
Less withholding tax 5%	£ 6,287
Total 'cash' receivable	£ 119,470

Franked Investment Income

This is a qualifying distribution together with the accompanying tax credit received by a UK resident company from another UK resident company. A UK company is not liable to Corporation Tax upon receipt of any such qualifying distribution. The recipient company can utilise the tax credit to 'frank' its payments of dividends (or other distributions); this is to the extent of its franked investment income. Where there is a surplus of franked investment income received over 'franked' payments made the tax credit portion of the surplus can be carried forward for franking future distributions or alternatively used by the Company to obtain relief against charges on income, capital allowances, trading losses and other income expenses of that accounting period.

C. ACT Situations

Restrictions on ACT Offset

There is a restriction on the extent to which ACT can be set against Corporation Tax where there has been an 'excessive distribution'. This can arise, for example, where, in a particular accounting period, a company makes distributions to the shareholders which bear no relation to the profits of that period and, thereby, utilises profits from earlier periods. To prevent this the set-off of ACT against Corporation Tax is restricted to the maximum ACT which would have been payable if the Company had made a franked payment equal to the whole of its taxable profits for this accounting period.

e.g.

a company has taxable income in an accounting period of		£ 100,000
Corporation Tax thereon		£ 52,000
Post-tax 'profits'		£ 48,000
Dividends are paid in the period totalling		£ 75,000
ACT thereon		£ 38,636
Corporation Tax at 52%		£ 52,000
ACT paid	£ 38,636	
ACT restriction 34/66 of 65,000	£ 34,000	
ACT surplus	£ 4,636	
Mainstream Corporation Tax		£ 18,000

A surplus of ACT in one period can be carried back to the two preceding accounting periods, or it may be carried forward to the next accounting period. In certain cases ACT can be 'surrendered' to subsidiaries by its parent (see the summary of provisions relating to groups).

ACT cannot be credited against a Corporation Tax Liability due in respect of capital gains. Clearly large irrecoverable surpluses of ACT are not financially beneficial to companies.

D. Other Items

(1) Capital Allowances and Balancing Charges

Depreciation and amortisation provided for in accounts cannot be deducted from profits for tax purposes. Instead, companies (and individuals and partnerships) are entitled to deduct capital allowances where capital expenditure has been incurred. Capital allowances are available is respect of expenditure incurred on plant. machinery, industrial buildings, research, ships, mining, expenditure, patents, know-how, etc. but not in respect of a series of other items including premises like shops, offices or hotels.

Plant Machinery and Equipment (including Motor Vehicles)

If used in a trade, these attract 100% first year allowance so that the whole of the expenditure is deductible in computing the trading profits for the same accounting period in which the expenditure is incurred. If and to the extent that a first year allowance is not claimed (or not available, e.g. because some anti-avoidance provision applies) writing down allowances are available of 25% of the unrelieved balance in any accrued accounting period.

With cars, the 100% first year allowance is not available but the 25% writing down allowances are. These allowances are limited where the car costs more than £5,000 to a maximum of £1,250 per annum for each car.

New ships may be freely depreciated, if and to the extent that the 100% first year allowance is not claimed in the first year as a first year allowance then the unused balance may be claimed in a later year.

On disposal of any item of plant the sale proceeds must be deducted from the total 'pool' of unrelieved capital expenditure on plant and machinery. Should the proceeds of sale be more than the 'pool', then the excess of sale proceeds over such unrelieved expenditure is subject to a balancing charge. Balancing allowances (i.e. final allowances of unrelieved expenditure) are usually only given on the cessation of a trade.

Industrial Buildings

The expression 'industrial building' is defined and includes buildings in use as a factory, mill or for the purpose of manufacturing, storage and other specified trades.

Expenditure incurred after 12th November 1974 qualifies for an additional allowance of 50% writing down allowance at a given rate of 4% per annum of the initial cost unless the expenditure was incurred prior to 6th November 1962 in which case only 2% may be claimed.

(2) Charges on Income

As a general rule, yearly interest annuities, patent royalties and any annual payments made under deduction of tax are deductible in computing profits of an accounting period. The general rule is, however, subject to a series of complicated exceptions.

(3) Trading in the UK – Branch or Company

Apart from commercial factors, the following has to be considered, as to whether it is more tax-efficient or not to operate in the UK through a subsidiary UK company here or whether to establish a branch office of the overseas company. Both subsidiary and branch will have to comply with the requirements of the Companies Acts 1948 and 1967. The following factors should inter alia be considered:

(a) A company resident in the UK is within the charge to Corporation Tax on all its profits whereas a non-resident company trading through a branch in the UK is chargeable to Corporation Tax on the profits attributable to that branch.

(b) A UK resident company is liable to pay ACT when it makes a distribution. A non-UK resident recipient can only get an equivalent tax credit if a Double Tax Treaty entitles him to such a credit so that the case of a UK resident company may result in a loss of tax from the point of view of the company and its shareholders together, as compared with an operation through a branch.

(c) There is a greater likelihood that, if the operation in the UK is conducted through a branch, then any losses will be available for relief against the taxable profits of the foreign company in the overseas jurisdiction where it is resident.

(d) A resident company receives more generous treatment in respect of taxes incurred outside the UK and the tax available as a credit against the UK liability.

(e) A non-resident company is not a close company (see later) and need not therefore concern itself with the taxation of undistributed profits.

(f) It is a criminal offence for a UK resident company (inter alia) to transfer its business or any part thereof to a non-resident (see special situations, Section V).

E. Computation and Adjustment of Profits

Income

ICTA 1970 s.250 (1) provides that the amount of any income for the purposes of corporation tax is to be computed, subject to one or two modifications, in accordance with income tax principles. Basically, what has been stated in Section III with regard to income tax principles applies also to companies. In making assessments of corporation tax, income is computed according to and assessments are made under the Schedules and Cases referred to in Section III. However, corporation tax will be levied as indicated above and not in the manner applicable to income tax; specifically the preceding year basis never applies to the taxation of a company's income.

Trading Losses

Generally, trading losses (but not any other losses) may be:

(i) carried forward and set against future profits of the same trade or

(ii) carried back against the profits of one or more previous periods (not in the aggregate exceeding the duration of the accounting period in which the loss was incurred) or

(iii) set against profits (of whatever description, i.e. including chargeable gains) of the period in which the loss was incurred and for the previous period or periods just described.

CAPITAL GAINS

The gains and losses are computed according to Capital Gains Tax rules.

CAPITAL LOSSES

These are in the first instance set against capital gains with any balance thereafter being carried forward for set-off against capital gains in one or more later periods. As indicated above, capital gains can also be relieved by set-off against trading losses in the same accounting period or the previous accounting period but capital losses cannot be similarly set against trading profits.

F. Groups

Groups of companies receive special benefits with regard to ACT, dividends, interest, losses and transfers of assets. For these purposes a group consists of a parent company and a company in which the parent holds a majority of the ordinary share capital ('a 51% subisidiary'); some provisions only apply when the parent owns 75% or more of the ordinary share capital of another company ('a 75% subsidiary'). A company resident outside the UK, can never be a member of a group for any of these purposes, so that, where the parent is a non-resident, there is no group at all.

ACT

A parent beneficially entitled to more than 50% of a 51% subsidiary's profits available for distribution and which would be entitled to more than 50% of the subsidiary's assets on liquidation can surrender its surplus ACT to the subsidiary, thereby reducing the subsidiary's mainstream corporation tax liability.

INTEREST

A parent may receive charges on income from a 51% subsidiary without the subsidiary deducting income tax.

LOSSES

In a group of companies consisting of a parent and one or more 75% subsidiaries, the losses of one group member may be offset against the profits of one or more others made in the same accounting period, provided that the group relationship has existed throughout the accounting periods and the accounting periods coincide. If the accounting periods do not coincide then the profits and losses are apportioned on a time basis.

Transfer of assets

Assets may be transferred within a group consisting of a parent and one or more 75% subsidiaries without any immediate liability to corporation tax on chargeable gains. However, if within 6 years after such a transfer, the acquiring company ceases to be a member of the group, the charge to corporation tax on the gain which would have occurred if the disposal had been made to a third party, is retrospectively imposed.

Corporation Tax on chargeable gains

Where there is a parent company and 75% subsidiaries, a gain on an asset sold by one trading company may be 'rolled over' against the purchase of an asset by another group company, provided that the assets are of such a nature as to qualify for roll-over relief.

Capital Losses

There are no provisions for group relief.

N.B. – There are often specific requirements for group benefits, e.g. set periods of time within which a claim or election must be made to obtain the benefits of the provisions summarised above.

G. Close Companies

Brief Definition

ICTA 1970 s.282 defines a close company as a resident company which is under the control of five or fewer participators, or of participators who are directors (irrespective of their number). Participators include inter alia shareholders, persons interested in the capital or in voting rights of the company and loan creditors other than bankers. The rights and interests of associates of participators are taken into account in determining whether or not a company is a close company. Associates includes partners, close family and the trustees of settlements made by the participator or by a member of his close family.

ICTA 1970 s.302 (see also FA 1972 Schedule 7 (5)) defines control as a situation where a person can exercise (or can acquire) directly or indirectly control over the company. In particular, a person will have control if he has or can have –

- the greater part of the share capital, issued share capital or the voting power
- such portion of the issued share capital as would if all the company's income was distributed amongst the participators (ignoring any of his rights as a loan creditor) result in him obtaining the greater part of the income so distributed.

A company will also be a close company if, on the assumption that it is such a company, more that 50% of its income can be apportioned to 5 or less participators or to participators who are directors. With non-trading companies loan creditors can be treated as having interests.

ICTA 1970 s.283 provides that a company generally will not be a close company if the shares (not being preference shares) carrying at least 35% of the voting power of the company are beneficially held by the public and quoted on a recognised Stock Exchange.

The foregoing is no more than the briefest of outlines of the lengthy and complicated definitions and provisions on this particular subject.

H. Consequences of Being a Close Company

There are many consequences, some of which are:

ICTA 1970, s.284 extends the concept of distribution to virtually all benefits granted by a company at the company's expense to any participator and any of his associates, except (a) to the extent that the expense is made good by the participator and (b) if the benefit granted to a director or a higher paid employee of the company. In the latter case, the benefit is to the extent that the expense is not made good to the Company, almost certainly taxable under Schedule E.

ICTA 1970, s.286 imposes a charge to tax on the close company in respect of any loan granted by it to a participator or any of his associates.

The principal consequence of a company being treated as being a close company is that in certain circumstances (subject to some reliefs and exemptions) the whole or part of the Company's income (less any distributions made) can be apportioned upon some or all of the Company's shareholders. The rules and the mechanics of such an apportionment are extremely complicated. A measure of relief is provided in that where a company's income is comprised of trading or estate (i.e. rental) income. In such cases having taken account of the requirements of the Company's business, then the apportionment can only be made in respect of up to 50% of such company's estate or trading income. The basic aim behind apportionments is to ensure that it is never fiscally more advantageous for shareholders to arrange to have funds retained inside close companies rather than distributing them.

Another relief is provided by FA 1972 Schedule 16 para 9 (2) (3) which provides that where (prior to 26th October 1977) a trading company has trading or estate income of no more than £ 5,000 then none of such income can be apportioned. Marginal relief is allowed on such income between £ 5,000 and £ 15,000 to the extent of one half of the difference of the income between £ 5,000 and £ 15,000 (these figures are reduced where there are associated companies). On 26th October 1977 it was announced that these figures are to be increased to £ 25,000 and £ 75,000 respectively in respect of companies with accounting periods ending after 26th October 1977.

Again, it must be stressed that the rules and mechanics of apportionment are extremely complicated.

Section X: Miscellaneous

A. National Health Service

Under the National Health Service Act all persons are treated free or in some cases at a very reduced fee. Dental treatment attracts a flat rate contribution from the patient. Prescriptions for medicines require a contribution of 20p. per item from the patient.

The benefits are financed partly by National Insurance contributions and also, by subventions from general taxation revenues. Where an individual has taken up residence in the UK it is advisable for him or her to register all members of the family with a doctor convenient to the principal residence. In some areas, it may not always be possible to obtain a place on the list of the medical practitioner who is most conveniently placed for treatment because he already has the statutory number of patients on his books.

There are in existence a number of good medical insurance schemes, which the new resident should consider, for they provide attractive ancillary benefits and allow the individual to see as a private patient a consultant or specialist of choice. Such schemes can ensure speed of treatment and secure accommodation in a privately run hospital.

B. National Insurance Contribution

The contribution has to be paid in respect of anyone who is over 16 but under 60 (women) or 65 (men) and is resident in the UK or is employed by a UK employer. The contributions are normally paid by the employer in respect of any person who is on the payroll. Contributions are deducted together with income tax, under the PAYE procedures. The employer is responsible for collecting and paying over the whole contribution (called Class I contribution) although he may recover a specified proportion by way of employee's contribution.

The total amount of the contribution (which covers pension, redundancy, unemployment, sickness, industrial injury and permanent invalidity) depends on the employee's level of gross earnings. At present, the standard contribution is 14.5% and the employer contributes 8.75% and the employee has to pay 5.75%. For the tax year 1976/77, the earnings maximum is taken at £95 per week, i.e. remuneration above this level does not attract any requirement of further contribution.

Persons who are self-employed or non-employed are still liable to pay National Insurance contributions if resident in the UK, but are not required to make any contributions until either twenty-six weeks or fifty-two weeks have elapsed, depending on whether the person is self-employed or non-employed. The self-employed are liable at a basic of £ 2.41 per week (men) and £ 2.20 per week (for women). These contributions are called Class 2 but additional Class 4 Contributions are payable at 8% on profits made between £ 1,600 and £ 4,900 for fiscal year 1976/77 and are akin to an additional income tax and are in fact collected with Schedule D income tax.

Where employment is with a UK employer, then contributions have to be paid by both the employer and the employee from the commencement of the residence in UK. However, persons who are sent temporarily by an employer outside the UK to work in the UK *and* who are not ordinarily resident are entitled to defer commencement of Class I contributions for 52 weeks. There are special provisions for persons employed *outside* the UK and in the Isle of Man, and for mariners; and the details are set out in leaflets NI 38 and NI 24.

There are exemptions for working married women, (Leaflet NI 1), and for the self-employed with small earnings, (NI 27A) below £ 775.

Those who have come from member States of the EEC or countries which have reciprocal social security agreements with the UK are subject to special provisions and should apply for the relevant leaflets in respect of the country with which reciprocal arrangements exist. The following leaflets are available from the Department of Health and Social Security, Overseas Group, Newcastle-upon-Tyne, NE98 1YX.:

Austria	(Leaflet SA 25)	Jersey and Guernsey	(Leaflet SA 4)
Bermuda	(Leaflet SA 24)	Malta	(Leaflet SA 11)
Cyprus	(Leaflet SA 12)	Norway	(Leaflet SA 16)
European Economic Community	(Leaflet SA 29)	Sweden	(Leaflet SA 9)
		Switzerland	(Leaflet SA 6)
Finland	(Leaflet SA 19)	Turkey	(Leaflet SA 22)
Israel	(Leaflet SA 14)	Yugoslavia	(Leaflet SA 17)
Jamaica	(Leaflet SA 27)		

The Social Security package in more detail is as follows, including Health Service treatment already referred to above:

(1) State Pension

A flat rate retirement pension (which is, nowadays, adjusted frequently to take into account inflationary trends) is payable at age 65 for a man and age 60 for a woman.

The level of benefit depends, generally, on the amount of Class I contributions paid during the course of the working life, and everyone generally, as stated above, who is in employment, self-employed or non-employed has to pay contributions. At the present time, there is a transitional period, and from 6th April 1979 the new provisions will apply so that on reaching retirement age there will be the present flat rate benefit plus a new earnings related benefit linked with the Index of Prices. However, probably in 1978, employees will be able to contract, to some extent, out of the State Scheme where the employer operates an alternative scheme which is accepted by the authorities as providing as adequate benefits as those available under the State Scheme.

Leaflet NI 15 describes the workings of the Scheme and lists the countries (which includes the EEC) where there are reciprocal arrangements which may have the effect that contributions paid overseas may count towards a UK retirement pension.

(2) Unemployment Benefits

The National Insurance payment made weekly by the employer and employee helps to provide funds for unemployment benefits. The fact of unemployment must be registered by the individual attending the local employment office, and benefit begins with a flat rate minimum payment. Additional amounts are payable, depending on, firstly, the previous earnings of the individual, taking the average weekly pay during the previous income tax year, and, secondly, the number of dependants in the individual's family.

To justify for any benefit those who become contributors for the first time on or after 6th April 1975 must have paid in any one tax year since that date Class I contributions equal to contributions on earnings of at least 25 times the weekly lower earnings limit for that year. This lower limit for tax year 1975/76 was, for example £ 11,– i.e. below that figure no NIS contributions are required. Also at least 26 contributions should have been paid in the contribution period and the greater the contribution period then the higher the benefit.

In cases of genuine hardship, supplementary benefits are available, although the individual must expect to have his affairs looked at very closely to satisfy the authorities as to his real need and lack of other resources.

Benefit is available for a maximum of 312 days in any period of unemployment so far as the flat rate benefit is concerned (and this includes the benefit for the dependants in the family), and there is a time-limit of 156 days for the earnings-related element of the unemployment benefit. The aim is, of course, to encourage those who are without employment to seek fresh employment as soon as possible.

The National Insurance Leaflet NI 38 gives details of the countries overseas with which the UK has reciproval arrangements and in some cases residence or payments under a foreign scheme may count towards qualifying for benefit in the UK conversely if a person is absent from UK, benefits can be claimed abroad in EEC countries.

(3) SICKNESS BENEFIT

Benefits are provided for all persons in employment who fall sick. This has to be evidenced by a doctor's certificate, which has to be forwarded to the local Department of Health and Social Security office. Sickness benefit is payable for a maximum of 168 days after which time it is replaced by the Invalidity benefit. Leaflet NI 6 describes the conditions and benefits and Leaflet NI 38 should be referred to in respect of the reciprocal arrangement with other countries.

Most UK employers, for their salaried staff, have provisions in the contract of employment to the effect that, in each year, a maximum period is permitted for absence from work due to sickness without any reduction in salary. But after a certain period in any given year of days off work, the salary will be reduced commensurate with the level of State benefits received. Sometimes it will be provided that, after an even longer maximum period, the salary will be further cut irrespective of the level of sickness benefits paid by the State.

For permanent invalidity, fairly generous State benefits are payable. These are described in Leaflet NI 16A. Again NI 38 should be referred to for details of the reciprocal countries.

(4) INDUSTRIAL INJURY BENEFIT

To qualify, the employee must have been injured on disabled in the course of his regular employment. The contributions paid by way of National Insurance go towards providing the benefit. If incapacity continues then a disablement benefit is payable, depending on the extent of permanent disability, and is reviewed from time to time, depending on the condition of the employee and the extent of the disability. Leaflets available are NI 2 (prescribed diseases) NI 5 (injury) and NI 6 (disablement).

(5) REDUNDANCY BENEFIT

The employee makes no contribution towards the cost of this benefit, and it is borne partly by employers and partly by a State fund. The level of redundancy compensation is based on the length of time that the employee has been working for the particular employer, age and the level of previous earnings. The benefit has a minimum of one-half and a maximum of one-and-a-half weeks' pay for every year of employment, but there is a maximum of twenty years' employment and an earnings maximum of £ 80 per week, so that the total amount of redundancy pay that any single employee can claim is, at present, no more than £ 2,400.

It is the responsibility of the employer to make the payment within a specified time-limit and for the employer then to seek reimbursement as to half the cost from the State fund.

(6) MATERNITY GRANTS

Maternity Grants are available to contributors in the form of a lump sum payment – the details are in the Department of Health and Social Security Leaflet NI 17A.

(7) CHILD BENEFIT

Child benefit as from April 1977 is available for all children and Leaflet CH 5 deals specifically with the entitlement of persons coming to the UK from overseas.

The Leaflets described above can be obtained from the Department of Health and Social Security.

C. Employment Contracts

It should be mentioned that by law almost every employee has to be given a contract of employment giving details of all the terms of the employment, such as hours of work, permitted holiday, termination and general conditions of employment, including the level of remuneration and any scales for annual increases.

D. Work Permits

Except where the person seeking employment in the UK is a resident of an EEC country, all who seek permanent employment in the UK have to apply for a work permit, issued by the Department of Employment.

There is a restrictive attitude towards the issue of permits, particularly at times of fairly high domestic unemployment. Generally, permits will be issued where the prospective employee has a definite offer for a specific appointment with a UK employer and has all the appropriate technical skill, professional qualifications or experience. The intending worker should be between age 18 and 54, and the wages and conditions of employment must not be less favourable than what would be offered to a UK resident. The employer has to show that he has made adequate efforts to find a suitable employee for the job vacancy from the existing UK labour force – usually by having applied to the local Employment Office or Job Centre with details of the vacancy.

Immigration matters are regulated by the Immigration Act, 1971, which came into operation on 1st January, 1973. Persons who are connected with the UK in some way – e.g. by birth, descent or residence – may be accorded the right of permanent abode in UK.

Some persons who are self-employed (e.g. writers and artists – also, doctors and dentists) – and, also representatives or employees of foreign governments and overseas news agencies or broadcasting organizations – do not require work permits. Other categories of persons such as those who wish to acquire a business or set up in business in the UK will require to satisfy the Home Office that they are competent to do so and have the necessary experience. Such applications take 6 weeks or more to be considered and consent is not readily given by the Home Office. Once consent is given the situation is monitored by the Home Office.

Whilst nationals of EEC member States are exempt from the requirement of work permits, it is necessary for such individuals and others to have residence permits.

Commonwealth citizens who can prove that they have at least one grandparent born in UK are entitled to obtain from the British High Commission in their country of residence an entry certificate, which effectively dispenses with the requirement of a work permit and gives a right of entry to UK to seek employment.

A work permit holder is admitted, initially, for one year and has to obtain consent if he wishes to change his employment. On the expiry of the first year, the permit may be extended if the employment is still approved, and, after four years, a person can be granted approval for permanent residence and is then free to take up any employment.

When first arriving in UK, foreign nationals should present to the Immigration Officers a valid passport issued by the foreign Government (not an identity card), together with the work permit. Where a visa is needed (as is the case for nationals from some countries), the work permit will have specified this requirement.

The wife and all children aged under 18 of a person admitted for a limited period are, likewise, admitted for the same period, but are not subject to any employment restrictions. Where a person is accepted for permanent settlement, in addition to the immediate family of that person, permission will usually be given for elderly dependent parents and grandparents to be admitted. On application, requests for the admission of other dependent relatives may be granted. All such persons will need to have entry clearance letters issued by the Home Office, through either application by the dependent to a British Embassy or High Commission Office overseas or application to the Home Office in UK by the head of the family already in UK.

Visitors are usually admitted for a minimum of six months – and can apply for longer periods. Returning residents are readmitted for permanent residence if they were previously allowed full rights of permanent settlement when they left and if they have not been away for more than two years. There are special provisions for au pair girls: usually, they will be admitted for a maximum of two years.

The following is an extract from the Department of Employment leaflet OW5, which outlines the categories of workers for whom work permits may be issued:

'12 Except as indicated below, permits are issued only for work requiring a professional qualification, skill or experience. They are issued for workers in the following categories:

(i) persons holding professional qualifications;
(ii) administrative and executive staff;
(iii) skilled craftworkers and experienced technicians;
(iv) specialised clerical and secretarial staff;

(v) workers in commerce or retail distribution with special experience or qualifications relevant to the post offered;

(vi) exceptionally highly qualified senior staff in hotel and catering, for example, Departmental heads in appropriate establishments and qualified cooks who have evidence of acceptable training at approved hotel schools abroad. For other workers in the hotel and catering industry see leaflet OW 6;

(vii) resident domestic workers without children under the age of 16 – see paras 14 and 15;

(viii) certain workers in hospitals and similar institutions – see paras 15 and 16;

(ix) entertainers and sportsmen/women. Professional sportsmen/women taking part in competition will not normally require permits;

(x) Commonwealth trainees coming for a fixed period of training 'on the job' approved by the Department of Employment – see Leaflet OW 7;

(xi) foreign student employees coming to this country for employment in industry and commerce in a supernumerary capacity – see leaflet OW 9;

(xii) other persons only if, in the opinion of the Secretary of State for Employment, their employment is in the national interest.

Permits are not available for unskilled or semi-skilled jobs except for citizens of Malta and Dependent Territories (mostly colonies), non-patrial UK passport holders, hotel and catering workers and resident domestic workers, all of whom are subject to an overall limit.

13 Documentary evidence of the worker's qualifications, skills and experience is required in all cases and should be submitted with the application.

The following helpful booklets are available from the Overseas Labour Section of the Department of Employment, Ebury Bridge House, Ebury Bridge Road, London, SWIW 8PY:

'Immigration Act, 1971 – A General Guide for EEC Nationals and Other Non-Commonwealth Nationals',

'Immigration Act, 1971 – A General Guide for Commonwealth Citizens',

'Working in Britain – Right of Entry and Conditions of Employment for Nationals of Other EEC Member States',

'Employment of Overseas Workers in Great Britain' – OW 5.

E. Counter-Inflation Act, 1973

This gives the Government wide powers to control prices, pay, dividends and rents; Prices are 'controlled' by a Prices Commission, and dividend control is exercised by H.M. Treasury. In the case of the latter, dividends should not be more than 10% above the level of dividend declared in the previous year, but this provision does not apply to close companies, where, for taxation reasons, dividends have to be paid.

As regards pay, there is, at the time of writing, a flat rate limit of £ 6. per week for all employees earning below £ 8,500. per annum, and contractual increases normally payable under contracts of employment cannot be paid by the employer if the employee is receiving over £8,500. The present pay restraint policy was negotiated by the Labour Government with the Trade Union Congress, representing organized labour, and representatives of the Confederation of British Industry, representing employers. The period of 'restraint', better known as the 'freeze' was reviewed in August 1977 and continues in force.

As regards prices, manufacturers have to seek permission to increase their domestic UK prices and are generally only allowed to do this by way of compensation for rising costs of production. The policy is administered, so far as possible, so as not to increase profit margins on sales.

F. Equal Pay

No discrimination between men and women over terms and conditions of employment is permitted, by the Equal Pay Act 1970. There is legislative provision for the settlement of disputes between employer and employee.

G. Indirect Taxation

This may be summarised as follows:

(1) Value Added Tax (VAT)

This is chargeable, subject of a few exceptions, on the value of all goods and services supplied in the UK by a person carrying on business, whether as a company or sole trader or partnership. However, credit is allowed to a registered taxable person for VAT already incurred in respect of goods and services. Thus, a manufacturer, buying semi-finished goods produced by another, will put VAT, at the present Standard Rate of 8%, on his sale price, but will obtain credit, by way of a refund, from Customs and Excise, in respect of the VAT paid by him on the purchased semi-finished products used by him in his manufacture.

Whilst the Standard Rate is 8%, there is a 25% Higher Rate, at present applicable to petrol and some consumer durables falling into what is thought to be a 'luxury' category. Exclusion from the provisions for VAT can take two forms, being either zero rating or exemption. In the case of the former, a taxable person in the business of dealing with zero-rated items, so far as his sales are concerned, can obtain a refund of all VAT suffered on the product that he is buying, whereas, if an item is altogether exempt, then there can be no refund of VAT.

Important zero-rated items include all food, fuel and power, children's clothing and footwear, exports and transport. Some notable items in the completely exempt category are payments in respect of health, education, insurance and land.

(2) CAR TAX

In addition to being subject to VAT at 8%, there is a special car tax on all vehicles made or registered in the UK, the present rate being at 10% of the wholesale value.

(3) CUSTOMS AND EXCISE

So far as the EEC is concerned, imports from EEC countries will be completely free of Import Duty as from 1st July 1977, but, otherwise, manufactured goods are subject to Import Duty at various rates, depending on the item imported, and policies are adjusted to some extent to give protection to domestic industry. Raw materials, however, are usually free of Import Duty.

Excise Duty is the alternative tax, and goods subject to Excise Duty are free of Import Duty.

Excise Duty is frequently used as a regulatory mechanism to cut back spending in the UK and is charged, principally, on tobacco, beer, spirits, wine and hydrocarban oils.

(4) STAMP DUTY

This is one of the oldest forms of taxation exisiting in the UK and stems from the Stamp Act 1891, and successive legislation, enacted largely at a time when there was no income tax nor capital gains tax. The rules are simple. Stamp duty is levied at 2% on transactions in securities (other than government stocks which are exempt) but where the purchaser is a non resident the rate is 1%. With real estate the first £ 15,000 consideration is exempt from stamp Duty with the rate increasing at $^1/_2$% within each slice of £ 5,000 above £ 15,000 until the full 2% rate is arrived at on a consideration of £ 30,000. The buyer is normally the person responsible for paying Stamp Duty.

(5) RATES

This is a form of local taxation, not related, however, to income but to the ownership of housing. Funds from rates go to the local authority in charge of local government for the provision of local services, such as road maintenance, refuse disposal, sewerage, education subsidised council housing and law enforcement. The rate charge is usually fixed annually, varying considerably from district to district, based on the notional annual rental value of the domestic or commercial property. It should be emphasized that the local valuer fixes the notional rental value of the property, and, generally, this is below the true commercial rental that could be obtained from the property. The value does, however, reflect the type of accommodation and facilities available, so that extensions and improvements to the property attract a higher valuation. With most local authorities, it is possible to pay the rate demand on residential property by means of instalments throughout the rating year. Where premises are unoccupied, it is sometimes possible to obtain limited rate relief.

A fairly typical example would be a house in a London suburb the market value of which was probably £ 25,000 or more and which comprised three bedrooms and two reception rooms and where the rateable value would be around £ 380 (compared with a probable true commercial rental potential of over £ 1,000 per annum). If the local rate were fixed by the local borough council or corporation at 66p. in the pound, the rate payable for the full year would be £ 250.80.

H. English Land Law

The title to all land ultimately vests in the Crown. Subject to this there are two estates in land, freehold and leasehold. The freehold estate creates the fullest rights of ownership, use and occupation. The freeholder can also grant a lesser interest or lease in the land whereby another (the leaseholder) is entitled to use and occupation for a fixed period upon payment of a rent. The length of the period or lease, the limitations upon the use and occupation imposed upon the leaseholder and the amount of the rent would depend upon the terms by the parties. In addition to the payment of rent, the freeholder would normally require the leaseholder to enter into other obligations as to repair and maintenance as well as complying with the limitations as to use and occupation which the parties might have agreed. Breach of the lessee's obligations can entitle the freeholder, in certain circumstances, to repossess the property.

The origin of these forms of ownership are historic. Many noble families became entitled to large estates either from conquest or service to the Crown. Other estates came into the ownership of the Church. Where these estates encompassed existing or potential centres of population leases of large plots were granted to builders and speculators to develop them as residential for various classes of society. These building leases were originally granted for 99 years or even longer. These leasehold estates still comprise larges areas of London and other cities although they are beginning to be broken up as the character of the areas change and the larger leasehold houses become ripe for conversion into flats or multiple occupation. The late 19th and 20th century has seen the development of the purposebuilt flats which is invariably the subject to leasehold ownership. Added to the payment of an annual ground rent, the leasehold flat owner inevitably will have to pay a charge for communal services and a maintenance contribution which, in London, can be very high.

In addition to the evolution of the residential dwelling note should also be taken of the role of the lease in the development of commercial or industrial property. In this case the property having been built by the freehold owner or developer for the purpose of investment, it is let to the commercial tenant at a rack rental calculated on the annual value of the property and upon an economic return on the initial investment. Such leases are usually granted for far shorter periods than residential building leases, 21 years being the normal, and at the present time such leases invariably contain a provision whereby the annual rent can be reviewed periodically during the term of the lease. It should also be noted that social legislation in the 20th century has limited the right of a landlord to obtain possession of his property either residential or commercial at the expiration of the lease and in the former case not only is the tenant given security of tenure but also the law limits the amount of rent that can be charged in certain circumstances.

The negotiation for the sale or letting of property is normally dealt with by an estate agent. The documentation for the leasing conveying or transfer of the land is handled by a solicitor it being usual for the Landlord and Tenant or Vendor and Purchaser as the case may be, each to instruct their own. It is the task of the Vendor's or Lessor's solicitor to draw up the written lease or contract and for the tenant's or purchaser's solicitor by investigation to satisfy himself that there are no onerous rights, obligations of convenants affecting the property and also that there are no onerous impositions charges or planning obligations imposed by the local authority. The former matters are dealt with by enquiry of the Lessor or Vendor's solicitor and the latter by enquiry and searches in local authority registers. Once the Purchaser's solicitor has satisfied himself on these matters, the parties enter into a binding commitment by 'exchange of contracts'. This is effected by each party signing a copy of the contract, which copies are then physically exchanged between the Vendor's and Purchaser's solicitors. Until this physical exchange has taken place the transaction is regard as being 'subject to contract' and before such exchange, either part can withdraw from the deal without obligation. It is also normal for the purchaser to pay to the Vendor's solicitor or agent a deposit of 10% of the purchase price upon exchange of contracts.

After exchange of contracts the Purchaser's solicitor makes further investigations as to the title of the property to satisfy himself that the Vendor is actually entitled to sell it. Title to the property can either be registered or unregistered. In the former case, the title is guaranteed by the Land Registry, a government department who issue a certificate of registration to the owner of a land. This certificate is handed over by the owner upon transfer and the purchaser then lodges it at the Land Registry in order that his title to the land can be registered. It is eventually intended that the whole of England and Wales will be covered by the system of land registration but at the present time there are still large areas of England and Wales where the title is unregistered and in such areas a purchaser's solicitor has to trace back the title of a vendor and if necessary any predecessors in title to it and be sure that such persons have had uninterrupted rights of ownerships and occupation without challenge for at least 15 years.

Unlike other jurisdictions, there is almost no title insurance, it being the responsibility of the solicitor acting for the Purchaser to investigate the title and to report to the Purchaser that the title is in order, if such is the case.

Completion of the sale and purchase of the property usually takes place 4 weeks after exchange of contracts, the Purchaser's solicitor having carried out his investigation within this four week period. Upon completion the balance of the purchase price is paid by the Purchaser and in return the Purchaser will receive the documents of title which in the case of registered land will comprise a transfer signed by the Vendor and a Land Certificate and in the case of unregistered land the various title deeds of the property comprising a Conveyance executed by the vendor and all earlier conveyances.

If the Purchaser's solicitor is for some reason not satisfied with Vendor's title for the property and completion may be delayed until the Vendor's solicitor can make good the remedy|or if the defect is irremediable this may result in the Purchaser being entitled to repudiate the contract.

Persons coming to the UK who are non-resident for EC purposes will find their local borrowing position restricted. They will only be able to borrow limited amounts from a building society insurance company or a bank. These are the three traditional means of financing house purchase in the UK. See Section VIII.

I. Scottish Land Law

Scotland has a different legal system from England and it is much closer to the Roman-Dutch continental systems.

Section XI: Tax Planning for Migrants. Check Lists

The editors felt that readers might appreciate having a conclusion in the form of two check lists – Part A being for the visitor, intending resident and immigrant and Part B for the intending non-resident and emigrant.

The intention behind the check lists is *not* to supplant the individual sections of this work but to supplement them and to be forms of aide-memoire. Before looking at the check lists it is essential that the reader has some knowledge of and some acquaintance with the realities described in the earlier sections. The check lists merely draw the attention to the reader to some of the relevant points to be considered. *Readers must look to the individual sections and elsewhere if necessary for any detail.*

Neither check list is fully comprehensive in itself and there is some cross-referencing and some duplication. Occasionally an item on a check list may suggest an answer to the problem – nonetheless reference should still be made to the individual section for an overall view.

Part A

CHECK LIST FOR VISITORS INTENDING RESIDENTS AND IMMIGRANTS

1. General

1.1 Why is he visiting, coming to or present in the UK in a particular tax year.

Will he be present (if so why) in the UK over several tax years.

What has been his pattern of visits to and stays in the UK (and the reasons for these) in the past.

What is the projected pattern of visits and stays in the UK over the next four years.

It is appreciated that it is very easy to be a resident in the UK for tax purposes with all the connotations that this implies?

Is he coming to the UK with the fixed intention of remaining permanently in the UK? Or is the stay temporary for a period of years or how long?

Are the differences appreciated between:
Domicil
Residence for tax purposes
Residence for Exchange Control purposes

1.2 Answers to 1.1.

These will in part (or whole) determine whether he becomes:

- domiciled in the UK (see 2 post)
- resident for tax purposes
- ordinarily resident
- resident for Exchange Control purposes

2. Domicil

2.1 Acquisition of Domicil of Choice/Revival of Domicil of Origin

An individual coming to the UK with the intention of remaining there permanently i.e. to end his days there will almost certainly acquire a domicil of choice in the UK.

If the individual had a UK domicil of origin which was subsequently displaced by a foreign domicil of choice then it is likely (more often than not) that the UK domicil of origin will revive. In the eyes of the UK Revenue a UK domicil is most adhesive.

2.2 Retention of a Foreign Domicil

An individual coming to the UK for a temporary purpose only e.g. for study work political pressures etc. will not normally acquire a UK domicil unless he forms the intention to remain in the UK permanently i.e. he intends to end his days there.

After an extended period of time an individual may have difficulty, particularly if he has no or few connections with his country of purported domicil, in sustaining his foreign domicil.

2.3 Domicil of Wives

Following the Domicil and Matrimonial Proceedings Act 1973 a wife is capable of having a separate domicil from that of her husband. The situations where this will actually arise are rare and it seems to be clear that there must be some form of actual severence between the spouses.

2.4 Measure of Intention

The measure of intention in 2.1 and 2.2 will usually be ascertained by looking at the facts of the situation – in particular

- reason for being and connections in the UK (see 1.1.)
- connections with and visits to the country of purported domicil

Examine:
domicil questionnaire – Appendix 2
P86 – Appendix 2
Part B 2.1

3. Residence for UK Tax Purposes

3.1 A. General Rules

If a person:

(i) is present in the UK for six months or more in a UK tax year, or

(ii) has a place of abode[1] (e.g. a flat or house) in the UK and visits the UK for one day in a UK tax year then he will be resident. There is *one* exception to this and it is if the person has a full time business occupation abroad. Incidental (narrowly construed) visits to the UK are permitted but clearly long 'holidays' and long business visits are not helpful, or

(iii) visits to the UK (with no place of abode) for four consecutive years averaging three months or more per tax year (6th April – 5th April)

then he will be treated (subject to any Double Tax Agreement) as *resident* in the UK.

3.1 B. Double Tax Treaties

With modern double tax treaties there are provisions for determining cases where a person is resident in both countries under each country's rules. Usually the criteria are:

i) permanent home. But if none or one in each *then*

ii) centre of vital interest (personal and economic relations). But if it cannot be determined *then*

iii) habitual abode. But if none or in both *then*

iv) nationality

3.2 Determination of Status

(a) In the UK one's residence status is determined after protracted correspondence with the UK Revenue – usually always after the event.

(b) Clearly if 3.1. A (iii) above periods are never exceeded then there are no problems.

(c) Where the 3.1. A (iii) periods are exceeded then any claim to non-residence will invariably rely on the Double Tax Treaty.

3.3 Date of Start of Residence

Strictly residence is on a whole tax year basis. But in certain circumstances 'new permanent residents' will be regarded as resident and ordinarily resident from the date of arrival (IR 20 paras 12 & 19)

4. Income and Capital Gains

4.1 Domicil and Ordinarily Residence – relation to income tax

A person being resident but

i) not domiciled in the UK *or*

ii) a British or Irish subject who is not ordinarily resident in the UK

will be subject to UK tax on his non-UK income upon the remittance basis i.e. when he receives it in the UK.

The exception to (i)-(ii) above is where a foreign-domiciled person receives emoluments from a foreign company in respect of duties performed in the UK. In such a case there is a deduction of 50% (or 25%) before such emoluments are subject to UK tax under Schedule E Case 1 or 2.

Consider

- what constitutes a remittance
- the particular meaning of foreign emoluments

If neither (i)-(ii) apply then a person will be subject to UK income tax upon the arising basis on all of his income i.e. when it accrues to him.

4.2 Personal Allowances

These should be full taken advantage of i.e. the total income subject to UK tax must be at least equal to the personal allowances.

4.3 Sources of income

list these:

a) project quantum of UK and non-UK income separately.

b) how much income is required to live on if the person will become resident.

c) will a tax treaty effect the position and deem residence status and income source to be different from the apparent situation.

d) if the remittance basis of taxation applies consider having separate bank accounts outside the UK for inter alia capital, income, interest etc. Pure capital can be remitted tax free. But N.B. the position of foreign currency gains.

Consider whether the overall situation is economically viable.

4.4 Capital Gains Tax ('CGT')

A. If an individual is

a) UK domiciled and resident or ordinarily resident in the UK

then he is subject of UK CGT on any capital gains that he realises with relief for losses.

b) Domiciled outside the UK and is resident or ordinarily resident in the UK

then (i) he is subject to UK CGT on any capital gains that he realises in the UK with relief for any losses realised in the UK.

(ii) with any foreign capital gains they are subject to UK Capital Gains Tax upon the remittance basis i.e. when the sale proceeds are brought into the UK. There is *no* relief for foreign losses.

B. Situs of Assets
Ascertain the location of the assets for CGT purposes. See FA 1965 s.43.

C. Extra statutory concession D 2
Certain gains realised in the tax year of arrival *prior to arrival* will be exempted provided certain conditions are satisfied.

D. Realisations of Gains
Prior to becoming resident and ordinarily resident consider realising any accrued capital gains but defer realising capital losses. Re-investment can be made immediately.

The reason for realisation is that the *acquisition cost* forms the base cost for CGT purposes.

N.B. foreign currency is usually a chargeable asset for CGT purposes.

5. Capital Transfer Tax ('CTT')

5.1 General

- CTT is the combination of a gifts tax and an estate duty.
- Residence is usually *immaterial* for CTT purposes.
- Domicil and location of assets can be crucial for CTT purposes.
- The CTT rates are steep and progressive.

5.2 Domicil & CTT
(i) – A foreign domiciled person is only liable to CTT in respect of his UK assets i.e. his foreign assets are not subject to CTT.
– Foreign assets are excluded property for CTT purposes (FA 1975 s.24).
(ii) A UK domiciled person or foreign domiciled person treated as being domiciled in the UK under FA 1965 s.45 will find that his world-wide assets are subject to CTT.
(iii) Has a spouse the same domicil as his or her spouse?

5.3 Loss of Foreign Domicil
Where this will occur consider placing beforehand the assets in a foreign trust; sooner rather than later as domicil is decided invariably with hindsight.

FA 1975 s.45 must be carefully studied – particularly s.45 (1)(b) in Appendix 5 and the table in Appendix 2.

If a foreign domiciled person (who is not treated under FA 1965 s.45 as being domiciled in the UK) forms a foreign trust and places non-UK assets in it then such property is excluded property for CTT purposes. FA 1975 Schedule 5 (2) (1) (a) – see Appendix 5.

5.4 Miscellaneous Points
Foreign domiciled individuals should keep the bulk of their assets outside the

UK. The position of the domicil of wives should be kept constantly under review.

Consideration should be given to making separate wills for UK and non-UK property.

UK domiciled or persons treated as being or about to be domiciled in the UK will to take advantage of the annual exemptions (see part B 4.1((c))

Check Finance Act 1975 s.45 position every year. Particularly the s.45 (1) (b) table in Appendix 2. Note FA 1977 s.49 – see Appendix 5

If the benefit justifies the annual costs consider forming a foreign company to hold UK situated property.

6. *Exchange Control* ('EC')

6.1 Stay of 3 years or more

If it is the intention to remain in the UK for three years or more then the individual *will be treated as a permanent resident* from the time of arrival and accordingly will be designated a UK resident. His immediate EC obligations are:

to convert all foreign currency and gold to £ sterling and remit it to the Scheduled Territories[2];

to lodge with or to have held to the order of a UK authorised bank or depository *all* non UK stock share and bond certificates (remember that on disposal the proceeds cannot be reinvested and must be converted into £ sterling at the official rates);

to arrange for *all* income arising outside the Scheduled Territories[2] to be remitted to the Scheduled Territories[2].

6.2 Stay of less than 3 years

Such an individual will only be temporarily resident in the UK and so retains his EC non-resident status. His access to UK financing directly or indirectly may be restricted and or subject to consent from the Bank of England.

After three years if such an individual is still present in the UK then his status is reviewed. Usually if he is going to remain in the UK (albeit temporarily) he will be designated a resident.

6.3 EC 27 Exemption

This exemption is given under EC Notice No 27 and cannot be applied for in connection with holdings of gold or £ sterling.

It only has a restricted application to a few categories of individuals. The normal UK resident cannot apply for it. To obtain the measure of exemption stringent criteria must be satisfied and this is particularly so where the individual is a British subject. A foreign national who has a measure of exemption under EC 27 who then loses his foreign nationality may well also lose his measure of exemption. Each case turns on its own facts.

It the measure of exemption is granted by the Bank of England then permission will be given to operate non-resident accounts but only with the permitted foreign source funds which are specifically declared in the application form for exemption under EC 27.

If the criteria cannot be wholly or only partially satisfied then consider 6.4

6.4 Prior to becoming an EC resident

A trust could be formed and the assets placed in the trust would retain their non resident status even after the individual became resident for EC purpose. There may also be other good reasons for forming a trust:

- continuity
- devolution
- confidentiality
- stability

N.B. Residence for EC purposes is quite separate and distinct to residence for tax (or any other) purposes.

Alternatively if EC 27 exemption cannot be obtained consider switching investments into good quality issues that are unlikely to require sale for investment reasons and are suitable for long term appreciation. There may also be CGT advantages in doing this.

7. UK Income Tax

7.1 Domicil, Residence and Ordinary Residence

a) is the person: UK or foreign domiciled, resident or not resident, ordinarily resident or not ordinarily resident

b) the three positions must be regularly reviewed.

7.2 UK Domiciled Individual

a) If resident and ordinarily resident he will be subject to UK income tax on his worldwide income.

With regard to his Schedule E earnings can he take advantage of the 25% or 100% deductions?

If his rates of tax are too high can he reduce his investment income by investing in lower yielding stocks?

Does his wife work and is it worthwhile having her earnings separately taxed?

b) If resident but *not* ordinarily resident (and a British subject or Irish citizen) some of his foreign income will be subject to UK income tax upon the remittance basis e.g. his investment income.

7.3 Foreign Domiciled Individual

a) The remittance basis re foreign income

Note: definitions of remittance, effect of preceding year basis of assessment, cessations of source

b) 50% (or 25%) Deduction

If the individual is employed by a foreign company in respect of his UK duties he will be able to obtain this deduction from his foreign emoluments *before* they are subject to UK tax under Schedule E case 1 or 2 (see 4.1 ante)

c) Worldwide Profession/Trade

Where an individual (whether foreign domiciled or not) is resident in the UK and carries on a worldwide activity then unless he can show (and this is difficult) that the activity was entirely carried on abroad he will invariably be subject to UK tax on the arising basis under Schedule D Case 1 or 2 and not on the remittance basis in respect of his 'overseas' earnings. Because of this the activity is often divided into two parts – a UK part re the UK activities and non-UK part re the non-UK activities and these are carried on through separate vehicles – usually partnerships or companies. This requires careful consideration.

d) Bank Accounts Abroad

It is often advantageous for the invidual to have abroad (i.e. outside the UK) separate bank accounts for separate sources of income and capital funds. It is often essential to do this to ensure that the UK Revenue will always accept that remittance of funds came from non-taxable monies i.e. capital (or monies that are taxable at a lower rate of tax e.g. foreign capital gains or earned income as opposed to investment income). Where different funds are mixed it is almost impossible to sort out the mixture to the satisfaction of the UK Revenues.

N.B. Foreign currency gains can be subject to CGT.

e) Foreign Income Accumulated Abroad

This may of course be subject to any EC regulations be used for holidays, travel, etc outside the UK.

f) Personal Allowances

There should always be sufficient income subject to tax in the UK to absorb the personal allowances.

8. *General Aspects*

Consider Part B 8 & 9 from the UK point of view.

Part B

CHECK LIST FOR INTENDING NON-RESIDENT AND EMIGRANTS

1. General

1.1 Requirements
- Is the individual (and any family he may have) really prepared to comply with the stringent requirements for obtaining full non-resident status.
- If emigrating then the requirements are more stringent if a foreign domicil is to be acquired. Can he make the 'clean cut' with the UK?

1.2 Motivation
Why is he going?
is he a fair or foul weather emigrant?
will he and (perhaps more important his family) he able to sever their ties with the UK
- emotional ties
- material ties
- social ties
- psychological ties

1.3 Lifestyle
- Will the emigrant be able to maintain his lifestyle on his income and very limited capital during the first four years?
- have the costs of settling in been properly estimated? currency debasement/inflation etc.
- has the tax structure in the new country of residence been properly evaluated? Is the tax base subject to virtual negotiation? If so is such uncertainty acceptable?

1.4 Advantages of non-residence and emigration
will any of the following benefits be obtained
- mitigation of tax liabilities - both capital and income
- new history starting - old history stops
- exchange control benefits
- increased earnings and savings
- better investment opportunities

1.5 Profitability

Is the whole exercise worth it? In financial as well as spiritual terms?

2. Domicil and Non-Residence

2.1 Do's and Don'ts and What Connections Remain with the UK and are with the Country of Residence and purported domicil

Directorships
Employment/occupation
Centre of economic interest
Business interests
Membership of clubs/associations
Place of abode available for accomodation
Property rented out
Relations
Education of children
History of past visits
Reasons for past visits
Reasons for future visits
Reasons for absence
Citizenship
Furniture etc., stored
Wills
Correspondences
Forwarding address
Documentation
Burial space
Voting

2.2 Residence

Consider:

- A 3.1 and 3.2
- Appendix 2. Form P 85 & IR 20 paras 13-18.
- The inadvisability of available accommodation in the UK.
- *Return visits* if not engaged in a full-time occupation outside the UK then return visits can be imprudent (if not fatal) – especially during the rump of the UK tax year, following departure and the subsequent tax year. There should be a 'clean cut'.
- Even if visits back to the UK are not detrimental for residence purposes they are not helpful for domicil purposes.

3. *Income and Capital Gains*

3.1 UK Income

Sources. See Form P.85. Check DTA position, dividends ('G' arrangements. N.B. Tax Credit position)

UK Government exempt securities
Interest (N.B. extra-statutory concession B.13)
Profits
Annuities
Rents (agents/tenants can be liable to account for tax)
Pensions
Royalties
Salaries directors fees

Rate of Tax

If rate of UK income tax is too high consider forming Investment Holding Company in Channel Island or elsewhere.

but consider: EC position, overall tax position, running costs.

Personal Allowances

Usually available in full in year of departure and any year of return.
ICTA 1970 s.27 proportional reliefs often available.
If UK citizenship not retained it is available under some DTAs.

Income Yield

Consider investment in UK government exempt securities to increase income.

3.2 Foreign Income

Sources (check DTA position)
dividends
interest
profits
annuities
rents
pensions
royalties
salaries directors fees

3.3 Viability

After taking into account withholding taxes, inflation and currency debasement is there sufficient:

- UK source income
- foreign income

3.4 Capital Gains Tax ('CGT')

The individual must be *not resident and not ordinarily resident in the UK* to avoid CGT.

Capital Gains
can any disposals resulting in capital gains be deferred until after the individual is not resident and not ordinarily resident. In these cases it is essential to be designated provisionally not resident and not ordinarily resident.

On sale of shares in a family company etc. prior to departure can it be arranged that equity consideration is received which can be disposed of later when full non-resident status is obtained.

Capital Losses
can these be realised before departure but if
- the loss is relatively small *and*
- the security was purchased with investment currency

Then is the benefit of taking the funds realised out without any s.40 EC 4 year restriction greater than the benefit obtained from 75% of the investment currency and the tax loss?

Extra-Statutory Concession D.2
gives exemption from CGT after departure for the balance of the tax year in which departure takes place provided certain conditions are satisfied.

Part A 4.3
see also IR 20 paras 11 & 78 in Appendix 1 (B).

4. Capital Transfer Tax ('CTT')

4.1 (a) Deemed Domicil
Domicil and the location of assets remain the two key criteria for CTT.

F (no. 1) A 1975 s.45 which provides that certain individuals are treated as being domiciled in the UK. Note FA 1977 s.49 – see Appendix 5.

(b) Holding Action until s.45 provisions do not apply?
- transfer between husband an wife during lifetime and on death (i.e. amend Wills leaving dutiable property to spouse and excluded property to other beneficiaries)
- utilisation of exempt UK Government Securities exclusion (F (No. 1) A 1975 Schedule 7 (3))
- term assurance – hard currency policies

(c) Gifts
Still essential to utilise the normal exemptions and relief:
- £ 2,000 annual exemption
- £ 100 small transfers
- in consideration of marriage
- out of income
- charities
- maintenance of dependants

– Transfers between spouses but N.B. Domicil and Matrimonial Proceedings Act 1973. Also F (No. 1) A 1975 Schedule 6 (2) (3).

4.2 Creation of Foreign Trusts

(a) life interest in possession to Settlor or his or her spouse *or*

(b) utilise exempt UK Government securities exclusion. N.B. Capital Gains Tax position on any disposals.

After s.45 deemed domicil period consider advance and re-settlement... but N.B. Schedule 5 para 11 (4).

4.3 Position of Assurance Policies

Some policies written under trust or MWPA may be regarded as trusts or liable otherwise to CTT. Previously they may well have been free of estate duty.

4.4 Accountability for CTT – F (No. 1) A 1975 ss.25 and 27 liabilities of:

- recipients
- beneficiaries
- trustees
- settlor

5. Existing Trusts

A. Export Operations:

- Trust law
- UK Revenue attitude
- CGT position – FA 1965 s.42
- Income Tax position
- Trust breaking
- UK former Trustees position – indemnities
- exempt UK Government securities

B. Exchange Control Aspects:

- redesignation
- payment of income

C. CTT Transitional reliefs:

only applicable to those persons who are UK domiciled
F (No. 1) A 1975 Sched. 5 para 14 (4) as amended by FA 1976.

6. Looking Ahead

6.1 Expectations

- sources
- switching

- generation hopping
- assignment of reversions

6.2 Ark (lifeboat)

- associations
- contacts
- connections
- EC
- ICTA 1970 s.478 – transfer of 'income' abroad
- FA 1965 s.41 – capital gains tax
- ICTA 1970 s.482
- Transfer of trade/business/company abroad only with Treasury Consent
- applies only to companies – not to partnerships or trading trusts
- forms of consent – Treasury Consents
- – General Consents
- change of residence of principal shareholders and directors may assist
- penalties
- ICTA 1970 s.485 Transfers at overvalue or undervalue

6.3 General

investments: are the assets deployed so as to satisfy the investment fiscal and political criteria?

education: is it suitable; can it be maintained?

7. *Exchange Control*

7.1 Emigration

Allowance per family unit (husband wife and children under 18) is £ 40,000 to an RNST territory or the Overseas Sterling Area. The allowance to an EEC Territory is now £ 80,000. Additional allowances can sometimes be obtained in hardship cases. Where an emigration allowance of £ 5,000 or £ 20,000 has been granted prior to 27th October 1977, application can be made to have the balance of the new allowances remitted.

The emigrant must check that he takes full advantage of the following allowances/concessions:

- household goods
- personal effects
- motor car for family (personal but not business use)
- foreign currency allowance
- sterling cash allowance

Foreign Currency Securities – These are not restricted and can be taken out. Do not realise any until after re-designation ***unless*** it is more advantageous to gain the benefit of the premium.

Annuities and Assurance Policies – Consider the position carefully. With insurance policies the Bank of England's practice can vary in each case.

All remaining assets (or their sale proceeds) are restricted under EC Act 1947 s.40 for 4 years. At the end of that period under current practice the s.40 restrictions are lifted.

Income from the Scheduled Territories is freely remittable to any country of destination.

Back-to-back loans
- practical difficulties in arrangement
- substantial investment currency margin usually required.

7.2 Repatriation
Does the individual qualify? It is usually preferable for an individual to be 'repatriated' rather than 'emigrated'.

7.3 EC 27 Exemption
Assets exempted under EC 27 are not effected by Exchange Control. So neither 7.1 nor 7.2 can apply to those assets.

8. Dropping Zone ('DZ')

8.1 Consider placing part of assets in a financial centre or low tax area e.g. Jersey
- Guernsey
- Isle of Man
- Switzerland

May be essential to utilize DZ if the proposed country of residence is politically or economically unstable or has or will have strict EC likely to inhibit funds being remitted out.
Consider
- the costs of a DZ operation
- availability of local expertise in DZ – in depth

DZ Alternatives:
trust and company structures
joint accounts
nominee names
wills

Ensure that devolution of any assets in the DZ are adequately provided for – consider the use of Trusts for this purpose if no other.
In some financial centres Wills must conform with the law of the country of domicil or nationality or place of execution.

i.e. it may not be a simple matter of just proving a Will (or having it resealed) but also an affidavit from an attorney resident in the country of domicil may have to be obtained.

8.2 Ensure that any DZ operation is properly linked-in with the taxation of income and assets and any Exchange Control Restrictions in the countries of origin and country of residence.

8.3 Confidentiality: is it real or imagined?

9. Country (State/Territory) of New Domicil

9.1 Residence permit
Work permit
Police Registration
Social Security
Insurance
Medical and Dental facilities

9.2 Language(s)
Customs
Education
Social Life
Xenophobia
Democracy
Justice

9.3 i) Political and economic stability
ii) cost of living
iii) rent or buy place of abode?
iv) occupation – Union Membership etc.
N.B. Consider 9.1 9.2 and 9.3 above from the viewpoint of the ***family unit as a whole.***

9.4 Exchange Control
UK
Country of Residence
Assets located elsewhere
Import Licences – re-exportation.

9.5 Taxation
a) Country of Residence
National Taxes
Regional Taxes
Municipal Taxes

Treatment of foreign income and foreign assets – remittance basis or worldwide basis types of taxes, income taxes, capital taxes (acquisition values!), VAT/ TVA, turnover taxes etc., any concession/tax holidays/special deals

b) At what stage regarded 'resident' and 'domiciled' (if appropriate) for tax purposes
c) Country of payment of income – income and capital taxes
d) Double Tax relief (if any)
e) tax assessment collection and practice
f) possible future fiscal and exchange control developments.

9.6 Domicil Aspects

Acquisition and *retention* of foreign domicil

What is the real state of intention and how is it evidenced?

Is it clear?

Real settled intention – not phoney confused or muddled

N.B. Take care that the domicil of origin does not revive

9.7 Divorce

– recognition of divorce

– legitimacy, illegitimacy and adoption

9.8 Devolution of Assets

Wills i) different Wills for different countries

ii) legitimacy/enforced heirship (an alien concept to English Law)

iii) CTT – s.45 3 year period

iv) DTA or unilateral relief for death duties

v) how will local taxes affect the position

Intestacies

Community of property

Trusts – are these recognised?

Joint accounts

Nominees

Bearer shares

Gifts inter vivos – donations tax, gifts tax

9.9 Care

advice on the foreign situation may be

– outdated

– inaccurate

– subject to sudden change

– grounded on local taxes or evasion techniques and do not reflect true legal position

1. This is widely construed. See IR 20 para 28 & 29
2. The UK Channel Islands Isle of Man Eire Gibraltar

Appendix 1

A. Legislation

ICTA 1970, S.27

Non-Residents

1. Subject to the provisions of this section, no relief under this Chapter shall be given in the case of any individual who is not resident in the United Kingdom.

2. Subsection 1 above shall not apply in the case of any individual who satisfies the Board that he or she:-

(a) is a British subject or a citizen of the Republic of Ireland; or

(b) is a person who is or has been employed in the service of the Crown, or who is employed in the service of any missionary society or in the service of any territory under Her Majesty's protection; or

(c) is resident in the Isle of Man or the Channel Islands; or

(d) has previously resided within the United Kingdom, and is resident abroad for the sake of his or her health, or the health of a member of his or her family resident with him or her; or

(e) is a widow whose late husband was in the service of the Crown:

Provided that no such relief as aforesaid shall be given so as to reduce the amount of the income tax... payable by that individual below the amount which results from applying the fraction A/B to the amount which would be payable by him by way of income tax... if the tax were chargeable on his total income from all sources (including income which is not subject to income tax charged in the United Kingdom), where:-

: A is the amount of his income subject to income tax charged in the United Kingdom; and

: B is the amount of his total income.

3. For the purposes of the proviso to subsection 2 above as it applies to an individual whose income includes income eligible for double taxation relief:-

(a) in computing the amount of the income tax payable by the individual, the tax chargeable in respect of the income eligible for double taxation relief shall be disregarded;

(b) in computing the amount of his income subject to income tax charged in the United Kingdom, the income eligible for double taxation relief shall be disregarded; and

(c) in computing his total income from all sources, including income which is not subject to income tax charged in the United Kingdom, income eligible for double taxation relief shall be included, and the income tax which would be chargeable on that total income shall be computed without regard to the double taxation relief available in respect of the income eligible for double taxation relief;

and accordingly, where this subsection applies, the amount of the tax chargeable in respect of the income eligible for double taxation relief shall not be affected by subsection 2 above -

: Provided that this subsection shall not operate so as to make the tax payable by an individual for a year of assessment higher than it would have been if the double taxation relief had not been available.

4. In subsection 3 above 'income eligible for double taxation relief' means any dividends, interest, royalties or other profits which are chargeable to income tax but in respect of which relief (other than credit) is available under an Order in Council under section 497 of this Act (double taxation agreements),... so as to limit the rate of income tax so chargeable (but not so as to confer an exemption

and make it income which is not subject to income tax charged in the United Kingdom).

5. Any claim which an individual is entitled to make by virtue of subsection 2 above shall be made to the Board.

S.49 – BRITISH SUBJECTS ETC. TEMPORARILY ABROAD

Every British subject or citizen of the Republic of Ireland shall, if his ordinary residence has been in the United Kingdom, be assessed and charged to income tax notwithstanding that at the time the assessment or charge is made he may have left the United Kingdom, if he has so left the United Kingdom for the purpose only of occasional residence abroad, and shall be charged as a person actually residing in the United Kingdom upon the whole amount of his profits or gains, whether they arise from property in the United Kingdom or elsewhere, or from any allowance, annuity or stipend, or from any trade, profession, employment or vocation in the United Kingdom or elsewhere.

S.50 – RESIDENCE OF PERSONS WORKING ABROAD

1. Where a person works full-time in one or more of the following, that is to say, a trade, profession, vocation, office or employment, and the condition mentioned in subsection 2 below is satisfied, the question whether he is resident in the United Kingdom shall be decided without regard to any place of abode maintained in the United Kingdom for his use.

2. The said condition is that no part of the trade, profession or vocation is carried on in the United Kingdom and all the duties of the office or employment are performed outside the United Kingdom.

3. Where an office or employment is in substance one of which the duties fall in the year of assessment to be performed outside the United Kingdom there shall be treated for the purposes of this section as so performed any duties performed in the United Kingdom the performance of which is merely incidental to the performance of the other duties outside the United Kingdom.

S.51 – TEMPORARY RESIDENTS IN UNITED KINGDOM

1. A person shall not be charged to income tax under Schedule D as a person residing in the United Kingdom, in respect of profits or gains received in respect of possessions or securities out of the United Kingdom, who is in the United Kingdom for some temporary purpose only and not with any view or intent of establishing his residence therein, and who has not actually resided in the United Kingdom at one time or several times for a period equal in the whole to six months in any year of assessment, but if any such person resides in the United Kingdom for the aforesaid period he shall be so chargeable for that year.

2. For the purposes of Cases I, II and III of Schedule E, a person who is in the United Kingdom for some temporary purpose only and not with the intention of establishing his residence there shall not be treated as resident in the United Kingdom if he has not in the aggregate spent at least six months in the United Kingdom in the year of assessment, but shall be treated as resident there if he has.

FA 1973 – S.38 – TERRITORIAL EXTENSION OF CHARGE TO INCOME TAX, CAPITAL GAINS TAX AND CORPORATION TAX

1. The territorial sea of the United Kingdom shall for all purposes of income tax, capital gains tax and corporation tax (including the following provisions of this section) be deemed to be part of the United Kingdom.

2. In this section and in Schedule 15 to this Act:–

(a) 'exploration or exploitation activities' means activities carried on in connection with the exploration or exploitation of so much of the seabed and subsoil and their natural resources as is situated in the United Kingdom or a designated area; and

(b) 'exploration or exploitation rights' means rights to assets to be produced by exploration or exploitation activities or to interests in or to the benefit of such assets; and

(c) references to the disposal of exploration or exploitation rights include references to the disposal of shares deriving their value or the greater part of their value directly or indirectly from such rights, other than shares quoted on a recognised stock exchange (within the meaning of the Corporation Tax Acts); and

(d) 'shares' includes stock and any security as defined in section 237 (5) of the Taxes Act; and

(c) 'designated area' means an area designated by Order in Council under section 1 (7) of the Continental Shelf Act 1964.

3. Any profits or gains from exploration or exploitation activities carried on in a designated area or from exploration or exploitation rights shall be treated for the purposes of income tax or corporation tax as profits or gains from activities or property in the United Kingdom; and any gains accruing on the disposal of such rights shall be treated for the purposes of Part III of the Finance Act 1965 as gains accruing on the disposal of assets situated in the United Kingdom.

4. Any profits or gains arising to any person not resident in the United Kingdom from exploration or exploitation activities carried on the United Kingdom or in a designated area or from exploration or exploitation rights, and any gains accruing to such a person on the disposal of such rights, shall for the purposes of corporation tax or capital gains tax, be treated as profits or gains of a trade, or gains accruing on the disposal of assets used for the purposes of a trade, carried on by that person in the United Kingdom through a branch or agency.

5. In relation to exploration or exploitation rights disposed of by a company resident in a territory outside the United Kingdom to a company resident in the same territory or in the United Kingdom, sections 273 to 275 and 278 to 279 of the Taxes Act (transfer within group and company ceasing to be member of group) shall apply as if in section 272 of that Act (definition of 'group' etc.) subsections 1 (a) and 2 were omitted.

6. Any emoluments from an office or employment in respect of duties performed in a designated area in connection with exploration or exploitation activities shall be treated for the purposes of income tax as emoluments in respect of duties performed in the United Kingdom.

7. This section shall have effect for the purposes of income tax and capital gains tax for the year 1973–74 and subsequent years of assessment and for the purposes of corporation tax for the financial year 1973 and subsequent years.

8. Schedule 15 to this Act shall have effect for supplementing this section.

DOMICILE AND MATRIMONIAL PROCEEDINGS ACT 1973

Husband and Wife

1. (1) Subject to (2) below, the domicile of a married woman as at any time after the coming into force of this section shall, instead of being the same as her husband's by virtue only of marriage, be ascertained by reference of the same factors as in the case of any other individual capable of having an independent domicile.

(2) Where immediately before this section came into force a woman was married and then had her husband's domicile by dependence, she is to be treated as retaining that domicile (as a domicile of choice, if it is not also her domicile of origin) unless and until it is changed by acquisition or revival of another domicile either on or after the coming into force of this section.

Minors and Pupils

3. (1) The time at which a person first becomes capable of having an independent domicile shall be when he attains the age of sixteen or marries under that age; and in the case of a person who immediately before 1st January 1974 was incapable of having an independent domicile, but had then attained the age of sixteen or been married, it shall be that date.

(2) This section extends to England and Wales and Northern Ireland (but not to Scotland).

4. (1) Subsection (2) of this section shall have effect with respect to the dependent domicile of a child as at any time after the coming into force of this section when his father and mother are alive but living apart.

(2) The child's domicile as at that time shall be that of his mother if –

a) he then has his home with her and has no home with his father; or

b) he has at any time had her domicile by virtue of paragraph (a) above and has not since had a home with his father.

(3) As at any time after the coming into force of this section, the domicile of a child whose mother is dead shall be that which she last had before she died if at her death he had her domicile by virtue of subsection (2) above and he has not since had a home with his father.

(4) Nothing in this section prejudices any existing rule of law as to the cases in which a child's domicile is regarded as being, by dependence, that of his mother.

(5) In this section, 'child' means a person incapable of having an independent domicile; and in its application to a child who has been adopted, references to his father and his mother shall be construed as references to his adoptive father and mother.

(6) This section extends to England and Wales, Scotland and Northern Ireland.

B. Revenue Practice

The following are the principal extracts of IR 20.

It must be stressed that the contents of IR 20 have no binding force and do not affect an individual's right of appeal on any point concerning the liability to tax. Nonetheless the vast majority of all cases are determined in accordance with IR 20.

General

6. The terms 'resident' and 'ordinarily resident' are not defined in the United Kingdom Income Tax Acts, but guidance as to the meaning of these words has been given in decisions by the Court. These show that both expressions are used in their everyday sense and do not have any special or technical meaning. The term 'domicile', on the other hand, is always used in its strictly legal sense (see paragraphs 31-34).

7. In the Income Tax Acts, 'resident' and 'ordinarily resident' are always used to describe a situation in a tax year, and not in relation to some longer or shorter period. The question that generally has to be decided is whether or not a person is resident (or ordiniarly resident) in the United Kingdom in a particular tax year. It is not practicable to do more in this booklet than set out the main principles which are followed in answering this question because each case depends on its particular facts.

8. If a person is to be regarded as resident in the United Kingdom for a given tax year he must normally be physically present in the country for at least part of that year. He will always be resident if he is here for six months or more in the year. *There are no exceptions to this rule.* Six months is regarded as equivalent to 183 days, whether or not the year is a leap year. For this purpose a count is made of the total number of days spent in the United Kingdom during the year whether the stay is of one period only or a succession of visits. Under present practice days of arrival and days of departure are normally ignored. If the person is here for less than six months, the decision whether or not he is resident depends on other circumstances (see paragraphs 13-30).

9. 'Ordinarily resident' is broadly equivalent to habitually resident; if a person is resident in the United Kingdom year after year, he is ordinarily resident here. It follows that a person may be resident but not ordinarily resident in the United Kingdom for a given tax year – if, for instance, he normally lives outside the United Kingdom but visits here in that year for six months or more. Or he may be ordinarily resident but not resident for a given tax year – if, for instance, he usually lives in the United Kingdom but has gone abroad for a long holiday and does not set foot in the United Kingdom during that year.

10. A person may be resident (or ordinarily resident) in two or more countries at the same time. He cannot claim to be not resident (or not ordinarily resident) in the United Kingdom merely because in that tax year he is resident (or ordinarily resident) in another country. Where, however, a person is

regarded as resident both in the United Kingdom and in a country with which the United Kingdom has a double taxation agreement there may be special provisions in the agreement for treating the person as a resident of one only of the countries for purposes of the agreement.

11. Strictly speaking, each tax year must be looked at as a whole, and a person is to be treated as either resident or not resident for the whole year: he cannot be regarded as resident for part of the year and not resident for the remainder. Thus a person who is ordinarily resident in the United Kingdom and who goes abroad for a period which does not include a *complete* tax year (eg, if he was abroad for the period from July 1970 to March 1972) is regarded as remaining resident and ordinarily resident throughout. But it is the practice, by concession, to split the year if the person:-

(a) is a new permanent resident, provided that he has been not ordinarily resident in the United Kingdom; or

(b) has left the United Kingdom for permanent residence abroad, provided that he becomes not ordinarily resident in the United Kingdom; or

(c) subject to certain conditions (see paragraph 18) is taking full-time employment abroad.

Where the year is split in this way, the day of departure from, or arrival in, the United Kingdom falls into the period of residence and ordinary residence here.

Husband and Wife

12. A wife's residence and ordinary residence status is not governed by her husband's status but is determined by her own circumstances. If, for example, a husband is employed abroad full-time and his wife goes out to join him, but later returns to the United Kingdom without having been away for a complete tax year, she is regarded as remaining resident and ordinarily resident here although he may be not resident and not ordinarily resident. If the residence status of husband and wife differ they may be treated as separate persons for tax purposes if it is to their advantage - see paragraph 88.

LEAVING THE UNITED KINGDOM

13. A person who has been ordinarily resident here is treated as remaining resident and ordinarily resident if he goes abroad for short periods only.

14. If a person goes abroad permanently but has accommodation (eg a house or apartment) available for his use in the United Kingdom, he is regarded as resident here for any tax year in which he visits the United Kingdom, however short the visit may be: and he is regarded as remaining ordinarily resident if he comes here in most years. The circumstances in which accommodation is regarded as available are set out in paragraphs 28 to 30.

15. Even if a person who has taken up permanent residence abroad has no accommodation available in the United Kingdom he is regarded as continuing to be resident and ordinarily resident here if he returns here for periods which amount to an *average* of three months a year.

16. If a person claims that he has ceased to be resident and ordinarily resident in the United Kingdom, and can produce some evidence for this (for example that he has sold his house here and set up a permanent home abroad), his claim is usually admitted provisionally with effect from the day following his departure. Normally this provisional ruling is confirmed after he has remained abroad for a period which includes a complete tax year and during which any visits to this country have not amounted to an annual average of three months.

17. If, however, he cannot produce sufficient evidence, a decision on his claim will be postponed for three years and will then be made by reference to what actually happened in that period. During the three intervening years, his tax liability is computed provisionally on the basis that he remains resident in the United Kingdom. He therefore continues to receive the various income tax reliefs due to a resident of the United Kingdom (see paragraph 60) except for any tax year in which he does not set foot in the United Kingdom. His liability is adjusted, if necessary, when the final decision is made at the end of three years.

18. If a person goes abroad for full-time service under a contract of employment and:-

(a) all the duties of his employment are performed abroad or any duties he performs here are incidental to his duties abroad (see paragraphs 37 to 39); ***and***

(b) his absence from the United Kingdom in this employment is for a period which includes a complete tax year; *and*

(c) interim visits to the United Kingdom do not amount to six months or more in any one tax year or three months or more on average,

he is normally regarded as not resident and not ordinarily resident in the United Kingdom from the day following the date of his departure until the day preceding the date of his return. On his return he is regarded as a new permanent resident.

COMING TO THE UNITED KINGDOM

New Permanent Residents

19. A person whose home has previously been abroad and who comes to the United Kingdom to take up permanent residence here is regarded as resident and ordinarily resident from the date of his arrival.

Visitors – General

20. A person whose home is abroad and who comes to the United Kingdom only as a visitor will not be treated as resident or ordinarily resident here except in the circumstances described in the following paragraphs.

21. As mentioned in paragraph 8, a visitor who stays for six months in a tax year will always be regarded as resident here. A visitor who has accommodation available here will be regarded as resident for any year in which he comes to the United Kingdom, however short his visit may be (but see paragraphs 29 and 30 below): if he visits in four or more consecutive years, or intends to do so, he will be treated as ordinarily resident also. A visitor who has no accommodation available will be regarded as becoming resident and ordinarily resident after his visits for four consecutive years have averaged three months or more a year. If it is clear when he first comes that he proposes to make such visits, he may be treated as resident and ordinarily resident in the United Kingdom from the start. A person who only visits the United Kingdom occasionally will not become ordinarily resident, but he will be resident for any year in which he visits amount to six months or more in aggregate.

22. The general principles described above are applied in the case of *all* visitors to the United Kingdom. There are additional principles applicable to visitors in certain special categories, and these are set out in the following paragraphs.

Visits for Education

23. A person who comes to the United Kingdom for a period of study or education which is expected to last for more than four years will be regarded as resident and ordinarily resident from the date of his arrival. If the period is not expected to exceed four years, he may be treated as not ordinarily resident, but this will depend on whether

(a) he has accommodation available here (see paragraph 28); or

(b) he intends to remain here at the end of his period of education; or

(c) he proposes to visit the United Kingdom in future years for average annual periods of three months or more.

If, despite the original expectation, he remains in the United Kingdom for more than four years, he will be treated in any event as ordinarily resident as from the beginning of the fifth tax year of his stay. His residence position will in any case be decided on the lines set out in paragraph 21.

24. If a parent or guardian of a child comes to the United Kingdom in connection with the child's education, the practice described in paragraph 23 is also applied to him.

Visits for Temporary Employment

25. A person who comes to the United Kingdom to work for a period of at least two years is treated as

resident here for the whole period from the day of arrival to the day of departure. He is not usually regarded as having become ordinarily resident here until he has been here at least three years, unless it is already clear that he intends to be here for three or more years (in which event his ordinarily resident status will normally follow the rules in paragraphs 26 and 27 below). In general, any other person coming to this country for employment will not be treated as resident unless he spends six months or more here in a tax year, or unless he has accommodation available (see paragraph 28).

Visits for Prolonged or Indefinite Residence

26. If a person comes to the United Kingdom for some purpose other than employment he may be ordinarily resident from the date of his arrival if it is clear that he intends to remain here for a long period – say three or more years – or if he has accommodation available: he is then treated as a new permanent resident.

27. If he has no definite intention as to the length of his stay, he is normally regarded as ordinarily resident from the beginning of the tax year in which the third anniversary of his arrival falls. A person who does not decide to stay here permanently until he has been here a little while is normally regarded as ordinarily resident from the beginning of the tax year in which he takes that decision.

Available Accommodation

28. Where a person's residence position turns on whether or not he has available accommodation, the question is whether any accommodation is *in fact* available for his use. *For this purpose ownership is immaterial* – a person does not have to own or rent a house, apartment or other accommodation for it to be available for his use: contrariwise, a house he owns and lets out on a long lease under the terms of which he has no right or permission to stay in it will be ignored. A house owned or rented by one spouse will usually be considered available for the use of the other. But any accommodation rented for use during a temporary stay here *may be* ignored if the period of renting is less than two years for furnished accommodation or one year for unfurnished accommodation.

29. Even if the accommodation is owned or held on a long lease, it may be ignored if the person is working full-time in a business, profession or employment carried on wholly abroad. But such accommodation is *not* ignored where the person owns a business, or is a partner in a business, carried on mainly abroad but which has a branch or permanent establishment in the United Kingdom; and this is so even though he himself does not work here.

30. If a person is employed abroad and some of his duties are performed in the United Kingdom it may be possible to ignore available accommodation provided that his duties in the United Kingdom are merely incidental to his duties abroad: the circumstances in which duties are regarded as merely incidental to the main duties of the employment are outlined in paragraphs 37 to 39.

PART IV. UNITED KINGDOM INCOME TAX ON EARNINGS FROM AN OFFICE OR EMPLOYMENT

Basis of Liability

35. Income tax on earnings from any office or employment is charged under one or more of three 'Cases' – I, II or III – of Schedule E. The diagram at the end of this booklet shows how the various Cases apply.

36. The term 'earnings' as used in this booklet includes salaries, fees, pay, wages, overtime pay, leave pay, bonus, commission, perquisites, tips, gratuities or other extra earnings. Earnings are treated as received in the United Kingdom if they are

(a) paid, used or enjoyed in this country; or

(b) sent or brought here in any form.

38. To determine whether duties in the United Kingdom are 'incidental' it is necessary to consider both the nature of the duties in the United Kingdom and their relation to the duties abroad. If the

overseas representative of a United Kingdom employer comes to the United Kingdom merely to report to his employer or to receive fresh instructions, the duties so performed in the United Kingdom will usually be regarded as incidental to the duties carried out abroad. But there are many circumstances in which the duties in the United Kingdom are not incidental to the overseas duties: for instance, a company director who, though usually working abroad, attends directors' meetings in the United Kingdom: or a member of the crew of a ship or aircraft; or a courier or similar employee who visits many countries in the course of his work. Although it is primarily the nature of the duties, rather than the time spent on them, which determines whether or not they can be regarded as incidental to the overseas duties, duties performed in the United Kingdom for periods amounting to more than three months in a year are not so treated.

39. If an overseas employee visits the United Kingdom for periods of training which do not exceed three months in the year, such periods are treated as incidental to his duties abroad if he does no productive work while he is here.

40. The duties of seafarers and members of aircraft crews are treated as performed in the United Kingdom if

(a) the voyage or flight does not extend to a place outside the United Kingdom; or

(b) the person concerned is resident in the United Kingdom and part of the voyage or flight begins or ends in this country.

Exemption under Double Taxation Agreements

41. Under many double taxation agreements

(a) earnings from an employment, and

(b) profits or earnings in respect of personal (including professional) services,

performed within the United Kingdom by a person who for the purposes of the agreement is a resident of the overseas country, are, subject to certain conditions, exempt from United Kingdom tax. One of the usual conditions is that the employer is, or that the services are performed on behalf of, a resident of the country with which the agreement was made. Another is that the person should not be present in the United Kingdom for more than 183 days in the tax year.

42. Most double taxation agreements also provide that a professor or teacher who comes to the United Kingdom for a period of not more than two years to teach at a university, college, school or other educational institution is exempt from United Kingdom tax on his earnings from the teaching post. Temporary absences from the United Kingdom during this period are treated as part of the period. If the professor or teacher stays in the United Kingdom for longer than two years he is not entitled to exemption and is liable to tax on the whole of the earnings. Under some agreements exemption is conditional on the earnings being taxed in the home country.

43. Most agreements provide that a student or business apprentice from the overseas country who is receiving full-time education or training in the United Kingdom is exempt from United Kingdom tax on payments made to him from sources outside the United Kingdom for his maintenance, education and training.

Special Classes of Employees

44. The information is this booklet needs to be supplemented for the following special groups of people who are employed overseas:–

(a) Those in the service of the Crown. They should write to HM Inspector of Taxes, (Public Departments 8).

(b) Those working in the Republic of Ireland. They should write to the Inspector of Foreign Dividends.

(c) Those ordinarily employed in this country but absent for a period from their employment (eg on leave). They should write to the Inspector of Taxes who normally deals with their tax affairs.

PART VII. RELIEF AND EXEMPTION UNDER DOUBLE TAXATION AGREEMENTS

Persons not Resident in the United Kingdom

54. A person who is resident of a country with which the United Kingdom has a double taxation agreement may be entitled to exemption or partial relief from United Kingdom income tax on certain kinds of income from United Kingdom sources and may also be exempt from United Kingdom tax on the disposal of assets. The conditions of exemption or relief vary from agreement to agreement and it is not possible to set them out in detail here. However, the agreements normally provide a measure of relief from United Kingdom tax on pensions (other than United Kingdom Government pensions), purchased annuities, royalties, dividends (but see paragraph 57) and, in some cases, interest. In some agreements it is a condition of the relief that the income is subject to tax in the other country.

55. A pension in respect of governmental service paid by the Government of one country to a person resident in the other is usually to be taxed only by the paying Government. However, under the agreements between the United Kingdom and Australia, Canada and New Zealand the pension is generally taxed in the country of residence only.

56. Relief in respect of royalties, interest or dividends may not be due where the person is engaged in any trade or business through a permanent establishment in the United Kingdom.

PART VIII. PERSONAL ALLOWANCES

60. A person who is resident in the United Kingdom is entitled to certain personal reliefs and allowances, based on personal and family circumstances. A person who is not resident and who is a British subject or who satisfies certain other requirements (see paragraph 61) may claim a proportion of the personal allowances and reliefs which he could have claimed had he been resident here: if he makes such a claim he will also be entitled to a tax credit in respect of any dividends he receives from United Kingdom companies paid on or after 6 April 1973 (see paragraph 57). A similar claim to proportionate allowances and reliefs may be made by residents or nationals of many of the countries with which the United Kingdom has concluded a double taxation agreement (see Annex C) – whether or not such persons will also be entitled to a tax credit in respect of dividends will depend on the terms of the agreement. As regards the personal allowances and reliefs of married women see paragraphs 86 to 88.

61. To qualify for proportionate personal allowances and reliefs, a person resident abroad must show that he or she:

(a) is a British subject or a citizen of the Irish Republic; or

(b) is or has been employed in the service of the British Crown; or

(c) is employed in the service of a missionary society; or

(d) is employed in the service of any territory under the protection of Her Majesty; or

(e) is resident in the Isle of Man or the Channel Islands; or

(f) has previously resided within the United Kingdom and is resident abroad for the sake of his or her health, or the health of a member of his or her familiy resident with him or her; or

(g) is a widow whose husband was employed in the service of the British Crown; or

(h) is a resident of and/or a national of a country with which there is a double taxation agreement providing for such reliefs

62. The relief due to a non-resident under the preceding paragraphs is given by:

(a) first calculating the tax (other than surtax) that would be payable if the claimant's total income were chargeable to United Kingdom tax and if he were granted those personal allowances to which he would be entitled if he were resident in the United Kingdom, and then

(b) restricting the tax (other than surtax) payable by him to the proportion of the tax ascertained as in (a) which his liable income (ie that part of his total income which is liable to United Kingdom income tax) bears to his total income. The tax payable cannot, however, be reduced below that which would be payable on the liable income were it the sole income of a United Kingdom resident.

'Total income' means total income from all sources including wife's income whether liable to United Kingdom income tax or not. It also includes any tax credit to which he may be entitled in respect of dividends paid by United Kingdom companies. If United Kingdom tax has already been paid on the liable income, any excess of the amount paid over the tax payable as in (b) is refunded.

PART IX. NEW PERMANENT RESIDENTS IN THE UNITED KINGDOM: SPECIAL PROVISIONS

Gains on the Disposal of Assets

64. If the person has not been resident or ordinarily resident in the United Kingdom at any time in the preceding thirty-six months, gains are charged to tax (see paragraphs 50 to 53) only in so far as they are made on the disposal of assets on or after the date of arrival for permanent residence.

Earnings from an Employment wholly Abroad

65. Earnings from an employment wholly abroad for a tax year in which a person is not resident in the United Kingdom are not liable to United Kingdom tax. In the year in which permanent residence begins, earnings for the part of the year before arrival are not charged.

Personal Allowances and Reliefs

74. For the year of arrival for permanent residence in the United Kingdom full personal allowances and reliefs are granted.

PART X. PERSONS LEAVING THE UNITED KINGDOM FOR PERMANENT RESIDENCE ABROAD: SPECIAL PROVISIONS

United Kingdom Government Securities

75. Interest on those United Kingdom government securities which are listed in Annex A is exempt from tax if it is payable after the date on which ordinary residence in this country ceases — that is, after the date of departure for permanent residence abroad (see paragraph 11).

Other United Kingdom Investment Income

76. In general, all other United Kingdom investment income remains liable to United Kingdom tax but relief or exemption may be due under a double taxation agreement (see paragraphs 54 to 58).

Income from Property in the United Kingdom

77. Profits from lettings of property in the United Kingdom remain liable to United Kingdom tax. Further information can be found in the Board's booklet on taxation of income from real property (No 530), obtainable from the Secretary, Board of Inland Revenue, or from any Tax Office in the United Kingdom.

Gains on the Disposal of Assets

78. In the year of a person's departure for permanent residence abroad tax is not charged on gains (see paragraphs 50 et seq) which accrue to him on the disposal of assets after the date on which ordinary residence ceases – that is, after the date of departure (see paragraph 11).

Investment Income from Overseas

81. The usual basis of liability to tax on investment income from overseas is outlined in paragraphs 46 to 49. A person who takes up permanent residence abroad is not liable on such income received through

a bank or paying agent after the date of departure, and any tax deducted can be reclaimed. Where income is not so received and the 'remittance basis' applies, the liability for the year of departure is calculated as in paragraph 80 above. Otherwise the liability for the year is based on the smaller of:-

(a) the proportion of the full amount of the income of the year of departure (or of the income of the preceding year, if that is the basis of assessment) which the period from 6 April to the date of departure bears to a complete income tax year: and

(b) the actual income arising for the period 6 April to the date of departure.

Personal Allowances and Reliefs

83. For the year of departure for permanent residence abroad full personal allowances and reliefs are granted.

87. A wife is treated as living with her husband unless:

(a) they are separated under an Order of a Court or by a Deed of Separation; or

(b) they are in fact separated in such circumstances that the separation is likely to be permanent.

88. If for a tax year a married woman is living with her husband but one of them is resident in the United Kingdom either for part or the whole of the year and the other is not resident for the year, they are regarded for income tax purposes as if they were permanently separated, and entitled to make separate claims, if it is to their advantage.

Other Claims

89. Claims to relief from United Kingdom income tax by a person who is not resident or not ordinarily resident in the United Kingdom in respect of:-

(a) income arising from sources outside the United Kingdom,

(b) interest on the United Kingdom government securities listed in Annex A, or

(c) income from United Kingdom sources covered by double taxation agreements (see paragraphs 54 to 58),

should be made to the Inspector of Foreign Dividends. In certain circumstances, arrangements can be made for relief to be given at the time when the income is paid.

90. Where however any income of the nature described in paragraph 89 is included in a claim made to the Chief Inspector (Claims) Foreign Division under paragraph 85, the repayment of United Kingdom income tax will normally be made in one sum. In certain circumstances, however, a separate claim must be made to the Inspector of Foreign Dividends in respect of items within (c) of paragraph 89; where this is necessary the claimant will be so advised.

91. A married woman living with her husband is entitled to claim the repayment referred to in paragraph 89 in her own name, but if her husband submits a claim under paragraph 85 to the Chief Inspector (Claims) Foreign Division, she does not need to lodge a separate claim except where necessary in respect of items within (c) of paragraph 89.

PART XII: APPEALS

92. In the great majority of cases, a person's residence, ordinary residence or domicile can be established, and any claim which he may make for relief from United Kingdom tax can be settled, by agreement between the person concerned (or his agents) and the Inland Revenue. If agreement cannot be reached, the law provides for the matter to be considered by an independent tribunal.

93. The procedure is, in general, for a formal decision in the case to be given by the Inland Revenue and for the person concerned to give notice of appeal against that decision. The law specifies the period within which the notice must be given; this period varies according to the issue which is in dispute. The appeal is heard by one of two bodies – either the General Commissioners or the Special Commissioners. In some cases the law directs which Commissioners shall hear the appeal but in others the person

concerned may choose. If a formal order is given, the Inland Revenue state the time within which any appeal must be made, and which Commissioners may hear the appeal.

94. Both the General Commissioners and Special Commissioners are independent of the Inland Revenue. The decision of either body of Commissioners on a question of fact is final, but an appeal against their decision may be made to the High Court on a question of law

C. Extra-Statutory Concessions

A14. RESIDENCE IN THE UNITED KINGDOM: YEAR OF ASSESSMENT AND CESSATION OF RESIDENCE

The Income and Corporation Taxes make no provision for splitting a tax year in relation to residence and an individual who is resident in the United Kingdom for any year of assessment is chargeable on the basis that he is resident for the whole year.

But where an individual:-

(a) comes to the United Kingdom to take up permanent residence or to stay for at least three years; or

(b) comes to the United Kingdom to take up employment which is expected to last for a period of at least two years; or

(c) ceases to reside in the United Kingdom if he has left for permanent residence abroad;

liability to United Kingdom tax which is affected by residence is computed by reference to the period of his residence here during the year. It is a condition that the individual should satisfy the Board of Inland Revenue that prior to his arrival he was, or on his departure is, not ordinarily resident in the United Kingdom. The concession would not apply, for example, where an individual who had been ordinarily resident in the United Kingdom left for intended permanent residence abroad but returned to reside here before the end of the tax year following the tax year of departure.

The concession has only limited application to changes of permanent residence between the United Kingdom and the Irish Republic and to income arising in the Irish Republic.

A30. OVERSEAS EMPLOYMENT – TRAVELLING EXPENSES

has been re-titled and amended to read:

30. OVERSEAS EMPLOYMENTS – REIMBURSED TRAVELLING EXPENSES BETWEEN THE UNITED KINGDOM AND OVERSEAS

Where a person holds an office or employment the duties of which are carried on wholly abroad and retains his place of abode in the United Kingdom the reimbursement by the person with whom he holds the office or employment of his expenses – including reasonable hotel expenses necessarily incurred – in travelling (whether alone or with his wife and family) to the country where his duties are performed and returning to the United Kingdom will not be assessed. Similarly, a person in receipt of 'foreign emoluments' (as defined in Section 181 (1) Income and Corporation Taxes Act 1970) for duties performed in the United Kingdom who retains his place of abode in his home country will not be assessed in respect of the reimbursement by the person with whom he holds the office or employment of travelling expenses between that country and the United Kingdom.

B.13 UNTAXED INTEREST PAID TO NON-RESIDENTS

This concession has been amended in consequence of the unification of income tax and surtax and now reads as follows:

Where a person not resident in the United Kingdom receives interest (e.g. bank interest) without deduction of income tax and is not chargeable in the name of an agent under Section 78 of the Taxes Management Act 1970, no action is taken to pursue his liability to income tax except so far as it can be recovered by set-off in a claim to relief (e.g. for proporionate reliefs and allowances under Section 27 of the Income and Corporation Taxes Act 1970) in respect of taxed income from United Kingdom sources. The concession does not apply to the corporation tax chargeable on the income of the United Kingdom branch or agency of a non-resident company.

D.2 RESIDENCE IN THE UNITED KINGDOM: YEAR OF COMMENCEMENT OR CESSATION OF PERMANENT RESIDENCE

A person who is treated as resident in the United Kingdom for any year of assessment from the date of his arrival here but who has not been regarded at any time during the period of 36 months immediately preceding the date of his arrival as resident or ordinarily resident here, is charged to capital gains tax only in respect of the chargeable gains accruing to him from disposals made after his arrival in the United Kingdom. When a person leaves the United Kingdom and is treated on his departure as not resident and not ordinarily resident in the United Kingdom he is not charged to capital gains tax on gains accruing to him from disposals made after the date of his departure.

This concession applies to changes of permanent residence between the United Kingdom and the Irish Republic notwithstanding that in such cases the person is treated as resident for the whole of the year of assessment in which the change takes place.

Appendix 2

A. Domicil Questionnaire

Will you please supply the following information. Where the addressee is a married woman and the marriage took place before 1st January 1974, the information should be given for both herself and her husband.

	REPLY	
	Self	*Husband*
1. Date and place of birth.		
2. Country of father's domicile at date of your birth.		
3. Details of any changes of father's domicile during your minority. If father dead his full name and date and place of death.		
4. In what country you consider yourself domiciled, and on what grounds.		
5. Whether you have a place of abode in the country stated in 4 and, if so, the address.		
6. Details of any business and other connections in or with the country stated in 4.		
7. Whether you have a place of abode in the United Kingdom and, if so, the address whether a house, flat etc., and if rented the conditions of tenancy.		
8. If you are married, the place of residence of your wife and any children.		
9. Dates of arrival and departure for all periods spent in the United Kingdom during the past ten years		
10. If you were born abroad, please state your motive in coming to the United Kingdom, e.g. whether in connection with business or employment here, or the education of children etc.		

11. Your intentions regarding the future.

Where the addressee is a widow who was married before 1st January 1974, the following information is also required:

12. Where and when your late husband was born.

13. The country of his father's domicile at late husband's date of birth.

14. Details of any changes in his father's domicile during your late husband's minority.

15. Your late husband's full name and the date and place of his death.

B. Form P.86 (to be completed on arrival in the UK)

ENQUIRIES	REPLIES
1. (a) What is your nationality? (b) Where were you born?	1. (a) (b)
2. In what country do you usually reside?	2.
3. (a) When did you arrive in the United Kingdom? (b) If you are married and your wife has also come to the United Kingdom, when did she arrive?	3. (a) (b)
4. (a) Where and by whom were you employed during the five years prior to your arrival in the United Kingdom? please state the length of each employment. (b) Was any part of the duties of employment(s) referred to in 4 (a) performed in the United Kingdom? if the answer is 'yes' please give details in an accompanying letter. (c) Has the most recent employment referred to in 4 (a) continued (on leave or otherwise) since your arrival in the United Kingdom? If the answer is 'yes', please state when it is likely to cease, if this is known to you.	4. (a) (b) (c)
5. (a) Please state the dates of arrival and departure in respect of all periods spent in the United Kingdom during the five years prior to the date entered at 3 (a) above by — (i) yourself and if you are married (ii) your wife, (b) Did you (or if you are married, did your wife) retain any accommodation for your use in the United Kingdom at any time during the five years immediately prior to the date entered in 3 (a) above?	5. (a) (b)

6. (a) Have you (or. if you are married, has your wife) held any accommodation for your use in the United Kingdom since your arrival?	6. (a)
(b) (i) What is the nature of the accommodation and the address?	(b) (i)
(ii) is it owned or rented, if rented is it held furnished or unfurnished and what is the period of the tenancy agreement? (if accommodation has been held at more than one address, please give separate details in each case).	(ii)
7. (a) Do you propose to remain permanently in the United Kingdom?	7. (a)
(b) If not —	(b)
(i) How long do you expect to stay in this country? if possible, please state the probable date of departure.	(i)
(ii) If you are married, will your wife continue to reside here, and if so, at what address?	(ii)

C. P.85 Income Tax Repayment Claim Form

As you are leaving this country, further relief or payment of tax may be due to you. Will you please therefore give the information asked for in Section B overleaf and return this form as soon as possible to the address below.

If you consider that repayment may be due to you, please also complete Section A and attach the tax certificate (Parts 2 and 3 of Form P.45) unless you have already sent it.

If you want any repayment arising from the claim to be made to a nominee please enclose your signed authority giving the full name and address of the nominee in BLOCK letters.

District
Date
Stamp

A. CLAIM

I claim any repayment of tax to which I may be entitled for the.......................... year 197...

Usual signature ....
(If a woman, state whether single, widow, married etc.)

Address in United Kingdom ....
up to date of departure ....
including postal code, if any ....

Date.................................... 197...

B. ENQUIRIES	REPLIES
1. Are you a British subject, if so, where were you born?	1.
2. How long have you lived in the United Kingdom prior to your departure?	2.
3. What is the date or intended date of departure from the United Kingdom and to what country are you going?	3.
4. (a) Do you intend to remain abroad permanently?	4. (a)
4. (b) If not, do you intend to remain abroad for a period of at least one year from 5th April immediately following your departure?	(b)
5. If you are married, is your wife going too? If so, please give the date or intended date of her departure.	5.
6. (a) Will either of you or, if you are married, your wife retain accommodation in the United Kingdom after your departure?	6 (a)
(b) If so:	(b)
(i) What is the nature of the accommodation and the address?	(i)
(ii) is it owned or rented; if rented is it held furnished or unfurnished?	(ii)
(iii) do you expect to visit the United Kingdom again before 6th April next?	(iii)
7. Will either of you or, if you are married, your wife be receiving rents, premiums or other income from property in the United Kingdom? If so, please state for each property concerned:-	7.
(a) the nature of the payments:	(a)
(b) the address of the property:	(b)
(c) whether you (or your wife) will be receiving the income direct (whether in the United Kingdom or elsewhere), and, if so, the name and address of the payer	(c)
(d) whether you (or your wife) will be receiving the income through an agent, and, if so, the name and address of the agent. If the agent's usual place of abode is outside the United Kingdom state the name and address of the payer.	(c)
8. Will either of you or,if you are married, your wife have any other source of income in the United Kingdom after your departure? If so, please give particulars.	8.

9. If you are taking up employment abroad:	9.
(a) Will your employment be full-time?	(a)
(b) What is the period of your contract, if any?	(b)
(c) What duties, if any, of the employment will be carried out in the United Kingdom?	(c)
(d) Will your pay be paid to you abroad or in the United Kingdom (by credit to your account or otherwise)? If paid partly abroad and partly in the United Kingdom please give full details (in an accompanying letter, if necessary).	(d)
(e) If your employment is with the United Kingdom Government please state the name of the department and the nature of the employment.	(e)
10. If you are not taking up employment abroad, what is your reason for leaving the United Kingdom?	(10)

Signature.. Date...... 197...
Address Abroad ....
(if known)
(USE BLOCK LETTERS)..

Appendix 3: Income Tax

A. ICTA 1970

S.108 - SCHEDULE D

The Schedule referred to as Schedule D is as follows:

SCHEDULE D

1. Tax under this Schedule shall be charged in respect of -
(a) the annual profits or gains arising or accruing -
(i) to any person residing in the United Kingdom from any kind of property whatever, whether situated in the United Kingdom or elsewhere, and
(ii) to any person residing in the United Kingdom from any trade, profession or vocation, whether carried on in the United Kingdom or elsewhere, and
(iii) to any person, whether a British subject or not, although not resident in the United Kingdom, from any property whatever in the United Kingdom, or from any trade, profession or vocation exercised within the United Kingdom, and
(b) all interest of money, annuities and other annual profits or gains not charged under Schedule A, B, C or E, and not specially exempted from tax.

3. The provisions of paragraphs 1. . . above are without prejudice to any other provision of the Tax Acts directing tax to be charged under this Schedule, and the tax so directed to be charged shall be charged accordingly

S.122 - ASSESSMENT ON PRECEDING YEAR BASIS, BUT, IN CERTAIN CASES, ONLY ON SUMS RECEIVED IN THE UNITED KINGDOM

1. Subject to the provisions of this section and sections 123 and 124 below, income tax chargeable under Case IV or Case V of Schedule D shall be computed on the full amount of the income arising in the year preceding the year of assessment, whether the income has been or will be received in the United Kingdom or not, subject in the case of income not received in the United Kingom: -
(a) to the same deductions and allowances as if it had been so received; and
(b) to a deduction on account of any annuity or other annual payment (not being interest) payable out of the income to a person not resident in the United Kingdom; and
(c) to a deduction on account of any annual interest payable out of the income to a person not resident in the United Kingdom, being interest payable before 6th April, 1980, on a debt incurred on or before 26th March, 1974.

2. Subsection 1 above shall not apply: –

(a) to any person who satisfies the Board that he is not domiciled in the United Kingdom, or that, being a British subject or a citizen of the Republic of Ireland, he is not ordinarily resident in the United Kingdom,. . .

(b). . .

(c). . .

Any claim under paragraph (a) above shall be made to the Board.

3. In the cases mentioned in subsection 2 above, the tax shall, subject to sections 123 and 124 below, be computed: –

(a) in the case of tax chargeable under Case IV, on the full amount, so far as the same can be computed, of the sums received in the United Kingdom in the year preceding the year of assessment, without any deduction or abatement; and

(b) in the case of tax chargeable under Case V, on the full amount of the actual sums received in the United Kingdom in the year preceding the year of assessment from remittances payable in the United Kingdom, or from property imported, or from money or value arising from property not imported, or from money or value so received on credit or on account in respect of any such remittances, property, money or value brought or to be brought into the United Kingdom, without any deduction or abatement other than is allowed under the provisions of the Income Tax Acts in respect of profits or gains charged under Case I of Schedule D.

4. For the purposes of subsection 3 above, any income arising from securities or possessions out of the United Kingdom which is applied outside the United Kingdom by a person ordinarily resident in the United Kingdom in or towards satisfaction of:

(a) any debt for money lent to him in the United Kingdom, or for interest on money so lent; or

(b) any debt for money lent to him outside the United Kingdom and received in or brought to the United Kingdom; or

(c) any debt incurred for satisfying in whole or in part a debt falling within paragraph (a) or (b) above;

shall be treated as received by him in the United Kingdom (and, for the purposes of paragraph (b) of the said subsection 3, as so received from remittances payable in the United Kingdom).

5. Where a person ordinarily resident in the United Kingdom receives in or brings to the United Kingdom money lent to him outside the United Kingdom, but the debt for that money is wholly or partly satisfied before he does so, subsection 4 above shall apply as if the money had been received in or brought to the United Kingdom before the debt was so satisfied, except that any sums treated by virtue of that subsection as received in the United Kingdom shall be treated as so received at the time when the money so lent is actually received in or brought to the United Kingdom.

6. Where a person is indebted for money lent to him, income applied by him in such a way that the money or property representing it is held by the lender on behalf of or to the account of the said person in such circumstances as to be available to the lender for the purpose of satisfying or reducing the debt by set-off or otherwise shall be treated as applied by the said person in or towards its satisfaction if, under any arrangement between the said person and the lender, the amount for the time being of the said person's indebtedness to the lender, or the time at which it is to be repaid in whole or in part, depends in any respect directly or indirectly on the amount or value held by the lender as aforesaid.

7. For the purposes of subsections 4 to 6 above:–

(a) a debt for money lent shall, to the extent to which the money is applied in or towards satisfying another debt, be deemed to be a debt incurred for satisfying that other debt, and a debt incurred for satisfying in whole or in part a debt falling within paragraph (c) of the said subsection 4 shall itself be treated as falling within that paragraph; and

(b) 'lender' includes, in relation to any money lent, any person for the time being entitled to repayment.

Editors Note – see also FA.1974, s22 (1) (income arising from foreign pensions and annuities to a person other than one falling under sub-section 2 (a) of this section; s.23 (1) (income derived by a person other than one falling under sub-section 2 (a) of this section from any trade, etc. carried on abroad either solely or in partnership).

181. SCHEDULE E

(1) The Schedule referred to as Schedule E is as follows:

Schedule E

1. Tax under this Schedule shall be charged in respect of any office or employment on emoluments therefrom which fall under one, or more than one, of the following Cases

Case I: where the person holding the office or employment is resident and ordinarily resident in the United Kingdom, any emoluments for the chargeable period, subject, however, to the deduction or exception provided for in Schedule 2 to the Finance Act 1974 if the emoluments are foreign emoluments and to the deduction provided for in Schedule 7 to the Finance Act 1977 if in the chargeable period he performs the duties of the office or employment wholly or partly outside the United Kingdom;

Case II: where that person is not resident or, if resident, then not ordinarily resident in the United Kingdom, any emoluments for the chargeable period in respect of duties performed in the United Kingdom, subject, however, to the deduction provided for in Schedule 2 to the Finance Act 1974 if the emoluments are foreign emoluments;

Case III: where that person is resident in the United Kingdom (whether ordinarily resident there or not), any emoluments received in the United Kingdom in the chargeable period, being emoluments either for that period or for an earlier period in which he has been resident there, and any emoluments for that period received in the United Kingdom in an earlier period;

and tax shall not be chargeable in respect of emoluments of an office or employment under any other paragraph of this Schedule.

The emoluments referred to in Cases' I and II as foreign emoluments are emoluments of a person not domiciled in the United Kingdom from an office or employment under or with any person, body of persons or partnership resident outside, and not resident in, the United Kingdom.

2. Tax under this Schedule shall be charged in respect of every annuity, pension or stipend payable by the Crown or out of the public revenue of the United Kingdom or of Northern Ireland, other than annuities charged under Schedule C.

3. Tax under this Schedule shall also be charged in respect of any pension which is paid otherwise than by or on behalf of a person outside the United Kingdom.

4. Where

(a) any pension or annuity is payable in the United Kingdom by or through any public department, officer or agent of the government of a territory to which this paragraph applies (but otherwise than out of the public revenue of the United Kingdom or the public revenue of Northern Ireland) to a person who has been employed in relevant service outside the United Kingdom in respect of that service, or

(b) any pension or annuity is so payable to the widow, child, relative or dependant of any such person as aforesaid,

and the person in receipt of the pension or annuity is chargeable to tax as a person resident in the United Kingdom, the pension or annuity shall be chargeable to tax under this Schedule.

The territories to which this paragraph applies are

(i) any country forming part of Her Majesty's dominions,

(ii) any other country for the time being mentioned in section 1 (3) of the British Nationality Act 1948, and

(iii) any territory under Her Majesty's protection,

and in this paragraph 'relevant service' means the service of the Crown, or service under the government of a territory to which this paragraph applies.

5. The preceding provisions of this Schedule are without prejudice to any other provision of the Tax

Acts directing tax to be charged under this Schedule, and tax so directed to be charged shall be charged accordingly.

2. References in the Tax Act to Cases I, II and III of Schedule E shall be taken as referring to the Cases under which tax is chargeable under paragraph I of that Schedule.

SUPPLEMENTARY CHARGING PROVISIONS

182. VOLUNTARY PENSIONS

(1) Where

(a) a person has ceased to hold any office or employment, and

(b) a pension or annual payment is paid to him, or to his widow or child, or to any relative or dependant of his, by the person under whom he held the office or by whom he was employed, or by the successors of that person, and

(c) that pension or annual payment is paid otherwise than by or on behalf of a person outside the United Kingdom,

then, notwithstanding that the pension or payment is paid voluntarily, or is capable of being discontinued, it shall be deemed to be income for the purposes of assessment to tax, and shall be assessed and charged under Schedule E.

(2) For the avoidance of doubt, it is hereby declared that the expressions 'annuity' and 'pension' in Schedule E include respectively an annuity and a pension which is paid voluntarily or is capable of being discontinued.

183. OFFICES AND EMPLOYMENTS: SCOPE OF CHARGE

(1) Tax under Case I, II or III of Schedule E shall, except as hereinafter mentioned, be chargeable on the full amount of the emoluments falling under that Case, subject to such deductions only as may be authorised by the Tax Acts, and the expression 'emoluments' shall include all salaries, fees, wages, perquisites and profits whatsoever.

(2) Tax under Case III or Schedule E shall be chargeable whether or not tax is chargeable in respect of the same office or employments under Case I or II of that Schedule, but shall not be chargeable on any emoluments falling under the said Case I or II for the same or another chargeable period (or on any emoluments charged under Schedule E for a chargeable period earlier than the year 1956–57).

184. OFFICES AND EMPLOYMENTS: PLACE OF PERFORMANCE, AND MEANING OF EMOLUMENTS RECEIVED IN UNITED KINGDOM

(1) Where a person ordinarily performs the whole or part of the duties of his office or employment in the United Kingdom, then, for the purposes of Cases I and II of Schedule E his emoluments for any period of absence from the office or employment shall be treated as emoluments for duties performed in the United Kingdom, except in so far as it is shown that, but for that absence, they would have been emoluments for duties performed outside the United Kingdom.

(2) Where an office or employment is in substance one the duties of which fall in the chargeable period to be performed outside the United Kingdom, then, for the purposes of Cases I and II of Schedule E, there shall be treated as so performed any duties performed in the United Kingdom the performance of which is merely incidental to the performance of the other duties outside the United Kingdom.

(3) For the purposes of Cases I and II of Schedule E, but subject to paragraph 7 of Schedule 7 to the Finance Act 1977, the following duties shall be treated as performed in the United Kingdom, namely

(a) the duties of any office or employment under the Crown which is of a public nature and the emoluments of which are payable out of the public revenue of the United Kingdom or of Northern Ireland, and

(b) any duties which a person performs on a vessel engaged on a voyage not extending to a port outside the United Kingdom, or which a person resident in the United Kingdom performs on a vessel or aircraft engaged on a voyage or journey beginning or ending in the United Kingdom, or on a part beginning or ending in the United Kingdom of any other voyage or journey.

(4) For the purposes of Case III of Schedule E, emoluments shall be treated as received in the United Kingdom if they are paid, used or enjoyed in, or in any manner or form transmitted or brought to, the United Kingdom, and subsections (4) to (7) of section 122 of this Act (under which income applied outside the United Kingdom in payment of debts is, in certain cases, treated for the purposes of Cases IV and V of Schedule D as received in the United Kingdom) shall apply for the purposes of this subsection as they apply for the purposes of subsection (3) of the said section 122.

B. Extract from 'Tax Return Guide 1977–78'

This leaflet is sent to individual taxpayers by the Inland Revenue when requesting the completion of Annual Returns.

ALLOWANCES: YEAR ENDING 5 APRIL 1978

A pamphlet on personal allowances and reliefs is available from your Tax Office.

A. Wife

Conditions

Your wife must be living with you
or
If you are separated, you must be maintaining her by voluntary contributions. If you are separated and make payments to your wife under a Court Order, Decree of the Court or other binding agreement, do not claim here but see Note 56. If you make both voluntary contributions and payments under a Court Order or agreement, write to the Inspector and give him details.

In the year of marriage the allowance is normally reduced by $^1/_{12}$ × £ 350 (the difference between the single person's allowance and the married man's allowance) for each complete month (beginning on the sixth day of each calendar month) in that year prior to the date of marriage, if you are already entitled to the allowance by virtue of a previous marriage you will continue to receive the allowance. If you qualify for housekeeper allowance or additional personal allowance for children you may elect not to claim the married man's allowance for the year of marriage.

How to claim

Enter her Christian or other forenames. If you were married after 5 April 1976, enter the date of marriage and give her former surname

B. Age Allowance for Persons Born before 6 April 1913

Conditions

If you (or your wife for whom you claim under Note A) were born before 6 April 1913 you may be entitled to an increased personal allowance known as age allowance.

If your total income exceeds £ 3,250 the age allowance is reduced by two-thirds of the excess until it is no larger than the ordinary personal allowance

Special provisions apply for the year of marriage. A leaflet 'Income Tax and the Elderly' is available from the Inspector.

How to claim

Enter 'X' in the box provided.

C. Children

Conditions

You can claim for any child of your own (including a step-child or a child you have legally adopted) who is alive at any time between 6 April 1977 and 5 April 1978.

You may also claim for any child (including an illegitimate child or yours) who is in your custody and maintained by you.

But

- The full allowance is reduced by the amount by which the child's earnings and other income exceed £ 350; however if throughout the year the child is under 18 and unmarried and has earnings of £ 235 or less but has other income, the allowance is reduced by the excess of that other income over £ 115. The child's earnings should include casual, part-time and holiday jobs. Scholarship income and exempt interest (see Note 29) should be excluded.
- If the child is 16 or over on 6 April 1977, you can claim only if the child is receiving full-time instruction at a university, college or school

  or

  is being trained full-time for at least two years for a trade or profession.
- Where two or more people are entitled to claim for the same child (for example, where the parents are separated of divorced), the allowance is divided between them. If this applies to you, show against the child's name the proportion you claim.

How to claim

Enter the information required for each child for whom you are claiming. You should give accurate details of the child's earnings and other income for the year ended 5 April 1977 and the best possible estimate for the year ending 5 April 1978.

D. Additional Personal Allowance for Children

Conditions

You must have a child living with you for whom you are entitled to child allowance (or would be but for the amount of the child's income – see Note C).

You must be one of the following

- a man or woman entitled to the single person's allowance
- a married man whose wife is totally incapacitated throughout the year ending 5 April 1978.

You cannot have both this allowance and housekeeper allowance.

How to claim

Answer the questions on the Return.

E. Housekeeper

Conditions

The housekeeper must be female and she must be resident with you. You must come within one of the following categories.

- a widow or a widower

– an unmarried person who maintains his mother or some other female relative living with him to look after a brother or sister for whom child allowance is given.

Any other person entitled to claim an allowance for the housekeeper must normally give up his claim.

You cannot have this allowance as well as the additional personal allowance for children.

How to claim

If you come within one of the above categories and if your housekeeper lives in, enter the details asked for.

F. Dependent Relative

Conditions

You may claim only for

– a relative of yours (or your wife's) who is unable to work because of old age or infirmity

– your (or your wife's) mother if she is –

a widow, or

separated, or

divorced

The relative (including a person who when he was under the age of 16 was in your custody and maintained by you) must be maintained by you. If the total value of maintenance and payments towards keep is less than £ 75, the allowance may be reduced. If two or more people pay towards the keep of the relative, the allowance is shared. If the relative's income exceeds the amount of the basic National Insurance retirement pension the allowance is reduced by the excess.

How to claim

Enter the details asked for by showing in the spaces provided the amount of the relative's income from any state retirement pension or Old Person's pension (Note 16) any other taxable Social Security benefits (Note 17) other pensions (including those from a former employer) as well as any other income except gifts and benefits which are not taxable (Notes 17 and 19).

G. Daughter's Services

Conditions

Your daughter must be resident with you and looking after you (or your wife) because you are old or infirm.

You must be maintaining your daughter.

You cannot have this allowance as well as the housekeeper allowance. If you satisfy the conditions for both allowances, claim the houskeeper allowance because it is more.

How to claim

Enter the detail required.

H. Blind Person

Conditions

You (or your wife) must be a registered blind person. If registration is for a part year only, a proportion of the allowance may be claimed. The allowance is reduced if any tax-free disability payments are received on account of the blindness.

You cannot have this allowance and the allowance for a daughter's services. You will be given whichever allowance is the larger.

How to claim

Enter the details required. If you and your wife are blind, give the date of each registration.

J. Death and Superannuation Benefits

Conditions

Normally you will not need to claim for relief on contributions to superannuation schemes as this is given automatically when your employer deducts the amount of your contributions which qualify for relief from your pay before operating PAYE on the remaining net pay. However this system of automatic relief does not apply to contributions to two types of scheme providing superannuation or death benefits:

(1) Superannuation schemes and compulsory schemes providing benefits for your widow or orphans where relief is given on the contributions as though they were premiums paid on a life insurance policy.

(2) Superannutation and death benefit schemes run by trade unions to which a proportion of the member's contributions is allocated. Relief is given on that part of your contributions which is for death and superannuations benefits as though it were a premium paid on a life insurance policy. The amount allowable has been agreed with many trade unions.

How to claim

Enter the details required.

K. Retirement Annuity Payments

Conditions

You may claim a deduction from non-pensionable earnings for
- payments under a contract approved by the Board of Inland Revenue
- contributions to a trust scheme approved by the Board of Inland Revenue for the provision of a life annuity in old age.

The deduction is normally the amount paid in the year of assessment. But it may not exceed 15 per cent of your non-pensionable earnings or £ 2,250, whichever is the less. Within these limits, up to 5 per cent of these earnings, or £ 750 if less, can be paid under a separate contract to provide widow's benefits.

How to claim

Enter the details required.

Ask for a special form (by putting 'X' in the box) if
- you were born before 1916 and wish to claim a percentage deduction or overriding maximum greater than those stated above
- you wish to allocate a payment to a previous year
- in the case of a married woman with non-pensionable earnings, separate assessment has not been claimed and qualifying payments are made.

L. Life Insurance

Conditions

A deduction is normally given for premiums paid by you or your wife to insure your own or your wife's life (but not the life of any other person) or, in connection with certain superannuation schemes.

The allowable premium, that is the amount of the premium which qualifies for relief, must not exceed 1/6th of your income for tax purposes.

In the case of a personal accident policy which covers death and other risks (e.g. disablement and sickness) the allowable premium is restricted to the proportion of the premium attributable to the death risk.

Certain further restrictions apply in respect of policies taken out after 19 March 1968. The most important of these is that single premium endowment policies no longer qualify for relief and the gains may be chargeable to tax if you are liable to higher rate tax or to the investment income surcharge.

Relief is given in terms of tax equal to one-half the basic rate tax on the whole of the 'allowable' premiums (or where the total premiums paid in the year do not exceed £ 20, at the basic rate on the amount of the premiums or on £ 10, whichever is the less).

There are special rules for policies and contracts made before 23 June 1916.

Special provisions apply for the year of marriage or reconciliation.

How to claim

Enter separately for each policy the details required. If you are claiming for the first time enclose form LAPC if you have received this form from the insurance company. Do not ask the Insurance company for form LAPC unless requested by your Tax Office.

M. Allowances and Tax Rates[1]

Here are the amounts of the personal allowances and reliefs which applied for the income tax year 1977–78

Single person's allowance	£ 945
Married man's allowance	£1455 (maximum)
Single person's age allowance	£1250 (maximum)
Married man's age allowance	£1975 (maximum)
Wife's earned income allowance	£ 945 (maximum)
Children:	
not over 11 on 6 April 1977 (or born during the year ending 5 April 1978)	
1st child	£ 196
others	£ 170
over 11 but not over 16 on 6 April 1977	
1st child	£ 231
others	£ 205
over 16 on 6 April 1977 (if receiving full time education; or if being trained full time for not less than two years for a trade, etc.)	
1st child	£ 261
others	£ 235
Additional personal allowance	£ 510
Dependent relative allowance	£ 100
(£ 145 if you are a woman, other than a married woman living with her husband)	
Housekeeper allowance	£ 100

1. This departs from the Revenue text to take in the 'mini budget' further changes of October 1977.

Daughter's services allowance	£ 55
Blind person's allowance (each)	£ 180

Income tax rates. A basic rate of 34% on the first £6,000 of income left after deducting all allowances and reliefs. Then the following higher rates:

on the next £1000	40%
on the next £1000	45%
on the next £1000	50%
on the next £1000	55%
on the next £2000	60%
on the next £2000	65%
on the next £2000	70%
on the next £5000	75%
on the remainder	83%

There are also additional rates ('investment income surcharge') on the excess of investment income over £1500, as follows

if neither you nor your wife were born before 6 April 1913
10% on first £500
15% on the remainder

The limit is £2,000 in the case of individuals aged at least 65.

C. Summary of Conditions for Approval of Pension Schemes

The law relating to occupational pension schemes is contained in ICTA 1970 s.226 et seq, FA 1970 s.21-22 and 5th Schedule, FA 1971, s.21-22 and 3rd Schedule and FA 1973 s.15.

In addition to an automatic right of approval once the requirements of the legislation have been met, the Revenue do have discretionary powers to approve other schemes.

The main requirements for a scheme to be approved may be summarised as follows:–

(a) The scheme must be established for the sole purpose of providing retirement benefits, in the form of annuities and pensions, whether for the employee or any dependants, including permitted benefits for early retirement on the grounds of ill health or on death.

(b) The Scheme must be in connection with a trade or employment carried on in the UK or by a UK employer who is a contributor, with the administration of the scheme carried on by a person resident in the UK (e.g. a Trustee or committee).

The benefit provided by way of pension on retirement should be at an age not earlier than 55 for a woman and 60 for a man – and in no event at an age later than 70.

Where a scheme is not approved the penalty is that the employers' contribution will be regarded as part of the taxable earnings of the employee and the employers', contribution will not be tax deductible.

There are strict provisions relating to the level of benefit – e.g. a pension payable to a widow on the death of a former employee who dies after retirement date cannot exceed two-thirds of the pension payable to the employee. Also, the aggregate value of benefits arising to the employee on retirement. are not to exceed two-thirds of the final remuneration after 40 years, and the total value of any lump sum payment has to be restricted to a maximum $1^1/_2$ times final remuneration after 40 years of service or can be calculated at $^3/_{80}$ths of final salary for each year of service subject to the same maximum.

Amongst other advantages of having one scheme approved pre-eminent are the provisions that the funds own investment income is free of income tax and capital gains tax and the contributions made by the employees are deductible from earnings liable to tax under Schedule E.

When an employee leaves his employment and thereby obtains (in some cases)'a refund of his contributions they are taxed at the rate of one-half of the basic rate of tax then prevailing.

The FA 1971 introduced substantial benefits for the self employed and generally those persons who were not able to joint occupational schemes, and the requirements are closely similar to those specified above. Thus to a high rate tax payer the provisions that up to 15% of taxable earnings can be contributed free of tax to a tax sheltered retirement plan is of considerable benefit.

Appendix 4

A. Scope of the Liability to Income Tax under Schedule E – from 6 April 1974

Type of Emoluments	UK Residence Status of Employee in the Year of Assessment	Duties of Employment Performed Wholly or Partly in the UK		Duties of Employment Performed Wholly Outside the UK
		Emoluments for Duties in the UK	Emoluments for Duties outside the UK	
Foreign Emoluments	Resident and ordinarily resident	Case I LESS a deduction under Sch.2 of 50% or 25%	Case I LESS a deduction under Sch.2 of 50% or 25%	Case III
	Resident but not ordinarily resident	Case II LESS a deduction under Sch.2 of 50% or 25%	Case III	Case III
	Not resident	Case II LESS a deduction under Sched.2 of 50%	No liability	No liability
Other Emoluments*	Resident and ordinarily resident	Case I	Case I	Case I LESS deduction under Sch.2, from emoluments for qualifying periods of absence from the UK of the whole, for an absence of 365 days or more, or one-quarter for other absences
	Resident but not ordinarily resident	Case II	Case III	Case III
	Not resident	Case II	No liability	No liability

* *Editors Note:* This part of the table is subject to slight amendment under FA 1977.

B. Principal Extracts of IR 25[1]

CHAPTER 1 – INTRODUCTION

Changes Made in the Finance Act 1974

1.1. The Finance Act 1974 changed the law relating to the taxation of foreign earnings and foreign pensions of persons resident in the United Kingdom. With a few minor exceptions, the remittance basis of taxation has ceased to apply from 6 April 1974, and its place has been taken by the arising basis, subject to certain deductions in charging the income to tax. This leaflet describes the effect of these changes. If has no binding force and does not affect the taxpayer's rights of appeal in respect of his own liability to tax.

Residence etc.

1.2. The Finance Act 1974 has not altered the rules relating to the meaning of 'resident' and 'ordinarily resident' for tax purposes, nor the meaning in law of 'domicile'. These concepts, and their application to persons coming to and leaving the United Kingdom to work here or abroad, are outlined briefly in Appendix 1, and are explained more fully in Board of Inland Revenue *Leaflet I.R. 20* obtainable from any tax office.

Double Taxation Relief

1.3. The rules governing the relief to which a person may be entitled under the terms of a double taxation agreement (or under the United Kingdom's provisions for unilateral relief) have not been affected by the new foreign income provisions. Where credit is due for foreign tax paid on the overseas income it will be computed (subject to the normal rules regarding limits on credit) by reference to the foreign tax attributable to the full amount of overseas income chargeable to United Kingdom tax *before* taking into account the deductions mentioned in paragraphs 2.6, 3.11, 3.13, 6.1, 6.7 and 7.1 of this leaflet.

1.4. The double taxation agreements vary and detailed information about them can be found in the Board's leaflet on double taxation relief (IR 6) obtainable from the Secretary, Board of Inland Revenue, Somerset House, London WC2R 1LB; from the Inspector of Foreign Dividends, 1, Blagdon Road, New Malden, Surrey, KT3 5BB; or from any tax office.

Overseas Income which cannot be Remitted

1.5. Where, because of the laws of an overseas country or the executive action of its Government or the impossibility of obtaining foreing currency in that territory, a person is unable to remit his overseas income to the United Kingdom he may claim not to be taxed until such time as it can be remitted.

Meaning of 'Emoluments'

1.6. The term 'emoluments' as used in this leaflet means any kind of pay for a job. It includes salaries, fees, pay, wages, overtime pay, leave pay, bonus, commission, perquisites, tips, gratuities and foreign service or cost of living allowances; and the provision of benefits in kind and expenses allowances to directors and to employees whose total emoluments are at the rate of £2,000 (from 6 April 1975, £5,000) a year or more.

Statutory References

1.7. Statutory references in this leaflet are to the Finance Act 1974 except where otherwise stated.

---

1. *Editor's Note:* These extracts do not take into account the FA 1977 changes nor new Revenue practice.

Enquiries

1.8. Enquiries by taxpayers (or their agents) about the application of the Finance Act 1974 provisions to their particular circumstances should be made to the Inspector of Taxes who normally deals with their tax affairs.

CHAPTER 2 – OFFICES AND EMPLOYMENTS CARRIED ON ABROAD

Basis of Liability

2.1. From 6 April 1974 a person who, in a tax year, is *both resident and ordinarily resident* in this country is liable to income tax on the whole of his emoluments for that year from an office or employment, wherever they arise and whether or not they are received in or remitted to the United Kingdom. Where however the employment is carried on *wholly* outside the United Kingdom a special deduction is given in charging the emoluments to tax (paragraphs 2.6 and 2.7).

2.2. The pre-1974-75 rules have not been changed for persons who are resident *but not ordinarily resident* in this country – for example persons who normally live and work abroad and come here for a fairly short period. These people will, as before, be liable to income tax on the whole of their emoluments for duties performed in this country. Their emoluments for duties performed abroad will continue to be taxed here only to the extent that they are received or remitted here.

2.3. Similarly, a person who is *not resident* here – an example would be a person who normally lives and works abroad and comes here to work for so short a period that he does not become resident – will, as before, be liable to Unted Kingdom tax on his emoluments for duties performed in this country (unless exempt under a double taxation agreement). His emoluments for duties performed abroad will continue to be exempt from United Kingdom tax.

2.4. It can be seen from the above description of the scope of the liability to income tax under Schedule E that the liability depends on the *residence status* of the director or employee in the relevant tax year; whether he is domiciled in any part of the United Kingdom or not is normally irrelevant. There are however special rules for taxing the emoluments of a person who is both *domiciled* outside the United Kingdom *and* working for an overseas concern. These rules are described in Chapter 3 ('Foreign Emoluments').

2.5. If emoluments are chargeable to income tax on the arising basis they cannot, in addition, be charged to tax on the remittance basis; they may therefore be remitted to the United Kingdom without additional tax liability being incurred. Emoluments are chargeable on the arising basis even though they may qualify for a 100 per cent deduction. This is because this deduction (and the one quarter deduction where appropriate) is given *in charging* the emoluments to tax; the deduction does not take any part of the emoluments outside the scope of the arising basis (paragraphs 2.6 and 2.7.).

The Special Deduction

2.6. This affects only emoluments for jobs carried on abroad by persons who are both resident and ordinarily resident in the United Kingdom. To qualify for the special deduction the emoluments must be in respect of an office or employment the duties of which are performed *wholly* outside the United Kingdom. In addition, the holder of the office or employment must be absent from the United Kingdom for a *'continuous period'* (paragraph 2.9). If these two conditions are met the deduction given in charging the emoluments to tax is equal to *one quarter* of their amount.

2.7. In certain circumstances the emoluments will qualify for a *100 per cent* deduction: that is to say, no United Kingdom income tax will be payable on them. The 100 per cent deduction will be due where the continuous period spent abroad by the director or employee – whether this period has spanned a complete tax year or not – includes 365 or more days on which he held one or more offices or employments the duties of which are performed wholly abroad. Such days are referred to in the legislation as 'qualifying days'.

2.8. Where the emoluments qualify for a deduction, the amount of the deduction – whether it be one quarter or 100 per cent – is calculated by reference to the amount of the emoluments *after* the deduction of expenses which qualify for relief under other provisions of the Taxes Acts. These 'expenses' include:

capital allowances on machinery or plant used for the purposes of the employment;

expenses incurred wholly, exclusively and necessarily in performing the duties;

fees and subscriptions to professional bodies;

annual contributions paid under certain approved and statutory pension schemes.

Visits back to the United Kingdom

2.9. The legislation prescribes *no minimum length* for a period of absence from the United Kingdom to qualify for the 'one quarter deduction'. Thus a person on a foreign employment, provided that its duties were carried on wholly abroad, would not forfeit the one quarter deduction however many times or for whatever length or time he returned to the United Kingdom; each period of absence abroad would be treated as a separate continuous period. Similarly, if a person left the United Kingdom and returned the same day the time spent abroad would be treated as a continuous period of absence from the United Kingdom for the 'one quarter deduction'.

Example
A is appointed a director of an overseas company on 1 January 1976. His duties consist solely of attending board meetings on 3 consecutive days a month. Each month he travels abroad on the day preceding the meetings and returns to the United Kingdom on the day after the meetings. Each of his trips abroad constitutes a *separate continuous period* and his fees qualify for the 'one-quarter deduction'.

2.10. The length of return visits to the United Kingdom is relevant in this context only for determining whether or not the emoluments qualify for the *'100 per cent deduction'*. In this connection, return vistis to the United Kingdom are treated as not breaking a period of continuous absence from the United Kingdom if *during* his period of absence the director or employee has spent in the United Kingdom not more than 63 *consecutive* days *or* a total period not greater than one sixth of the total period of absence. For this purpose, a day of arrival in the United Kingdom counts as a day on which he is present in the United Kingdom, and a day of departure from the United Kingdom counts as a day spent abroad.

2.11. A day spent in the United Kingdom during the period of overseas employment will count as a 'qualifying day' (for the purpose of reckoning 365 or more qualifying days) provided the director or employee held on that day one or more offices or employments the duties of which are performed wholly outside the United Kingdom. This would be the case where, for example, the employee returned to the United Kingdom on leave and resumed his duties abroad before the periods referred to in paragraph 2.10 had expired.

Example
B leaves the United Kingdom on 1 January 1975 to take up employment abroad. The employment

begins on 1 January 1975 and ends on 2 March 1976 when B returns permanently to the United Kingdom. He spends his leave in the United Kingdom from 1 July 1975 to 31 July 1975 (31 days) and 1 December 1975 to 3 January 1976 (34 days), arriving in the United Kingdom on 1 July 1975 and 1 December 1975 and departing on 1 August 1975 and 4 January 1976 respectively.

The total period of absence is from 1 January 1975 (day of departure counts as a day absent from the United Kingdom) to 1 March 1976 (2 March 1976, as a day of arrival, counts as a day present in the United Kingdom) inclusive i.e. 426 days. Each of these days is a 'qualifying day'. Days spent in the United Kingdom during this period were 65 (31 and 34). Since these 65 days do not include more than 63 consecutive days, and do not amount to more than one-sixth of the total number of days in the continuous period (one-sixth × 426 =71), the '100 per cent deduction' is due.

Duties Performed wholly Abroad

2.12. Whether the duties of an office or employment 'are performed wholly outside the United Kingdom' is primarily a question of fact. If some duties were performed in the United Kingdom the office or employment would not, prima facie, be one the duties of which are performed *wholly* outside the United Kingdom and the emoluments would not therefore qualify for the special deduction. But if the duties performed in this country were merely *incidental* to the duties performed abroad the duties in the United Kingdom would be treated for this purpose as performed abroad.

Incidental Duties

2.13. In determining whether the duties in the United Kingdom were 'incidental' both the nature of the duties and their relation to the duties performed abroad would have to be considered. If, for example, the overseas representative of a United Kingdom employer returned to the United Kingdom merely to report to his employer or to receive fresh instructions, these duties would normally be regarded as incidental. But if, on the other hand, a company director who usually worked abroad attended board meetings in the United Kingdom his United Kingdom duties would not be regarded as incidental to his overseas duties.

2.14. Each case depends on its own facts and no firm rules can be laid down. But, although it is primarily the nature of the duties rather than the time spent on them which determines whether or not they can be regarded as incidental to the overseas duties, duties performed in the United Kingdom for periods amounting to more than three months in a year would not usually be considered to be 'incidental'. A visit to the United Kingdom solely for a period of training which did not exceed three months would normally be treated as incidental.

2.15. Days on which 'incidental' duties are performed will count as 'qualifying days' (paragraph 2.7); but they will not count as days spent abroad in determining whether the continuity of a period of absence has been broken (paragraph 2.10).

2.16. Pay for a period spent in the United Kingdom in which the only duties performed were incidental to the duties performed abroad will be attributed to the immediately preceding period of absence for 'special deduction' purposes.

Duties Performed both in and outside the United Kingdom

2.17. Where the duties of a single office or employment are performed both in and outside the United Kingdom an apportionment will be required to determine how much of the emoluments are attributable to the United Kingdom, duties. No such apportionment however will be necassary in the case of persons who are both resident and ordinarily resident in the United Kingdom; their emoluments are chargeable on the arising basis wherever the duties are performed.

Crown Servants

2.18. The duties of an office or employment under the Crown are normally treated as performed in the United Kingdom irrespective of where they are in fact performed. The emoluments cannot therefore qualify for the special deduction. On the other hand, an allowance paid to a Crown servant, which is certified to represent compensation for the extra cost of having to live outside the United Kingdom in order to perform his duties, is not taxable.

Seamen and Aircrew

2.20 There are special rules for determining whether the duties of seamen and aircrew are performed in or outside the United Kingdom. In the case of seamen, details can be obtained from HM Inspector of Taxes (Cardiff Marine), Pearl Assurance House, Greyfriars Road, Llandaff, Cardiff CF 1 13QP; and, in the case of aircrew, from the Inspector of Taxes dealing with the tax affairs of the person concerned.

Oil Rig Workers

2.21. The territorial sea of the United Kingdom is deemed for tax purposes to be part of the United Kingdom. Further, emoluments from an office or employment is respect of duties performed in a designated area in connection with exploration or exploitation activities are treated for income tax purposes as emoluments for duties performed in the United Kingdom. Thus a person who works on a rig situated in United Kingdom territorial waters or in designated area (that is, an area designated by Order in Council under Section 1 (7) of the Continental Shelf Act 1964) will be treated as performing his duties *in the United Kingdom.*

Two or more Jobs

2.22. Where a person has a job(s) in the United Kingdom and another job(s) abroad his emoluments for the latter will qualify for the special deduction if the duties are carried on wholly outside the United Kingdom. To qualify for the special deduction his overseas job must however be a separate job quite distinct from his United Kingdom job. If the duties carried on abroad are part of his United Kingdom job the special deduction cannot be given.

2.23. The 100 per cent deduction would be due even though during the continuous period of absence the director or employee had more than one job or had changed his job *provided* that the continuous period of absence included 365 days or more on which he held an office or employment the duties of which 'are performed wholly outside the United Kingdom'.

Example
C leaves the United Kingdom on 1 January 1975 to take up employment abroad. The employment begins on 1 January 1975 and ends on 31 March 1975. He remains abroad and commences another employments there on 11 April 1975. He then returns to the United Kingdom on leave from 1 October 1975 to 31 October 1975 (31 days) returning abroad on 1 November 1975. The employment ends on 20 January 1976 and he returns permanently to the United Kingdom on 1 February 1976. The total period of absence is 1 January 1975 to 31 January 1976, i.e. 396 days. Days spend in the United Kingdom during this period amount to 31, and the total period of absence therefore counts as a continuous period. The number of 'qualifying days' included is 90 (1 January 1975 to 31 March 1975) plus 285 (11 April 1975 to 20 January 1976) = 375. Since the continuous period includes 365 or more 'qualifying days', the '100 per cent deduction' is due.

2.24. If a person who is resident and ordinarily resident in the United Kingdom has a United Kingdom job and also one or more overseas jobs which qualify for the special deduction, he may be required to shew that the amount of the emoluments from his foreign job(s) would have been what they are even if he did not have his United Kingdom job. That is to say, he would have to shew that he was getting no more than the commercial rate for the job(s). This requirement is designed to prevent tax avoidance by the diversion to the overseas job of part of the pay for the United Kingdom job.

Example

D is resident and ordinarily resident in the United Kingdom. He is employed by UK Ltd and carried on the duties of this employment in the United Kingdom and also, from time to time, abroad. His emoluments for this job, on which he spends the bulk of his time, are £7,000 a year (Job 1). D has also an employment with UK (S) Ltd, a United Kingdom subsidiary of UK Ltd; the duties of this employment are performed wholly abroad and he usually spends about 3 months in the year on it, for which he is paid £2,000 (Job 2). In addition, he has a directorship with UK (F) Ltd, a foreign subsidiary of UK Ltd, which involves his attendance at board meetings in Paris about six times a year. The emoluments of the directorship are £1,000 a year (Job 3).

It would be open to the Inspector to require D to shew that either the £2,000 (Job 2) or the £1,000 (Job 3) or both, were no more than normal commercial rates of pay. If D could not do so, the emoluments of that job(s), would be treated as attributable to duties carried on in the United Kingdom and would not therefore qualify for the one quarter special deduction.

Whether the Inspector would consider it appropriate to invoke this power would depend on all the circumstances, in particular the relative time devoted to the employments or directorships and the duties performed.

Leave Spent in the United Kingdom

2.25. A period of leave which is taken in the United Kingdom and exceeds 63 consecutive days or one sixth of the total period of absence will break the continuous period of absence from the United Kingdom for purposes of the 100 per cent deduction. In that event, the periods before and after the break will fall to be considered separately.

2.26. Where a person receives pay for a period of leave in the United Kingdom which *immediately follows* a period of continuous absence from the United Kingdom (terminal leave) the *leave pay* is 'attributed' to that period of continuous absence. This has the effect that the terminal leave pay will qualify for the same special deduction (one quarter or 100 per cent as appropriate) as the emoluments for the continuous period spent abroad.

2.27. Days which a person spends in the United Kingdom on terminal leave cannot count as part of a continuous period of absence from the United Kingdom unless he resumes his absence abroad before the expiry of 63 consecutive days or one sixth of the total period of absence.

Example

E leaves the United Kingdom on 1 July 1975 to take up employment abroad. He returns to the United Kingdom on 1 June 1976 on terminal leave. The employment ends on 31 July 1976. Although there are 397 qualifying days' (1 July 1975–31 July 1976), the continuous period of absence is only 336 days (1 July 1975–31 May 1976). The earnings of the employment, including any terminal leave pay, therefore attract only the 'one quarter deduction'. If, however, he had returned abroad on 1 July 1976 and commenced a fresh employment which lasted until 31 December 1976 (E returning to the United Kingdom on 1 January 1977) the total period of absence (1 July 1975–31 December 1976) would be 550 days. The 30 days leave in the United Kingdom in June 1976 would not break continuity, and the '100 per cent deduction' would therefore be due for the pay (including terminal leave pay) of both employments.

Leave Spent Abroad

2.28. Leave spent outside the United Kingdom will not break a continuous period of absence from the

United Kingdom and the pay for the leave period will qualify for the special deduction. For purposes of the 100 per cent deduction a leave day spent abroad counts as a 'qualifying day'.

Expenses which can be Claimed

2.29. The Schedule E expenses rules apply to overseas employments in the same way as they apply to United Kingdom employments.

2.30. Expenses incurred in travelling to and from the place of employment and the United Kingdom will not be allowable if the emoluments qualify for the special deduction; the travelling expenses would not have been incurred ***in the performance*** of the duties carried on wholly abroad. On the other hand, if the duties of the office or employment are performed partly in the United Kingdom and partly abroad the special deduction will not be due but the expenses necessarily itourred in travelling to and from the United Kingdom in the performance of the overseas duties will be allowable.

2.31. Where a director or employee is ***reimbursed*** his expenses (including reasonable hotel expenses) incurred in travelling (whether alone or with his wife and family) to the place of employment overseas and returning to this country income tax will not be charged on the reimbursement (see Appendix 4).

Transitional Arrangements

2.32. A period of absence of an overseas employment which began before 6 April 1974 will be taken into account in calculating the number of days of absence from the United Kingdom and the one quarter or 100 per cent deduction, as appropriate, will be given in charging to tax the foreign earnings ***arising after 5 April 1974.***

2.33. A person who becomes liable to tax after 5 April 1974 on the arising basis in respect of emoluments previously chargeable on the remittance basis will not be taxed on remittances made after 5 April 1974 of the emoluments for earlier years.

Example

F left the United Kingdom on 1 October 1973 to take up employment abroad. The employment began on 1 October 1973 and ends on 31 December 1974. He returns to the United Kingdom on 1 January 1975. The emoluments for the period of employment are £3,000 (£200 per month); £400 was remitted to the United Kingdom before 6 April 1974 and £2,600 on 1 January 1975.

The emoluments for the period 1 October 1973 to 5 April 1974 are chargeable on the remittance basis and the assessment for the year 1973–74 is therefore £400.

The continuous period of absence from the United Kingdom from 1 October 1973 to 31 December 1974 included 365 or more qualifying days. Thus, a 100 per cent special deduction will be due in respect of the emoluments for the 9 months from 6 April 1974 to 31 December 1974, i.e. £1,800. (The £1,800 can be remitted to the United Kingdom without attracting any further tax liability.)

The £2,600 remitted after 5 April 1974 includes £800 which relates to emoluments for the period 1 October 1973 to 5 April 1974. The £800 will not be taxed even though the emoluments for that period were chargeable on the remittance basis.

CHAPTER 3 – FOREIGN EMOLUMENTS

Definition

3.1. 'Foreign emoluments' is the term used in the Taxes Acts to denote:

'emoluments of a person not domiciled in the United Kingdom from an office or employment under or with any person, body of persons or partnership resident outside and not resident in the United Kingdom.'

3.2. It is important to note that the following *are not foreign emoluments* and the rules about liability to income tax under Schedule E described in paragraphs 2.1. and 2.3 will therefore apply:

emoluments of an office or employment with a concern resident in the United Kingdom even though the holder of the office or employment is domiciled abroad;

emoluments of a person domiciled in the United Kingdom from an office or employment with a concern resident outside the United Kingdom;

emoluments of a person resident in the United Kingdom from an office or employment with a concern resident in the Republic of Ireland.

Basis of Liability

3.3. Before 6 April 1974, 'foreign emoluments' of persons resident in the United Kingdom, whether for duties performed in the United Kingdom or not, were chargeable to tax on the remittance basis; in the case of persons not resident in the United Kingdom, they were not subject to tax. This has been changed from 6 April 1974, as described in paragraphs 3.4 to 3.6.

Duties Performed in the United Kingdom

3.4. Foreign emoluments in respect of duties performed in the United Kingdom are now chargeable on the arising basis whether or not the director or employee is resident in the United Kingdom.

Duties performed outside the United Kingdom

3.5. Where the foreign emoluments are for duties performed outside the United Kingdom the basis of liability depends on the residence status of the director or employee. If he is *not resident* in the United Kingdom there will, as before 6 April 1974, be no liability. If he is resident in the United Kingdom *but not ordinarily resident* foreign emoluments for duties performed abroad will, as before, be chargeable on the remittance basis.

3.6. If he is both *resident and ordinarily resident* in the United Kingdom foreign emoluments for duties performed abroad will be chargeable on the arising basis unless the duties are performed *wholly* outside the United Kingdom. In that case the emoluments will be chargeable on the remittance basis.

Place of Performance of Duties

3.7. Whether the duties of an office or employment are performed in the United Kingdom is primarily a question of fact. But where duties performed in this country are merely incidental to duties performed abroad they are treated as if performed abroad. For example, a person domiciled in New York State and employed in the USA by an American Corporation who comes to the United Kingdom merely to attend a conference will not be regarded as performing duties in the United Kingdom. On the other hand, if duties of an office or employment are ordinarily performed in the United Kingdom, emoluments for a period of leave spent abroad will be treated as emoluments for duties performed in the United Kingdom.

One Job with Duties both in the United Kingdom and Abroad

3.8. Where the foreign emoluments are in respect of a single office or employment the duties of which are carried on both in the United Kingdom and elsewhere, an apportionment of the emoluments will be required. Apportionment of the foreign emoluments between the various duties is however of no significance and will therefore not be required if the director or employee is both resident and ordinarily resident in the United Kingdom; his emoluments will be chargeable on the arising basis wherever the duties are performed.

Payment of Tax

2.34. From 6 April *1975* PAYE will be applied in the ordinary way to emoluments from offices and employments carried on abroad if paid by an employer operating PAYE. Where it is clear that a 100 per cent deduction will be due the employer will be authorised to pay the emoluments wihout deduction of tax ('no tax' code). In other cases, the one quarter deduction (and any other reliefs due) will be given in the coding. It is therefore important for the tax office to be given details of the overseas employment as soon as possible so that the appropriate code can be issued.

2.35. If deduction of tax at source is not possible – for instance because the emoluments are paid abroad by a foreign company – the tax due will be collected by assessment. Where possible the tax office will make an assessment based on the estimated amount of emoluments for the current tax year, and the tax will then normally be payable in four instalments during the year. It is important for the tax office to be given details of the overseas employment as soon as possible so that the appropriate reliefs can be given in the assessment and the correct tax payments made. The estimated assessment will be adjusted after the end of the tax year when the emoluments and reliefs for the year are known.

Two or more Jobs

3.9. If the holder of an office or employment is both resident and ordinarily resident in the United Kingdom and performs duties in the United Kingdom he will be liable to tax on the whole of his foreign emoluments, including foreign emoluments for duties carried on wholly outside the United Kingdom, *unless,* in the case of the latter, he can shew that their amount would have been the same whether he performed duties in the United Kingdom or not. Thus, if he could shew that he was getting no more than the normal commercial rate for the office or employment the duties of which are carried on wholly abroad those emoluments would be chargeable on the remittance basis; otherwise, they would be chargeable on the arising basis.

3.10. The purpose of the 'two job' rule is to counter tax avoidance by the switching of pay between jobs.

Example

X, who is domiciled abroad, is employed by a foreign corporation, He has two separate employments. The only duties of one involve him in periodic visits to France and his emoluments for these duties are £2,000 a year. The bulk of his time however is spent in the United Kingdom in connection with the duties of his other employment and he is both resident and ordinarily resident in the United Kingdom. For the latter job he is paid £10,000 a year.

It would be open to the Inspector to require X to shew that the £2,000 was no more then the normal commercial rate of pay for the job. If X could not do so the emoluments of that job would not be treated as being for duties performed wholly outside the United Kingdom and the £2,000 would therefore be taxed on the arising basis instead of the remittance basis.

Whether the Inspector would consider it appropriate to invoke this power would depend on all the circumstances, in particular the relative time devoted to the employment and the duties performed.

The Standard Deduction

3.11. This deduction – which is broadly similar to that referred to in Chapter 2 as the 'special deduction' – is given in charging to tax those foreign emoluments which are chargeable on the arising basis (paragraphs 3.4 and 3.6). The deduction is equal in amount to one-half of the foreign emoluments *after* the deduction of 'expenses' which qualify for relief under other provisions of the Taxes Act (those mentioned in paragraph 2.8) and various other reliefs which the Board may allow (paragraph 3.13).

3.12. The standard deduction reduces from one half to one quarter for years after 1975–76, if the director or employee is resident in the United Kingdom in the relevant year and was also resident in the United Kingdom in any nine of the ten preceding years.

The 'Corresponding Payment' Deduction

3.13. In addition to the standard deduction of one half or one quarter, as appropriate, and the reliefs to which the director or employee may be entitled under the normal United Kingdom tax rules – for example, expenses incurred wholly exclusively and necessarily in the performance of his duties – the Board of Inland Revenue are empowered, where a claim is made, to give a deduction for 'corresponding payments'.

3.14. It is a condition of such a claim that the payments are made *out of the foreign emoluments* which are charged to United Kingdom tax. Moreover the Board, in exercise of their discretion to allow such claims, will in practice require the claimant to shew that he has not sufficient overseas income (on which United Kingdom tax is not chargeable) to enable him to make the payments without having recourse to the foreign emoluments.

3.15. Where the claimant has some overseas income (on which United Kingdom tax is not chargeable) but of an amount less than that of the payments for which relief is claimed, relief will be given only for that part of the payments which exceeds the amount of the overseas income.

3.16. 'Corresponding' superannuation contributions paid out of foreign emoluments will however be treated as reducing the foreign emoluments, whether there was overseas income available to make the payments or not.

3.17. The availability of capital out of which the payments could have been made will be disregarded.

Meaning of 'Corresponding Payment'

3.18. In general, a payment will be regarded as a corresponding payment only if it differs from a payment which qualifies for relief under United Kingdom tax rules, not in substance but solely because it is made under a foreign obligation or in accordance with a normal foreign practice. Examples of payments which may qualify for relief under this heading are alimony paid under a foreign court order; interest on a loan to purchase a sole or main residence in the employee's home country; premiums paid to certain foreign life assurance companies; and annual contributions to a foreign pension fund which corresponds to a United Kingdom pension fund in respect of which relief on contributions would be given.

Amount of Relief

3.19. The tax relief due in respect of a corresponding payment will be computed as far as possible by reference to the appropriate United Kingdom tax rules.

Payments by Employers – Retirement Benefits

3.20. In the case of 'foreign emoluments' employments, income tax will not be charged on payments by the employer which the Board are satisfied are made under a retirement benefits scheme – usually one established overseas – which corresponds to a United Kingdom scheme in respect of which exemption would be given.

Claims for Relief

3.21. Claims for 'corresponding payments relief' should normally be made on Form 11K (tax return form) issued by the tax office to persons in receipt of foreign emoluments. An appeal against the Board's ruling on a claim lies to the Special Commissioners.

Tax Equalisation Schemes

3.22. Some employers have arrangements under which an executive posted abroad does not himself have to bear his tax liability in the country of work insofar as it is greater than it would have been if he was working in, for example, his home country. It is paid for him (or reimbursed to him) by his employer.

3.23. Under United Kingdom tax rules that part of an employee's tax liability which is borne by his employer counts as an 'emolument' of the office or employment and is therefore taxable.

Information

3.26. A person in receipt of foreign emoluments for duties performed in the United Kingdom for the benefit of a person (including a company or partnership) who is resident or carries on a trade, profession or vocation here may be required – if the duties extend over a continuous period of not less than 30 days – to disclose the full amount of any emoluments paid to him *whether or not United Kingdom tax is chargeable on them.*

3.27. The person for whose benefit the duties in the United Kingdom are carried on may be required by the Inspector of Taxes to disclose the name and address of the recipient of the foreign emoluments as if the recipient were employed by him.

CHAPTER 6 – FOREIGN PENSIONS AND ANNUITIES

6.1. From 6 April 1974 a person who is resident, ordinarily resident and domiciled in this country will, in general, be liable to income tax on the whole of a pension from overseas (whether remitted here or not) less a special deduction of one-tenth of the amount of the pension.

6.2. A person who although resident in this country is not domiciled here, or who is a British subject or citizen of the Republic of Ireland and not ordinarily resident here, will continue to be subject to tax on so much of his pension as is remitted to this country, without the one-tenth deduction.

6.3. A person who is not resident in this country, will, as before, not be subject to United Kingdom tax on an overseas pension.

Basis of Assessment

6.4. An assessment on an overseas pension is normally based on the taxable income of the previous year. Thus, where paragraph 6.1 applies, the amount to be assessed for 1974–75 is the full amount of the pension arising in the year ended 5 April 1974 less the one-tenth deduction, and, where paragraph 6.2 applies, the amount remitted in the year ended 5 April 1974. Income for the year ended 5 April 1974 will have been returned on the remittance basis (instead of the arising basis which now generally applies for 1974–75) and the Inspector of Taxes may therefore issue a supplementary return form to establish the correct amount assessable for 1974–75 under the new rules.

SPECIAL CASES

Pensions from the Republic of Ireland

6.5. The general principle is that a United Kingdom resident is taxed in the United Kingdom on income derived from the Republic of Ireland in the same way as he would be taxed on similar United Kingdom income. Thus pensions from the Republic of Ireland will continue to be taxable in full without the one-tenth deduction mentioned in paragraph 6.1.

Compensation Payments for Victims of Nazi Persecution

6.6. Certain compensation payments to the victims of Nazi persecution have been exempt from United Kingdom tax since 1961. This exemption will continue.

6.7. From 6 April 1974, the rules set out in paragraphs 6.1 and 6.2 will apply to payments under any special provision of the law of the Federal Republic of Germany or Austria for victims of Nazi persecution which do not qualify for the exemption mentioned in paragraph 6.6 except that the deduction allowable in cases falling within paragraph 6.1 will be *one-half* of the amount of the pension and not one-tenth.

Certain Overseas Public Service Pensions

6.8. From 6 April 1974 the rules set out in paragraphs 6.1 and 6.2 will apply to an overseas public service pension for which HM Government has assumed responsibility under the Overseas Pensions Act 1973 if the pensioner (of in the case of a widow her late husband) became entitled to it before 6 April 1973. Any increase in such a pension and any such pension to which a pensioner becomes entitled after 5 April 1973 will be taxed in full like any other pension from a source in the United Kingdom.

6.9. If a pensioner was entitled to a pension from the Government of Malawi, Trinidad and Tobago or Zambia before 6 April 1973 and that pension was exempt from United Kingdom tax under the terms of the double taxation agreement with that country, it will continue to be exempt from United Kingdom tax, as long as the double taxation agreement contains such an exemption, even though HM Government has assumed responsibility for it.

6.10. Certain overseas public service pensions and annuities, which are not payable out of the public revenue of the United Kingdom,but are payable in the United Kingdom by or through any public department, officer, or agent, (including the Crown Agents and High Commissions), of the overseas government concerned, are chargeable under Schedule E if the recipient is resident in the United Kingdom. The basis of assessment under Schedule E is the income arising in the year of assessment. From 6 April 1974, a deduction of one-tenth of the amount of the pension will be given in charging such pensions to tax.

Transitional Arrangements

6.11. A person who becomes liable to tax after 5 April 1974 on the arising basis in respect of a pension or annuity previously chargeable on the remittance basis will not be taxed on remittances made after 5 April 1974 of pensions for years prior to 1973–74.

CHAPTER 7 – TRADES, PROFESSIONS AND VOCATIONS CARRIED ON ABROAD

7.1. From 6 April 1974, a person[1] who is resident in this country and derives income from a trade[1] carried on *wholly* abroad either solely or in partnership will, in general, be liable to income tax on the whole of this income, (whether remitted or not) less a special deduction of one-quarter of the amount of the income.

7.2. If, however, such a person is not domiciled in this country, or is a British subject or citizen of the Republic of Ireland and not ordinarily resident here, he will, as before, be subject to tax on so much of his income for the overseas trade as he remits to this country, without the one-quarter deduction.

1. *Editor's Note:* A 'person' in IR 20 means an individual not a company. Also where in the text there is a reference to 'a trade', the comments also apply to professions and vocations.

7.3. A person who is not resident in this country will, as before, not be liable to United Kingdom tax on his income from a trade carried on wholly abroad.

7.4. A person resident in the United Kingdom will continue to be subject to tax on the full amount of income arising from a trade not carried on wholly abroad, without the special deduction of one quarter.

Computation of Income and Capital Allowances

7.5. Income from an overseas trade to which paragraph 7.1 applies will be computed in the same way as income from a trade carried on in this country, i.e. under the normal rules of Case I of Schedule D Similarly, the normal rules for computing capital allowances and balancing charges will apply except that a deduction will be made of one-quarter (as in charging the profits). Capital allowances may not be claimed for a year before 1974–75.

Losses

7.6. Relief may be claimed for losses (including any capital allowances which cannot be given because of a lack of profits) incurred in a trade to which paragraph 7.1 applies. The amount of the loss, restricted by one-quarter (in the same way as profits are), may be set against any *overseas* earned income (excluding any which has, exceptionally, remained assessable on the remittance basis) of the same or the following year. (Earned income in this context includes income from trades, professions or vocations, pensions and salaries and wages.) Losses (restricted by one-quarter), including any balance remaining after set off against other overseas earned income, may also be carried forward and set against subsequent profits in the same trade or against income from shares in a company to which the business has been transferred. Relief cannot be claimed against any income arising *in the United Kingdom.*

7.7. The first trading losses qualifying for relief will be those incurred in 1973–74, i.e. the losses of the year to 5 April 1974 or of the accounts year ending in the year to 5 April 1974.

7.8. Terminal losses of an overseas trade may be set against earlier years' profits of the same trade which have been assessed under the rule set out in paragraph 7.1., i.e. not assessed on the remittance basis.

Basis of Assessment

7.9. The assessment on an overseas trade etc. for any year of assessment is, in general, made on the income of the preceding year or of the account year ending in that preceding year . (There are special rules for the opening and closing years).

Returns

7.10. Income for the year ended 5 April 1974 will have been returned on the remittance basis instead of the arising basis which now generally applies for 1974–75; the Inspector of Taxes may therefore issue a supplementary return to establish the correct amount assessable for 1974–75 under the new rules.

Partnerships

7.11. In the case of an overseas trade carried on in partnership the income assessed under Case V will be the resident partner's share of the profits computed as in paragraph 7.5. Reliefs for capital allowances and losses apportioned to the resident partner's share will be given on the lines described in paragraphs 7.6 to 7.8.

APPENDIX 4: TRAVELLING EXPENSES TO AND FROM THE UNITED KINGDOM

1. On 16 July 1974 Mr.T. Dalyell (La-West Lothian) asked the Chancellor of the Exchequer if he would make a statement amplifying the announcement made on 24 June by the Chief Secretary of the Treasury, to the effect that he proposed to authorise the Inland Revenue to extend its present practice of not seeking to tax reimbursements of travelling expenses incurred by directors and employees in certain circumstances.

2. *Mr. Joel Barnett MP* the Chief Secretary to the Treasury, replied as follows:
Yes. The further concession will be that where the employer reimburses the employee the expenses incurred by the latter in travelling (whether alone or with his wife and family) to the place of employment overseas and returning to the United Kingdom the Inland Revenue will not seek to tax the reimbursement as income in the hand of the employees. This concession will extend also to directorships.

This futher concession is required because there are – in the context of the Government's proposals for the taxation of foreign incomes – two categories of person who are outside the scope of the Board of Inland Revenue's existing concessions relating to the taxation of travelling expenses, published as A5 (Director's travelling expenses) and A6 (Expenses allowances and benefits in kind). First, there is the person who takes up a new employment abroad lasting less than a year and, as will usually be the case, retains his place of abode in the United Kingdom. Second, there is the person with a continuing United Kingdom job and one or more overseas directorships or employments which are not within the same group as the company he works for in the United Kingdom. Both of these categories would come within the scope of the further concession referred to above.

3. The two published extra statutory concessions referred to in the Chief Secretary's statement are as follows:

A5. Directors' Travelling Expenses

The general rule is that the cost to a taxpayer of travelling to and from his place of business is not allowable as a deduction in computing his tax liability; consequently, the full amount of an allowance paid by a company to a director or senior employee in respect of such expenses is chargeable to tax under Chapter II of Part VIII of the Income and Corporation Taxes Act 1970. The rule is modified in the following types of cases:–

(i) A director (whether whole or part-time) of two or more companies within a group of parent and subsidiary or associated companies, whether or not entitled to separate remuneration from each of the companies of which he is a director, is regarded as having one place at which he normally acts as a director of companies within the group, and as entitled to a deduction (or a dispensation from assessment under Section 199 of the Income and Corporation Taxes Act 1970) for expenses necessarily incurred in travelling from that place to other places on the business of the group in the course of his duties as a director. The same principle is applied to an individual who is an employee of one company and a director of another company within the same group of companies. (By 'associated company' is meant a company on whose board the group is represented because of the group's shareholding or other financial interest.)

(ii) A director who gives his services without remuneration to a company not managed with a view to dividends (e.g. a company owning a hall or sports ground, or running a club) is not treated as assessable in respect of any travelling expenses paid to him.

(iii) Where a directorship is held as part of a professional practice (and not, for example, because of some direct or indirect financial interest in the company), expenses incurred by the director in carrying out his duties are allowed as deductions in assessing the profits of the practice under Schedule D, whether the practice is carried on alone or in partnership. Reasonable expenses paid to the director by the company are accordingly not assessed upon the director under Schedule E, provided no claim is made to a deduction under Schedule D.

'Travelling expenses' includes in all cases reasonable hotel expenses necessarily incurred.

A6 Expenses Allowances and Benefits in Kind

Under Chapter II of Part VIII of the Income and Corporation Taxes Act 1970, expenses allowances and benefits in kind received by directors and (with certain exceptions) by senior employees are assessable to tax as emoluments of the director or employee, subject to a deduction for expenses incurred which satisfy, the conditions laid down in Section 189 of the same Act. The following relaxations are made in practice: -

(a) No assessment is made in respect of removal expenses borne by the employer where the employee has to change his residence in order to take up a new employment or as a result of transfer to another post within an employer's organisation, provided that the expenses are reasonable in amount and their payment is properly controlled. 'Removal expenses' includes such related items as a temporary subsistence allowance while the employee is looking for accommodations at the new station.

(b) Under Section 196 (3) of the Income and Corporation Taxes Act 1970 living accommodation provided for an employee (as distinct from a director) in part of the employer's business premises is exempt from charge under Chapter II of Part VIII where certain conditions are satisfied. In practice the exemption is also allowed in the case of a full-time director of a company whose beneficial shareholding does not exceed 5 per cent of the ordinary share capital, unless his emoluments (including the value of benefits within the scope of Chapter II) exceed £2,000. The exemption does not apply to expenses of occupation such as heating, lighting, etc. met by the employer in respect of such accommodation, but the amounts charged under this head on an employee or director (within the above description) are restricted in the case of a patently old-fashioned and too large house.

Editors Note: - The above extracts do not take into account the FA 1977 changes nor new Revenue practice.

Appendix 5: Capital Transfer Tax

A. Legislation

F. (NO.1) A1975 – S.24 – EXCLUDED PROPERTY

1. The following provisions of this section apply for determining what is excluded property for the purposes of this Part of this Act, in addition to property which is excluded property by virtue of any of the provisions of Schedule 7 to this Act, and subject to paragraph 2 of Schedule 5 to this Act.

2. Property situated outside the United Kingdom is excluded property if the person beneficially entitled to it is an individual domiciled outside the United Kingdom.

3. A reversionary interest is excluded property unless:–

(a) it has at any time been acquired (whether by the person entitled to it or by a person previously entitled to it) for a consideration in money or money's worth; or

(b) it is the interest expectant on the determination of a lease treated as a settlement by virtue of paragraph 1 (3) of Schedule 5 to this Act.

S.45 – PERSONS TREATED AS DOMICILED IN THE UNITED KINGDOM

1. Except as otherwise provided, a person not domiciled in the United Kingdom at any time (in this section referred to as 'the relevant time') shall be treated for the purposes of this Part of this Act as domiciled in the United Kingdom at the relevant time if:–

(a) he was domiciled in the United Kingdom on or after 10th December, 1974 and within the three years immediately preceding the relevant time; or

(b) he was resident in the United Kingdom on or after 10th December, 1974 and in not less than seventeen of the twenty years of assessment ending with the year of assessment in which the relevant time falls; or

(c) he has, since 10th December, 1974, become and has remained, domiciled in the Islands and, immediately before becoming domiciled there, was domiciled in the United Kingdom.

2. For the purposes of subsection 1 (b) above the question whether a person was resident in the United Kingdom in any year of assessment shall be determined as for the purposes of income tax, but without regard to any dwelling-house available in the United Kingdom for his use.

3. In this section 'the Islands' means the Channel Islands and the Isle of Man.

S.46 – DISPOSITION FOR MAINTENANCE OF FAMILY*

1. A disposition is not a transfer of value if it is made by one party to a marriage in favour of the other party or of a child of either party and is:–

(a) for the maintenance of the other party; or

(b) for the maintenance, education or training of the child for a period ending not later than the year in which he attains the age of eighteen or, after attaining that age, ceases to undergo full-time education or training.

* *Editor's Note:* – see also S 49. FA 1977.

22. A disposition is not a transfer of value if it is made in favour of a child who is not in the care of a parent of his and is for his maintenance, education or training for a period ending not later than the year in which:-

(a) he attains the age of eighteen; or

(b) after attaining that age he ceases to undergo full-time education or training;

but paragraph (b) above applies only if before attaining that age the child has for substantial periods been in the care of the person making the disposition.

3. A disposition is not a transfer of value if it is made in favour of a dependent relative of the person making the disposition and is a reasonable provision for his care or maintenance.

4. A disposition is not a transfer of value if it is made in favour of an illegitimate child of the person making the disposition and is for the maintenance, education or training of the child for a period ending not later than the year in which he attains the age of eighteen or, after attaining that age, ceases to undergo full-time education or training.

5. Where a disposition satisfies the conditions of the preceding provisions of this section to a limited extent only so much of it as satisfies them and so much of it as does not satisfy them shall be treated as separate dispositions; and where a disposition satisfying those conditions is a disposal of an interest in possession in settled property, the interest shall not, by virtue of paragraph 4 (1) of Schedule 5 of this Act, be treated for the purposes of that Schedule as coming to an end.

6. In this section -

: 'child' includes a step-child and an adopted child and 'parent' shall be construed accordingly;

: 'dependent relative' means, in relation to any person, a relative of his, or of his spouse, who is incapacitated by old age or infirmity from maintaining him-self, or the mother of that person, or of his spouse, if the mother is widowed or living apart from her husband, or, in consequence of dissolution or annulment of marriage, a single woman;

: 'marriage' in relation to a disposition made on the occasion of the dissolution or annulment of a marriage, and in relation to a disposition varying a disposition so made, includes a former marraige; and

: 'year' means any period of twelve months ending with 5th April.

SCHEDULE 5 PARA 2 SETTLED EXCLUDED PROPERTY

(1) Where property comprised in a settlement is situated outside the United Kingdom -

a) the property (but not a reversionary interest in the property) is excluded property unless the settlor was domiciled in the United Kingdom at the time the settlement was made; and

b) section 24 (2) of this Act applies to a reversionary interest in the property but does not otherwise apply in relation to the property.

(2) In determining whether property comprised in a settlement which became so comprised before 10th December 1974 is excluded property section 45 of the Act shall be disregarded.

SCHEDULE 5 PARA 4. INTERESTS IN POSSESSION

(2) Where at any time during the life of a person beneficially entitled to an interest in possession in any property comprised in a settlement his interest comes to an end, tax shall be charged, subject to the following provisions of this paragraph, as if at that time he had made a transfer of value and the value transferred had been equal to the value of the property in which his interest subsisted.

(3) If the person whose interest in the property comes to an end becomes on the same occasion beneficially entitled to the property or to another interest in possession in the property tax shall not be chargeable under this paragraph, except in the case mentioned in sub-paragraph 10 (b) below.

SCHEDULE 7 PARA 3. GOVERNMENT SECURITIES FREE OF TAX WHILE IN FOREIGN OWNERSHIP

3.-(1) Where securities have been issued by the Treasury subject to a condition authorised by section

22 of the Finance (No. 2) Act 1931 (or section 47 of the Finance (No. 2) Act 1915) for exemption from taxation so long as the securities are in the beneficial ownership of persons neither domiciled nor ordinarily resident in the United Kingdom the securities are excluded property–

(a) if they are not settled property and are in the beneficial ownership of such a person; or

(b) if they are settled property and such a person is beneficially entitled to an interest in possession in them.

(2) If the securities are settled property and no interest is possession subsists in them the condition of sub-paragraph (1) (b) above shall be treated as satisfied if it is shown that all known persons for whose benefit the settled property or income from it has been or might be applied or who might become beneficially entitled to an interest in possession in it are persons neither domiciled nor ordinarily resident in the United Kingdom.

(3) Section 45 of this Act does not apply for the purposes of this paragraph.

FINANCE ACT 1977 S.49. PERSONS DOMICILED IN THE CHANNEL ISLANDS OR THE ISLE OF MAN

49.–(1) In section 45 of the Finance Act 1975 (which in subsection 1 (c) provides that certain persons domiciled in the Channel Islands or the Isle of Man are to be treated as domiciled in the United Kingdom) after subsection (2) there shall be inserted–

(2A) Subsection (1) (c) above does not apply to–

(a) a person with a domicile of origin in the Islands; or

(b) a person who, when he became domiciled in the Islands as there mentioned, was incapable of having an independent domicile.'

(2) Subject to subsections (3) and (4) below, property situated outside the United Kingdom is excluded property for the purposes of Part III of the said Act of 1975 if–

(a) the person beneficially entitled to it is domiciled in the United Kingdom by virtue only of subsection (1) (c) of the said section 45; and

(b) it is shown that the property directly or indirectly represents–

(i) emoluments resulting from the carrying on by him of an office or employment in the Islands at a time when (disregarding that section) he was domiciled there; or

(ii) profits resulting from the carrying on of a business there at such a time either by him or by a company of which he then had control.

(3) Paragraph (b) (i) of subsection (2) above does not apply to a person's emoluments from an office or employment under or with a person with whom he is connected; and paragraph (b) (ii) of that subsection does not apply to profits from the carrying on of a business which consists wholly or mainly of one or more of the following, that is to say–

(a) dealing in securities, stocks or shares or in land or buildings situated outside the Islands; or

(b) making or holding investments, being, in the case of investments consisting of land or buildings, land or buildings situated outside the Islands.

(4) Subsection (2) above does not apply in relation to settled property; but where at the time when a settlement was made the settlor was domiciled in the United Kingdom by virtue only of section 45 (1) (c) of the said Act of 1975 any property comprised in the settlement is excluded property for the purposes of Part III of that Act if–

(a) it is situated outside the United Kingdom; and

(b) it is, or directly or indirectly represents, property that was excluded property by virtue of that subsection at the time when it was settled.

(5) In this section–

'business' includes a business carried on in the exercise of a profession or vocation;

'the Islands' means the Channel Islands and the Isle of Man;

and for the purposes of subsection (2) above a person has control of a company if he has the control of powers of voting on all questions affecting the company as a whole which if exercised would yield a majority of the votes capable of being exercised thereon.

F (NO 1) A 1975, S. 45 (1) (b) TABLE

	Husband	Wife
56/57		
57/58		
58/59		
59/60		
60/61		
61/62		
62/63		
63/64		
64/65		
65/66		
66/67		
67/68		
68/69		
69/70		
70/71		
71/72		
72/73		
73/74		
74/75		
75/76		
76/77		
77/78		
78/79		
79/80		
80/81		
81/82		
82/83		
83/84		
84/85		
85/86		

B. Rates

SCALES OF CTT RATES

The tables below show the new scales in the case of transfers etc. made after 26 October 1977.

First Table – transfers made on death or within 3 years before the transferor's death

New scale Portion of value	*Rate*	*Cumulative tax to bottom of range*
£000s	%	£
0– 25	0	–
25– 30	10	0
30– 35	15	500
35– 40	20	1,250
40– 50	25	2,250
50– 60	30	4,750
60– 70	35	7,750
70– 90	40	11,250
90– 110	45	19,250
110– 130	50	28,250
130– 160	55	38,250
160– 510	60	54,750
510–1010	65	264,750
1010–2010	70	589,750
over 2010	75	1,289,750

Second Table – other transfers

New scale Portion of value	*Rate*	*Cumulative tax to bottom of range*
£000s	%	£
0– 25	0	–
25– 30	5	0
30– 35	7½	250
35– 40	10	625
40– 50	12½	1,125
50– 60	15	2,375
60– 70	17½	3,875
70– 90	20	5,625
90– 110	22½	9,625
110– 130	27½	14,125
130– 160	35	19,625
160– 210	42½	30,125
210– 260	50	51,375
260– 310	55	76,375
310– 510	60	103,875
510–1010	65	223,875
1010–2010	70	548,875
over 2010	75	1,248,875

Appendix 6: Capital Gains Tax

FA 1965, S.20 – Capital Gains Tax

1. Subject to any exceptions provided by this Act, a person shall be chargeable to capital gains tax in respect of chargeable gains accruing to him in a year of assessment, during any part of which he is resident in the United Kingdom, or during which he is ordinarily resident in the United Kingdom.

2. Subject to any such exceptions a person shall also be chargeable to capital gains tax in respect of chargeable gains accruing to him in a year of assessment in which he is not resident and not ordinarily resident in the United Kingdom but is carrying on a trade in the United Kingdom through a branch or agency, and shall be so chargeable on chargeable gains accruing on the disposal:–

(a) of assets situated in the United Kingdom and used in or for the purposes of the trade at or before the time when the capital gain accrued; or

(b) of assets situated in the United Kingdom and used or held for the purposes of the branch or agency at or before that time, or assets acquired for use by or for the purposes of the branch or agency;

Provided that this subsection shall not apply to a person who, by virtue of the provisions of Part XVIII of the Income and Corporation Taxes Act 1970 (double taxation agreements), is exempt from income tax chargeable from the year of assessment in respect of the profits or gains of the branch or agency.

7. In the case of individuals resident or ordinarily resident but not domiciled in the United Kingdom, capital gains tax shall not be charged in respect of gains accruing to them from the disposal of assets situated outside the United Kingdom (that is chargeable gains accruing in the year 1965–66 or a later year of assessment) except that the tax shall be charged on the amounts (if any) received in the United Kingdom in respect of those chargeable gains, any such amounts being treated as gains accruing when they are received in the United Kingdom; and accordingly losses accruing on the disposal of assets situated outside the United Kingdom to any such individual shall not be allowable under this Part of this Act.

S.42 – Non-Resident Trusts

1. This section applies as respects chargeable gains accruing to the trustees of a settlement if the trustees are not resident and not ordinarily resident in the United Kingdom, and if the settlor, or one of the settlors, is domiciled and either resident or ordinarily resident in the United Kingdom, or was domiciled and either resident or ordinarily resident in the United Kingdom when he made his settlement.

2. Any beneficiary under the settlement who is domiciled and either resident or ordinarily resident in the United Kingdom during any year of assessment shall be treated for the purposes of this Part of this Act as if an apportioned part of the amount, if any, on which the trustees would have been chargeable to capital gains tax under section 20 (4) of this Act, if domiciled and either resident or ordinarily resident in the United Kingdom in that year of assessment, had been chargeable gains accruing to the beneficiary in that year of assessment; and for the purposes of this section any such amount shall be apportioned in such manner as is just and reasonable between persons having interests in the settled property, whether the interest be a life interest or an interest in reversion, and so that the chargeable gain is apportioned, as

near as may be, according to the respective values of those interest, disregarding in the case of a defeasible interest the possibility of defeasance.

3. For the purposes of this section:-

(a) If in any of the three years ending with that in which the chargeable gain accrues a person has received a payment or payments out of the income of the settled property made in exercise of a discretion he shall be regarded, in relation to that chargeable gain, as having an interest in the settled property of a value equal to that of an annuity of a yearly amount equal to one-third of the total of the payments so received by him in the said three years; and

(b) if a person receives at any time after the chargeable gain accrues a capital payment made out of the settled property in exercise of a discretion, being a payment which represents the chargeable gain in whole or part then, except so far as any part of the gain has been attributed under this section to some other person who is domiciled and resident or ordinarily resident in the United Kingdom, that person shall, if domiciled and resident or ordinarily resident in the United Kingdom, be treated as if the chargeable gain, or as the case may be the part of the chargeable gain represented by the capital payment, had accrued to him at the time when he received the capital payment.

4. In the case of a settlement made before 6th April, 1965:-

(a) subsection 2 of this section shall not apply to a beneficiary whose interest is solely in the income of the settled property, and who cannot, by means of the exercise of any power of appointment or power or revocation or otherwise, obtain for himself, whether with or without the consent of any other person, any part of the capital represented by the settled property; and

(b) payment of capital gains tax chargeable on a gain apportioned to a beneficiary in respect of an interest in reversion in any part of the capital represented by the settled property may be postponed until that person becomes absolutely entitled to that part of the settled property, or disposes of the whole or any part of his interest, unless he can, by any means described in paragraph (a) above, obtain for himself any of it at any earlier time;

and for the purposes of this subsection, property added to a settlement after the settlement is made shall be regarded as property under a separate settlement made at the time when the property is so added.

5. In any case in which the amount of any capital gains tax payable by a beneficiary under a settlement in accordance with the provisions of this section is paid by the trustees of the settlement such amount shall not for the purposes of taxation be regarded as a payment to such beneficiary.

6. This section shall not apply in relation to a loss accruing to the trustees of the settlement.

7. In this section 'settlement' and 'settlor' have the meaning given by section 454 (3) of the Income and Corporation Taxes Act 1970 and 'settled property' shall be construed accordingly.

Appendix 7: Exempt Government Stocks

Treasury $10^1/_2\%$	14 July, 1978
Exchequer 5%	26 September, 1976–78
Treasury 3%	17 September, 1979
Treasury $10^1/_2\%$	1 November, 1979
Treasury Conv. 9%	3 March, 1980
Treasury $9^1/_2\%$	14 May, 1980
Funding $5^1/_4\%$	15 June, 1978–80
Exchequer 13%	25 November, 1980
Treasury $11^1/_2\%$	15 January, 1981
Treasury $9^3/_4\%$	1 April, 1981
Exchequer $12^3/_4\%$	23 November, 1981
Treasury $8^1/_2\%$	15 January, 1980–82
Treasury 3%	15 February, 1982
Treasury 14%	16 March, 1982
Treasury 12%	17 March, 1983
Funding $5^1/_2\%$	15 January, 1982–84
Treasury $8^1/_2\%$	10 July, 1984–86
Funding $6^1/_2\%$	1 May, 1985–87
Treasury $7^3/_4\%$	26 January, 1985–88
Treasury 13%	14 January, 1990
Treasury $8^1/_4\%$	15 June, 1987–90
Funding $5^3/_4\%$	5 April, 1987–91
Treasury $12^3/_4\%$	22 January, 1992
Treasury $12^1/_2\%$	14 July, 1993
Funding 6%	15 September, 1993
Treasury $13^3/_4\%$	23 November, 1993
Treasury $14^1/_2\%$	1 March, 1994
Treasury 9%	17 November, 1994
Treasury $12^3/_4\%$	15 November, 1995
Treasury 9%	15 March, 1992–96
Treasury $15^1/_4\%$	3 May, 1996
Exchequer $13^1/_4\%$	15 May, 1996
Treasury $8^3/_4\%$	1 September, 1997
Treasury $6^3/_4\%$	1 May, 1995–98
Treasury $15^1/_2\%$	30 September, 1998
Treasury $9^1/_2\%$	15 January, 1999
Treasury Conv. 9%	3 March, 1980
Treasury 8%	5 October, 2002–06
Treasury $5^1/_2\%$	10 September, 2008–12

Treasury $7^3/_4$%	26 January, 2012–15
War $3^1/_2$%	on or after 1 December, 1952 (see Note 3 below)

Notes

1. The above stocks are quoted on the principal Stock Echanges in the UK, and the Registrar is the Bank of England. Application must be made by the non-resident holder for interest to be paid gross to the Inspector of Foreign Dividends, Lynwood Road, Thames Ditton, Surrey, KT7 ODP.

2. They can be purchased through a stockbroker or by direct application to the Director of Savings. Harrogate, Yorkshire. In the case of the latter, the current market price will be applied to any purchase or sale, but there is a limit on dealings of £5,000. nominal per day each stock. Stocks acquired through the Director of Savings pay interest gross, so no application to the Inspector of Foreign Dividends is required.

3. Interest on this stock is paid gross to all holders.

Appendix 8: Double Taxation Agreements (Taxes on Income)

Territory

Antigua
Australia
Austria[1 2]
Barbados
Belgium[1]
Belize (formerly British Honduras)
Botswana
British Solomon Islands
Brunei
Burman
Canada
Cyprus
Denmark[1 2]
Dominica
Falkland Islands
Faroe Islands[1 2]
Fiji
Finland[1 2]
France[1]
Gambia
Germany[1 2]
Ghana
Gilbert Islands and Tuvalu
Greece[1 2]
Grenada
Guernsey
Hungary
Indonesia
Ireland
Isle of Man
Israel
Italy[1]
Japan
Jersey
Kenya
Lesotho

Territory

Luxembourg[1 2]
Malawi[2]
Malaysia
Malta
Mauritius
Montserrat
Netherlands[1 2]
Neth. Antilles[1 2]
New Zealand
Nigeria
Norway[1 2]
Pakistan
Philippines
Poland
Portugal[1]
Rhodesia[2]
Romania
St. Christopher
St. Lucia
St. Vincent
Seychelles
Sierra Leone
Singapore[1]
South Africa[1]
South West Africa[1]
Spain
Sudan
Swaziland[1]
Sweden[1 2]
Switzerland[1 2]
Tanzania
Trinidad and Tobago
Uganda
USA[2]
Zaire
Zambia

New Treaties are believed to be under consideration with Brazil, Czechoslovakia and Korea.

1. Residents of these countries may claim reliefs under TA 1970, s.27.
2. Residents of these countries exempt on interest arising in UK.

Bibliography

Revenue Law, *Pinson,* Sweet & Maxwell

Tax Handbook 1977/78, Butterworths (contains all Income Tax, Corporation tax and Capital Gains Tax legislation)

Simon's Taxes (Encyclopaedia), Butterworths (the leading 6-volume work on Income Tax, Capital Gains Tax, Corporation Tax and Case Law (with an up-dating service))

Elements of Capital Transfer Tax, *D.J. Hayton and J. Tiley,* Butterworths

Exchange Control, *A. Parker,* Jordans (with an up-dating service)

The Law of Partnership Taxation, *P. Lawton, D. Goldberg and R. Fraser,* Oyez

Taxation of Overseas Income and Gains, *A. Sumption,* Butterworths

Belasting van Bedrijven in het Verenigd Koninkrijk, *E. de Vries,* Kluwer

Practical Tax Saving, *A.J. Nelson Jones and B. Smith,* Butterworths

Tax Planning, *P. Lawson and A. Sumption,* Oyez

Executive Remuneration, *Geoffrey Newman,* Guild Press (Jersey)

Practical Capital Transfer Tax Planning, *R.P. Ray,* Butterworths

N.B.

(i) There are various modestly priced booklets put out by the Taxation Publishing Co. and by Tolleys. In addition various banks, large firms of accountants and other institutions put out (often free) booklets dealing with various aspects of UK taxation.

(ii) The Inland Revenue has various helpful free guides, inter alia:

CTT	1	–	Capital Transfer tax
CGT	8	–	Capital Gains Tax
IR	25	–	Taxation of Foreign Earnings and Foreign Pensions: FA 1977
IR	20	–	Liability to Tax for Residents and Non-Residents
IR	28	–	Starting in Business
IR	22	–	Personal Allowances
IR	19	–	The New Unified Tax System
IR	27	–	Taxation of Income from Real Property
IRI (1976)		–	Extra-Statutory Concessions at 30th September 1976

Index

GPSR Compliance

The European Union's (EU) General Product Safety Regulation (GPSR) is a set of rules that requires consumer products to be safe and our obligations to ensure this.

If you have any concerns about our products, you can contact us on ProductSafety@springernature.com

In case Publisher is established outside the EU, the EU authorized representative is:

Springer Nature Customer Service Center GmbH
Europaplatz 3
69115 Heidelberg, Germany

Batch number: 10844827

Printed by Printforce, the Netherlands